DEMYSTIFYING
Organizational Learning

This book is dedicated to Chris Argyris and the late Donald A. Schön, who showed us the way, and to Leah, Nurit, and Rinat, who keep us on track.

DEMYSTIFYING
Organizational Learning

Raanan
LIPSHITZ
University of Haifa

Victor J.
FRIEDMAN
Emek Yezreel College

Micha
POPPER
University of Haifa

SAGE Publications
Thousand Oaks ■ London ■ New Delhi

For information:

Sage Publications, Inc.
2455 Teller Road
Thousand Oaks, California 91320
E-mail: order@sagepub.com

Sage Publications Ltd.
1 Oliver's Yard
55 City Road
London EC1Y 1SP
United Kingdom

Sage Publications India Pvt. Ltd.
B-42, Panchsheel Enclave
Post Box 4109
New Delhi 110 017 India

Printed in the United States of America

Library of Congress Cataloging-in-Publication Data

Lipshitz, Raanan.
Demystifying organizational learning / Raanan Lipshitz, Victor Friedman, Micha Popper.
    p. cm.
Includes bibliographical references and index.
ISBN 1-4129-1377-2 (cloth) — ISBN 1-4129-1378-0 (pbk.)
   1. Organizational learning. 2. Organizational learning—Case studies.
I. Popper, Micha, 1947- II. Friedman, Victor, 1952- III. Title.
HD58.82.L57 2007
658.3′124—dc22   2006002940

This book is printed on acid-free paper.

06   07   08   09   10   10 9 8 7 6 5 4 3 2 1

Acquisitions Editor:	Al Bruckner
Editorial Assistant:	MaryAnn Vail
Production Editor:	Diane S. Foster
Copy Editor:	Robert Holm
Typesetter:	C&M Digitals (P) Ltd.
Proofreader:	Gail Fay
Indexer:	Molly Hall
Cover Designer:	Candice Harman

Contents

Preface

The idea of this book emerged through our attempts to make sense of organizational learning, connect it to our experience of this phenomenon in everyday life, and help others understand and practice it. Each of us began this journey at different points in time and for somewhat different reasons. A long-standing interest in organizational learning and set of common concerns brought us together to develop the multi-facet model and later this book.

Raanan Lipshitz was drawn to organizational learning after reading Chris Argyris and Donald Schön's (1974) *Theory in Practice: Increasing Professional Effectiveness* and meeting Schön when Schön spent a year in Jerusalem working on *The Reflective Practitioner*. Later he was helped by both in the transition from the military to academia when he spent 2 years in the (now defunct) Center for Applied Social Studies at Boston University.

Victor J. Friedman was a student of Argyris and Schön's during his doctoral studies in the 1980s. Their ideas deeply influenced him on both a personal and professional level. People who have watched Argryis in action are usually struck by two reactions. The first is that there is something extremely important and powerful in his ideas. The second is that only Chris Argyris or a few select masters can really put these ideas into practice. Thus, a central professional challenge for Friedman has been to make these ideas more easily accessible and actionable for both the individual and organizational levels.

Micha Popper, having worked for many years with managers and commanders, felt that many of them do learn from their experience and improve themselves on the personal level. On the organizational level, however, too many mistakes were repeated, as if the manager's personal learning had left no trace beyond his or her own tenure. This phenomenon was especially salient in organizations in which individuals were assigned for relatively short terms. The gap between individual learning and organizational learning became very apparent in these cases. Such issues illuminated the need to conceptually link individual level and organizational level learning.

The sudden explosion of interest in and writing about organizational learning that began in the 1980s led us to wonder whether this concept was not simply being used as a new way of repackaging ideas from organizational change, organizational development, participative management, and the quality movement. This concern stimulated us to ask a number of questions: Is organizational learning a distinct phenomenon? How does individual learning actually become organizational? How can organizational learning be conceptualized so as to distinguish it from organization change?

Another concern involved what we saw as a growing gap between the rhetoric and the practice of organizational learning. We repeatedly encountered managers, students, and even researchers who were inspired by these ideas but had no idea what to do with them. The more they became popularized, the less they seemed to be clearly understood and rigorously applied. This concern led us to the realization that much of the literature on organizational learning, learning organizations, and knowledge management tends to mystify rather than clarify this phenomenon. We were concerned that this tendency could lead to disillusionment and cynicism about something we felt was critically important.

This insight led us to seek answers to another set of questions: What are the sources of mystification? How can organizational learning be approached in a way that demystifies the phenomenon? How can its complexity be unpacked so as to achieve both clarity and comprehensiveness? How can organizational learning be conceptualized in ways that are relevant to both scholars and practitioners? What accounts for productive learning?

The answers to these questions were generated gradually over a 15-year period in bits and pieces through our research, teaching, and consulting. Our feeling that the work of Argyris and Schön focused too narrowly on the interpersonal level led us to the concept of organizational learning mechanisms. Our research and attempts to foster organizational learning in a variety of organizations led us to unpack these processes and theorize about cultural, psychological, policy, leadership, and contextual influences. These insights then led to further cycles of testing and conceptualization.

Our sense about mystification grew stronger in the process of writing the book. As ideas on how to counter this dysfunctional tendency jelled, writing the book became a learning experience. Although we are all psychologists by training, we come from very different fields and theoretical outlooks. Lipshitz and Popper brought a wealth of research and experience on organizational learning in military, industrial, and health care organizations. Friedman has worked primarily on learning and change in education, the social service, and the public sector. In developing and applying the multi-facet model, we have tried to complement our own research and personal experience by drawing on examples from the literature on organizational learning in a wide variety of organizations.

Developing the model and writing the book have themselves been a team effort and an exciting, creative process. Each of the authors contributed pieces to the multi-facet model, which gradually emerged and evolved over time. Integrating our different viewpoints and sensibilities has required hours of stimulating, and sometimes very heated, discussions about every chapter. As a consequence, each chapter contains parts of all three of us. In the process, we have tried to practice what we preach about inquiry, issue orientation, transparency, integrity, and accountability. One of our colleagues who happened to read some of our critiques of each other's work was amazed at the depth and frankness of the criticism. That is what we truly appreciate about each other, and we hope that it has led to a better product.

This book is aimed at a mixed audience of researchers, consultants, managers, and students. The choice of this target audience stems largely from our own intellectual and research traditions, which are concerned with the relationship between theory and practice. We have attempted to develop a model that is both sophisticated and easily grasped. We have tried to illustrate our concepts and arguments with clear and concrete examples. We have consciously avoided abstract language, the cookbook approach, and inspirational rhetoric, but instead provide readers with useful tools for thinking and action.

We are indebted to a number of people who have contributed to this book. We are fortunate to have known and learned from Chris Argyris and the late Donald Schön, who have always been very generous with their ideas and their feedback. Yael Ben Horin-Naot, Michal Razer, and Neta Ron deserve special thanks for their works, which serve as basis for Chapters 10, 13, and 8, respectively. Others who deserve our thanks are Ariane Berthoin-Antal, Mary Crossan, Mark Easterby-Smith, Amy Edmondson, Shmuel Ellis, Shahaf Gal, William Isaacs, Giovan Francesco Lanzara, Wim Overmeer, Fernando Olivera, Moshe Sharir, Israel Sykes, Marilyn Paul, Tim Rogers, Jay Rothman, Shankar Sankaran, A. B. Rami Shani, Itzik Samuel, and Karl Weick, who were all kind enough to show interest in our work, critique it, give us support, or collaborate with us along the journey that culminated with this book. Al Bruckner, from Sage, deserves special thanks for his trust, quick response, and efficient treatment of our book.

PART I

Introduction

1

Demystifying Organizational Learning

It began when the CEO read a book by one of the leading gurus of organizational learning. The book touched a deep desire to transform her organization into something special, something that would not only serve the shareholders but also enable individuals to realize their potential. It was easy to lose sight of these deeper values in the daily struggle to keep one's head above water, but now she was determined to act on them.

The CEO contracted with a consulting firm experienced in the "learning organization" to facilitate the annual retreat of the executive team. Her team came away inspired after 3 intensive days of lectures, exercises, dialogue, and reflection. Many of them had never engaged their colleagues or even themselves so deeply or let themselves envision what they might accomplish. There were, of course, skeptics who had seen this all before. To them, it was little more than empty rhetoric, wishful thinking, and a diversion from the cold hard realities of organizational life. However, they kept their doubts to themselves and played along.

The HR Department was assigned to roll out an organizationwide program for becoming a learning organization. Vision and value statements began to appear in the CEO's addresses, in memos, on walls, and on the organization's Web site. A large investment was made in training. One division, which was selected for an intensive pilot program, embraced these ideas and experienced an upsurge of motivation and teamwork. A general training program in organizational learning was designed for all employees, but in practice it was carried out primarily at middle and supervisory levels. There was plenty of enthusiasm, and soon the language of organizational learning began to seep into normal organizational discourse.

Then things got stuck. The problem was not resistance to change or the ideas themselves. To the contrary, these ideas almost inspired many employees at all levels, though there were also plenty of skeptics. The problem was translating them into everyday action. The ideas, exercises, and tools that were so inspiring in training seemed to fall flat when transferred to the actual work. Learning projects were initiated but rarely carried through. After undergoing training, many employees had the feeling of being "all dressed up with nowhere to go." The gap between rhetoric and action provided an opening for those who knew all along that organizational learning was just another fad to be endured. Skepticism grew and even turned to cynicism.

What's more, the executive team's commitment to the program began to wane. The CEO continued to refer to the learning organization in her speeches, but when the organization encountered serious financial trouble, funding for training and projects was cut back and learning took a back seat to survival. On the individual level, many employees had been influenced by these ideas, and there were a few pockets of ongoing activity. The organization, however, was not transformed. And after a while, it shifted focus to implementing a new system for knowledge management.

We have encountered this story again and again in many variations in organizations large and small, in business, government, military, educational, and social services. In fact, we have been *in* this story as researchers, teachers, consultants, and organizational members ourselves. This story deeply concerns us because it reflects what we call the "mystification" of organizational learning (Lipshitz, Popper, & Friedman, 2002). According to *Webster's Collegiate Dictionary*, "mystify" means to "bewilder" or "make mysterious or obscure." And, indeed, we have observed that the more that is written and discussed about organizational learning, the less clarity and agreement there seems to be about what it means and how it can be put into practice in the everyday life of managers and their organizations (Berthoin-Antal, Dierkes, Child, & Nonaka, 2001).

We care deeply about the problem of mystification because we believe that the idea that organizations *learn* represents one of the most significant advances in management theory in the last 50 years. During the past decade, organizational learning has emerged as a critical concern for managers (Arthur & Aiman-Smith, 2002, p. 738; Senge, 1990). It has been called an "essential core competency" for managers, consultants, and researchers (Sugarman, 2001, p. 62). Today it would be hard to find any organization that does not aspire to be a learning organization (Gerhardi, 1999, p. 103). Nevertheless, organizational learning remains an elusive concept for managers and researchers alike (Arthur & Aiman-Smith, 2002; Crossan & Guatto, 1996; Crossan, Lane, & Roderick, 1999; Easterby-Smith, 1997; Garvin, 2000).

It may sound a bit strange (and bad for sales), but our purpose in writing this book is not to inspire you. There are already plenty of good inspirational works on organizational learning and the learning organization. We admire many of these works and have incorporated their ideas into our own practice, but our purpose is not to add another one. Rather, our goal is to present a set of ideas aimed at *demystifying* organizational learning so as to make it more accessible to managers, researchers, or consultants in their everyday practice. This means addressing three basic questions: How can organizations actually learn? What is the key for productive organizational learning? When is productive organizational learning likely to occur?

Our ongoing struggle with these questions has led us to develop a solid, research-based, and integrative multi-facet model of organizational learning that can help bridge the gap between theory and practice. This model draws on existing theory and research, practitioner accounts, and our own insights as researchers and consultants (Lipshitz, Popper, & Friedman, 2002). We believe that this model provides managers and researchers with conceptual tools that will enable them to more effectively initiate, enhance, support, and/or research organizational learning from any position within an organization.

The story told at the beginning of this chapter could apply to practically any innovation in management, but organizational learning presents a special, more extreme case of mystification and its consequences. Therefore, we begin this chapter with a look at the factors that have led to the mystification of organizational learning. Then we begin the task of demystification by briefly presenting the multi-facet model, the way in which each chapter develops this model, and how you might read this book.

❖ THE MYSTIFICATION OF ORGANIZATIONAL LEARNING

Both the academic and the popular literature on organizational learning have contributed to the process of mystification in five ways: (1) multiple parochial disciplines, (2) treating organizations like people (the problem of anthropomorphism), (3) splitting the field into visionaries and skeptics, (4) chic and mystique, and (5) actively mystifying the concept.

Multiple Parochial Disciplines

The mystification of organizational learning is partly produced by the multiplicity of viewpoints from which it has been studied. Twenty years ago, a survey of the field of organizational learning found that there was "considerable inconsistency in what is being observed and how it is being measured" (Fiol & Lyles, 1985, p. 811). Six years later, research on organizational learning still reflected a lack of cumulative and integrative work, little agreement on what organizational learning is, and few research-based guidelines for managers wishing to promote it (Huber, 1991). Despite the explosive growth in the literature, the field still lacks theoretical integration or convergence on what is meant by the term (Berthoin-Antal et al., 2001; Crossan et al., 1999; Garvin, 2000, p. 10; Snell, 2001). Operationally defining and measuring organizational learning has proven to be "excruciatingly hard to do" (Arthur & Aiman-Smith, 2002, p. 739) so that there is still a lack of cumulative empirical research (Lant, 2000). In other words, the more organizational learning is studied, the more obscure it seems to become. Indeed, some observers suggest that the learning organization resembles "a management Rorschach test" because one can see whatever one wants to see in this concept (Yeung, Ulrich, Nason, & Von Glinow, 1999, p. 10).

Why has it been so difficult to achieve conceptual clarity in the field of organizational learning? At least part of the answer appears to be that organizational learning has acted as a kind of conceptual magnet, attracting scholars from multiple parochial disciplines to focus on the same phenomenon—or different phenomena under the same name. The learning metaphor has offered fertile ground in which each discipline could stake its claim, generating its own terminology, assumptions, concepts, methods, and research. For example, the *Handbook of Organizational Learning and Knowledge* includes separate chapters for each of the following disciplinary perspectives on organizational learning: psychology, sociology, management science, economics, anthropology, political science, and history (Dierkes, Berthoin-Antal, Child, & Nonaka, 2001).

The existence of a variety of perspectives on organizational learning was identified early on by Argyris and Schön (1978), who concluded that the challenge was to "invent a productive synthesis of fragmentary approaches" (p. 331). Synthesis, however, has been difficult to come by. The more organizational learning and related phenomena have been observed and studied, the more conceptually complex and ambiguous they have become (Argyris, 1980; Barnett, 2001; Castillo, 2002; Ortenblad, 2002). Divergence begets divergence, giving rise to a secondary stream of organizational learning literature offering typologies and conceptual frameworks for making sense of the theoretical diversity.

The attraction of organizational learning for multiple parochial disciplines may be a reflection of the complexity and multidimensionality of the phenomenon itself (Berthoin-Antal et al., 2001). There are many ways of dividing up the field, inviting new perspectives and new typologies. Table 1.1 presents a sample of typologies that have emerged over the past 20 years and illustrates the diversity of ways in which the field can be conceptualized.

Table 1.1 is merely intended to compare these frameworks rather than offer an alternative typology. Our view is that adding another typology would only contribute to the mystification of organizational learning at this point in the development of the field. Pawlowsky (2001) expressed this view when he questioned whether "new contributions should be valued as increases in knowledge about organizational learning or whether they just add to the growing diversity." He then answered the question by stating that "the current growth of literature . . . coincides with a sense of ambiguity, lack of consensus . . . and even growing confusion" (p. 64). Even so, Pawlowsky himself suggested a new framework of five perspectives on organizational learning based on different theoretical traditions and assumptions.

Treating Organizations Like People

Much of the thinking on organizational learning assumes that organizations learn like people learn. This assumption entails anthropomorphism—attributing a human capacity (learning) to a non-human entity (organization) (Doving, 1996). There is, for example, a high degree of similarity between Kolb's model of how individuals learn from experience (Kolb, 1984) and the Shaw and Perkins model of organizational learning (Shaw & Perkins, 1992). The only substantive difference is the addition of "dissemination" in the latter (see Chapter 2 for a graphic comparison of these two models).

Table 1.1 Conceptual Frameworks for Organizational Learning

Shrivastava (1983)	Adaptive learning	Assumption sharing	Development of the knowledge base	Institutionalized experience effects (Learning curve)			Individualistic-normative
Wiegand (1996)	The James March approach (Behavioral)	The Chris Argyris approach (Individual as agent)	Knowledge-based	Theoretically eclectic	Theoretically integrative	Systemic thinking and systems theory	
Edmondson and Moingeon (1997)	Residues: Organizations as residues of past learning	Communities: Organizations as collectives of individuals who can learn and develop	Participation: Organizational learning through policies that engage individuals in contributing to the organization	Accountability: Organizational learning through development of individuals' mental models			
Easterby-Smith (1997)	Psychology and organizational development	Sociology and organization theory	Management science	Strategy	Production management	Cultural anthropology	
Pawlowsky (2001)	Organizational decision making	Systems theory	Cognitive knowledge	Cultural	Action learning		

It is, however, far from self-evident that organizations are actually capable of learning. Kolb's model is plausible because the human nervous system enables people to execute the processes specified by the model. It is not at all clear how organizations can perform the operations specified by Shaw and Perkins. Simply extrapolating from individual learning to organizational learning overlooks significant differences between the two. It also obscures the critical question of how the learning of individual organizational members becomes "organizational."

Researchers who take a behavioral approach to organizational learning solve the problem of anthropomorphism by more or less ignoring it or defining it away (e.g., Arthur & Aiman-Smith, 2002; Baum, Xiao Li, & Usher, 2000; Cyert & March, 1963). They define organizational learning in terms of outcomes (changes in standard operating procedures) but treat learning processes as a "black box." Nevertheless, they still draw heavily on anthropomorphic metaphors such as imitation, improvisation, experiential learning, and vicarious learning (Baum et al., 2000) or exploration versus exploitation (March, 1991).

Researchers who take a more cognitive approach to understanding organizational learning have attempted to look inside the black box. Argyris and Schön (1978) addressed the question of anthropomorphism directly by asking, "What is an organization that it may learn?" Recognizing that only individuals can act as agents of learning, they suggested that organizational learning occurs when individual members reflect on behalf of the organization. They linked learning to changes in mental "theories of action" that not only drive individual behavior but which can be inferred at the organizational level as well. The drawback of this latter solution to the problem of anthropomorphism is that the transition from individual to organizational learning remains unspecified.

Much of the practitioner-oriented literature on learning organizations uses anthropomorphic language that appeals to the imagination but masks complexity. For example, Garvin began his book on the subject by discussing how learning is an essential aspect of everyone's life. A few paragraphs later, he shifted effortlessly, and uncritically, from individual learning to organizational learning, offering a "few simple litmus tests" to help managers know whether their organizations are learning organizations: "Does the organization have a learning agenda? Is the organization open to discordant information? Does the organization avoid repeated mistakes? Does the organization lose critical knowledge when key people leave? Does the organization act on what it knows?" (Garvin, 2000, pp. 13–15).

It is immediately apparent that "organization" is treated here as a subject capable of "having a learning agenda," "being open to discordant information," "avoiding repeated mistakes," "losing critical knowledge," and "acting on what it knows." At first glance, these questions appear to be quite concrete and unproblematic, so the anthropomorphism might be easily overlooked or excused. However, difficulties arise as soon as one considers how a manager might actually answer these questions. How could any manager know whether the organization is open to discordant information, avoids repeated mistakes, loses critical knowledge, and acts on what it knows? For an organization of any size, these questions are enormously complex. Which percentage of organization members should be behaving this way, for example, in order to say that "the organization acts on what it knows?" Treating organizations as if they were human beings is a helpful heuristic for thinking about organizational learning. However, it has also added to its mystification by projecting human abilities onto the organization and obscuring the causal mechanisms through which organizational processes occur (Doving, 1996).

Visionaries and Skeptics

Almost from its beginning, the field of organizational learning has been characterized by a fundamental dichotomy between visionaries and skeptics. Several seminal works on organizational learning expressed doubts about the ability of organizations to learn (e.g., March & Olsen, 1976). Argyris and Schön (1978) focused on the limits to learning but argued that these limits could be overcome through a fundamental change in thinking and behavior that could be created through new kinds of consulting, teaching, and research (Argyris, 1980; Argyris, Putnam, & Smith, 1985). Over a decade later, Huber's evaluation of the literature still focused on the "obstacles to organizational learning from experience" (Huber, 1991, p. 95).

The visionary approach to organizational learning received its greatest thrust from Peter Senge's *The Fifth Discipline* (1990), which synthesized a number of innovative ideas into a vision of the "learning organization" in which "people continually expand their capacity to create the results that they truly desire, where new and expansive patterns of thinking are nurtured, where collective aspiration is set free, and where people are continually learning how to learn together" (Senge, 1990, p. 3). This unabashedly utopian message is reflected in the title of the first chapter of the book, taken from Archimedes: "Give me a lever long enough . . . and single-handed I can move the world."

Not surprisingly, the loftiness of Senge's vision added not only to the popularity of organizational learning but also to its mystification (Jackson, 2000). It projected a compelling image of the desired state—the learning organization—while leaving obscure the concrete steps that need to be taken to achieve it. Despite the publication of works intended to fill this gap by providing tools and techniques (e.g., Senge, Kleiner, Roberts, Ross, & Smith, 1994), research has shown very limited results (Ford, Voyer, & Gould-Wilkinson, 2000; Schein, 1996). Sugarman (2001) termed the learning organization concept an essential core competency, but his analysis of five case studies concluded that making such a change is "a huge accomplishment—even in just one segment of the whole [organization]" (p. 75). Garvin (2000, p. 5) pointed to the ongoing mystification stemming from the "reverential," "utopian," and "uplifting" rhetoric of organizational learning, which provides little "comfort to practical-minded managers."

According to Driver (2002), the visionaries are mainly practitioners and consultants looking to sell their advice to client organizations, whereas the skeptics are mostly academics looking to publish by setting forth an overly critical view. Some skeptics, particularly those with postmodernist orientation, view organizational learning and the learning organization as "a nightmare for [organizational] members" (Driver, 2002, p. 34). They view these concepts as rhetorical devices used by those in power to trap employees into a utopian vision so that they can be more effectively exploited:

> The "learning organization" is naught but a Hawthorne light bulb with a dimmer switch, intended to stimulate productivity regardless of its chameoleonic brilliance. It is a Machiavellian subterfuge, it is a pimp, and the employees, the hapless prostitutes. (Armstrong, 2000, p. 359)

This critique is rather mystifying in itself. The rich imagery and polemical tone shed more heat than light on the subject, leaving practitioners and scholars to wonder whether they are really prophets or prostitutes—and what it all means.

Chic and Mystique

The field of organizational learning has injected a rich new terminology that includes concepts such as "double-loop learning," "systems thinking," "mental models," "organizational memory," "competency traps," "dialogue," "tacit knowledge," "reflection," "defensive routines," "absorptive capacity," "knowledge creation," and so on. The jargon is very appealing and easy to adopt (chic) but difficult to really understand and use in an appropriate fashion (mystique) (Lipshitz, 2000). For example, Argyris and Schön (1974) introduced the concept *double-loop learning* to describe a particular and rare type of learning within the context of a specific theoretical framework. Nevertheless, this term is one of the mostly widely cited in all of the organizational learning literature, usually taken out of its original context and used loosely to refer to almost any type of far-reaching organizational change.

Lane, Koka, and Pathak (2002) described how the use of the concept *absorptive capacity* has tended to obscure rather than clarify its meaning. They described this tendency as the "reification" of absorptive capacity, treating a complex phenomenon as a distinct integral "something" that organizations possess or want to acquire. Reification also inhibits research into the relationships and dynamics a construct is meant to capture. As Lane and colleagues (2002) put it, reified concepts are used as a kind of "magic talisman" to be "waved at" problems rather than as rigorous conceptual tools.

When organizational learning was reframed as the "art and practice of the learning organization" (Senge, 1990), the term *learning* became a qualifier for those organizations that have a capacity for learning. This reframing lent itself to a kind of thinking that creates a false dichotomy between organizations that learn and those that do not. Furthermore, there are no clearly defined, operationalizable criteria for determining when an organization becomes a "learning organization." As a result, the concept of the learning organization has become reified, lending itself to public relations or image management.

Active Mystification

Why does the vision of the learning organization remain popular even while its meaning and practical application have remained largely obscure? One explanation is that obscurity may actually increase its appeal. As one observer put it, "Being a learning organization is a long-term guiding aspiration that can be glimpsed, but is not likely to be achieved in the near future" (Snell, 2001, p. 333). Jackson (2000, p. 207) attributed the power of Senge's approach to "the dramatic qualities of his socially rooted vision . . . [the] ability to inspire followers to see themselves actively engaged in building a learning organization." In other words, the appeal of this vision may have more to do with what it says to managers about the meaning of their work than what it actually does for the organization.

For many practitioners, the appeal of the "learning organization" may be more spiritual than instrumental. Senge's *The Fifth Discipline* was one of the first major management works to speak directly to a desire for spirituality and meaning in organizational life (Delbecq, 2000; Elmes & Smith, 2001; Vaill, 2000b). The book jacket of *The Fifth Discipline* states that it is "a remarkable book that draws on science, *spiritual wisdom* [our italics], psychology, the cutting edge of management thought, and on Senge's work with top corporations." Personal mastery, one of the five core disciplines, represents a "*quest* [our italics] for *continual* learning" on the part of the individual from which "comes the spirit of the learning organization." This spirit emanates from the "*transcendent* [our italics] values of love, *wonder* [our italics], humility, and compassion" (Kofman & Senge, 1993, p. 16). These quotations all reflect a shift from framing organizational learning in terms of organizational effectiveness to framing it as a spiritual quest.

Mystification plays a very important role in this reframing of organizational learning as spiritual quest. Like science, a spiritual quest is a search for knowing, but it differs from science because knowledge is revealed while remaining hidden.

> *Homo religiosus*, like cognitive man (scientist), seeks the lawful and the ordered, the fixed and the necessary. But for the former, unlike the latter, the revelation of the law and the comprehension of the order and interconnectedness of existence *only intensifies and deepens the questions and the problem* [our italics]. For while cognitive man discharges his obligation by establishing the reign of a causal structure of lawfulness in nature, *homo religiosus* is not satisfied with the perfection of the world under the dominion of law. For to him the concept of lawfulness is in itself the deepest of mysteries. (Soloveitchik, 1983, p. 7)

From the spiritual perspective, order, causal explanation, and instrumental concerns are not an end but rather a starting point from which to engage and experience deeper mysteries. The desired state of affairs for a spiritual consciousness is awe and wonder (Heschel, 1955). Thus, mystification plays an important role in keeping the learning organization as something that can be glimpsed but never fully achieved. Utopian visions and spirituality may have important roles to play in organizational theory and practice, but they also place a heavy burden on the practice of organizational learning.

If the ability to learn better and faster is important for organizations, then mystification might justifiably be added to Senge's (1990) list of seven organizational "learning disabilities." Mystification poses a threat to the long-term health of inquiry. It adds to the concept's allure while at the same time impeding theoretical integration and obscuring the links between theory and practice. If the concept of organizational learning continues to remain largely obscure, it is likely that researchers and practitioners will become frustrated and lose interest.

❖ DEMYSTIFICATION

Demystifying organizational learning requires a set of concepts that can guide the actions of managers and researchers who want to promote or study organizational learning in their everyday practice. These concepts must speak to people in a wide variety of organizational contexts and at all levels of management. They must avoid the pitfalls of multiple parochial disciplines and anthropomorphism. They must avoid chic jargon and provide a terminology that can be clearly connected to observable phenomena. They cannot be overly visionary nor overly skeptical, neither utopian nor a cookbook.

This book attempts to provide such a set of concepts in the form of an integrative "multi-facet" model of organizational learning (see Figure 1.1) that draws on existing theory and research, practitioner accounts, and our own insights as researchers and consultants. The "facets" in this model are five sets of factors that determine the extent to which learning is *organizational* and *productive*. These facets, each of which is described in detail in a separate chapter, include structure (Chapter 2), culture (Chapter 3), psychological climate (Chapter 4), contextual (Chapter 5), and leadership and policy (Chapter 6).

The model deals with multiple parochial disciplines by identifying the sound empirical findings of existing research, finding significant commonalities among seemingly divergent approaches, and combining them into a single conceptual framework (Barnett, 2001). It aspires to achieve a balance between clarity and complexity, being complete enough to accurately capture the factors that influence organizational learning and parsimonious enough to be easily grasped and used by both managers and researchers. For managers, these facets provide a set of criteria through which they can assess the actions they need to take to promote learning around a particular task in a particular organizational context. For researchers, the facets provide a set of factors that can be operationalized and studied empirically.

Figure 1.1   Facets of Organizational Learning

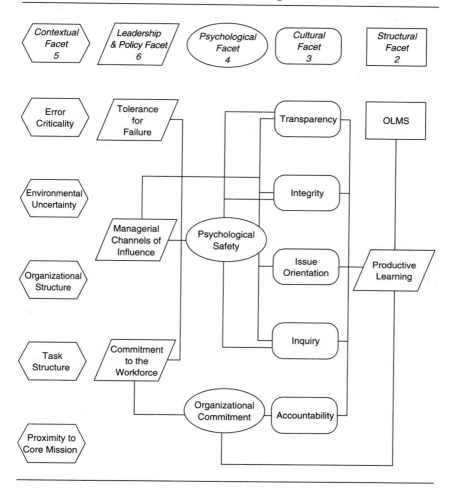

Before turning to the model, however, we need to clearly define the term *productive* organizational learning. Rather than attempt to produce definitive answers to the definitional dilemmas previously described our approach offers a pragmatic solution that builds on the definition of *organizational learning* as the detection and correction of error (Argyris & Schön, 1996). To this basic definition, we add the discovery and exploitation of opportunity. This definition, which includes both insight and action, views learning as a cyclical process involving the evaluation of past behavior, the discovery of error or opportunity, the invention of new behaviors, and their implementation. According to our definition, productive learning is a conscious and critical process of reflection intended to produce new perceptions, goals, and/or behavioral strategies (Doving, 1996).

Based on this definition, we posit two criteria for determining whether learning is productive or not. The more rigorous criterion is conclusively showing that learning results in intended organizational outcomes. Unfortunately, it is often difficult, if not impossible, to establish such a clear causal connection. The impact of new organizational knowledge can never be fully determined. Different stakeholders may hold very contradictory views about what constitutes usefulness and how knowledge contributes to the well-being of the organization. In addition, knowledge deemed worthless today may eventually prove critical for the organization's survival, and lessons deemed worthwhile today may turn out to be the seeds of disaster.

The more practical criterion is showing that learning results in organizational *action* based on *valid* knowledge. Knowledge is valid to the extent that it withstands critical evaluation and is not based on willfully distorted information or unquestioned interpretations. Critical evaluation focuses on the ends as well as the means of new knowledge. This criterion would at least require considering the productiveness of learning destructive or unethical practices. It is also based on the assumption that acquiring information or new knowledge is not enough. Knowledge must inform the behavior of organizational actors, even if such a link to intended outcomes cannot be clearly established (see Chapter 7 for an in-depth discussion of what we consider to be "actionable" knowledge).

❖ THE FACETS OF ORGANIZATIONAL LEARNING

The Structural Facet (see Figure 1.1)

The multi-facet model begins with the following question: How can we account for *organizational* learning without resorting to anthropomorphic metaphors? What organizational mechanisms fulfill the function of the central nervous system in human learning? Our answer to this question is to look at the *structures* that enable organizational members to jointly collect, analyze, disseminate, and apply information and knowledge. We call these structures "organizational learning mechanisms" (OLMs). They include the roles, functions, and procedures that enable organizational members to systematically collect, analyze, store, disseminate, and use information relevant to their own and other members' performance.

In the multi-facet model, OLMs are the fundamental building blocks of organizational learning. OLMs are concrete observable entities that provide a means for observing and specifying where and when organizational learning occurs. They also make a clear distinction between the individual and organizational levels of learning. Chapter 2 takes an in-depth look at this *structural facet* of organizational learning and presents four basic types of OLMs using real-world examples from the literature and our own research (Baird, Henderson, & Watts, 1997; Carroll, 1995; Cheney, 1998; DiBella, Nevis, & Gould, 1996; Dodgson, 1993; Gulliver, 1987; Lipshitz & Popper, 2000; Lipshitz, Popper, & Ron, 1999; Popper & Lipshitz, 1998).

The Cultural Facet (see Figure 1.1)

The existence of OLMs explains how organizations learn, but it does not account for *productive* learning. We argue that productive learning occurs when *organizational culture* supports both the creation of valid knowledge and taking action on that knowledge. Chapter 3 looks at the role of culture and how it affects organizational learning.

It is interesting that the literature takes a mainly negative stance toward organizational culture, regarding it as a *barrier* to organizational learning (e.g., De Long & Fahey, 2000; Ford et al., 2000; Tan & Heracleous, 2001).

In contrast, we argue that it is more useful to think of effective OLMs as "cultural islands" characterized by cultural norms more conducive to learning than those of the organization as a whole. Based on the literature and our own experience, we specify five norms that promote learning: inquiry, issue orientation, transparency, integrity, and accountability (Argyris & Schön, 1978, 1996; Beer & Spector, 1993; Davenport, De Long, & Beer, 1998; Davies & Easterby-Smith, 1997; DiBella et al., 1996; McGill, Slocum, & Lei, 1993). This chapter defines each of the five norms and illustrates them with examples drawn from real OLMs.

The Psychological Facet (see Figure 1.1)

The willingness of people to act on and internalize learning-oriented norms depends on the way in which they think and feel. Thus, Chapter 4 explores this *psychological facet* of organizational learning and its influence on behavior in OLMs. The model specifies two key factors that influence learning behavior: degree of psychological safety and commitment to the organization. Psychological safety engenders trust and enables people to face the risks of inquiry, transparency, and accountability (Edmondson 1999; Schein, 1996). Organizational commitment is particularly important for counteracting the dysfunctional effects of politics and game playing on learning.

The Leadership and Policy Facet (see Figure 1.1)

The leadership-policy facet, presented in Chapter 5, describes the *channels of influence* through which managers can foster organizational learning. These channels include the leadership behaviors and organizational policies that support the development of OLMs and learning-oriented cultural norms. Learning-oriented leadership and policies communicate a clear commitment to learning, tolerance for error, and commitment to the workforce. The literature on organizational learning, however, tends to emphasize the role of "heroic" leadership, usually from the CEO, in transforming their organizations. This emphasis inspires but also contributes to mystification because most managers are neither heroes nor in the position to transform their organization. Therefore, in this chapter, we address the ways managers at any level can promote learning without necessarily having to wait for an overall organizational transformation.

The Contextual Facet (see Figure 1.1)

Chapter 6 looks at the contextual facet of organizational learning. This facet includes those factors that have an important impact on organizational learning but are largely outside of managerial control. They include the degree of environmental and task uncertainty, task structure, proximity of the learning to the organization's core task, and the degree to which errors can be costly. We also treat the overall organizational structure as a contextual factor because for most managers it is more or less a given. These factors constitute both opportunities and constraints in regard to learning, and managers must take them into account.

Knowledge Dissemination

Chapter 7 completes the presentation of the multi-facet model, looking at how organizations disseminate knowledge and lessons learned. It examines different kinds of knowledge, mechanisms for knowledge dissemination, and barriers to effective dissemination.

❖ APPLYING THE MULTI-FACET MODEL

In order to overcome mystification, the multi-facet model creates specific and observable links between concepts and organizational action

(Lipshitz et al., 2002). Therefore, Chapters 8 through 13 provide in-depth case studies in order to shed light on how the model can be applied to analyze, guide, and study organizational learning in action. These case studies show that the model can be applied to a wide variety of organizations in industry, high tech, the military, and education. Each chapter is intended to provide an additional perspective on how the model can be used.

Inside an Organizational Learning Mechanism: The Case of Postflight Reviews in the Israel Defense Force Air Force

Chapter 8 provides an in-depth analysis of "after-action reviews," the most common form of organizational learning mechanism (OLM), using the example of postflight reviews in a combat squadron of the Israel Defense Force Air Force. Our objective in this chapter is to further demystify organizational learning by examining in detail the learning dynamics in after-action reviews: What goes on beneath the surface of the procedure-following activities? How do participants think and feel? How do they learn from the review process? How does the Israel Defense Force Air Force (IDFAF) actually learn?

Training Versus Organizational Learning

Chapter 9 builds on the OLM concept to take a critical look at the role of training in relationship to organizational learning. When individual organizational members acquire new knowledge or learn a new skill, it does not necessary add up to *organizational* learning. We call the former "learning *in*" an organization and the latter "learning *by*" an organization. On the other hand, training programs can evolve into, or generate, very effective OLMs. In this chapter, we describe how OLMs, and organizational learning, evolved out of training programs at Johnsonville Foods, Motorola, Dell, and Bell Laboratories.

High-Quality Learning

An obvious cause of failures of learning is a low-quality learning process. Chapter 10 presents a general conceptualization of high-quality organizational learning based on the distinctive characteristics of successful and unsuccessful postaccident reviews in an elite combat unit of the Israel Defense Force. This chapter demonstrates the mere existence of OLMs is insufficient, in and of itself, to ensure productive learning. It shows how cultural norms, leadership, and other factors influence the probability that lessons learned from after-action reviews will not be forgotten, thereby lowering the likelihood that past errors will not be repeated.

Demystifying the Learning Organization: The Case of Hewlett-Packard

As we pointed out before, demystifying the learning organization means stepping back from the false dichotomy between organizations that learn and those that do not. Hewlett-Packard is a company that is often seen as an exemplar of the learning organization. Organizational learning in such companies is often attributed to unique cultures that are both inspiring and difficult to imitate. In Chapter 11, we reanalyze two cases of organizational learning within HP: one that was discontinued and one that was sustained. We use the multi-facet model as analytical tool to show how key differences in the way learning was designed and managed can account for the different trajectories of these two projects. This chapter illustrates management's role in understanding and adapting to the contextual facet for ensuring the long-term viability of an organizational learning effort.

Demystifying the Learning Organization: The Case of Chaparral Steel

Chaparral Steel represents another famous hard-to-imitate exemplar of the learning organization. In Chapter 12, we argue that managers *can* learn from Chaparral Steel's example, but they need a framework for systematic comparison that enables them to identify both similarities *and* the key differences between their organizations and Chaparral. The multi-facet model presented in this book offers such a framework. Our reanalysis of existing studies of Chaparral will show how Chaparral implemented a unique configuration of OLMs. It will also identify features of Chaparral's learning culture, managerial policies, and leadership that make these OLMs effective. Finally, it will show how the particular design of learning at Chaparral was shaped, at least in part, by a specific set of contextual conditions. Such an analysis provides managers with a template for comparing their organizations with Chaparral so as to understand which principles can be adopted and which cannot.

Putting the Multi-Facet Model Into Practice

Chapter 13 illustrates how the multi-facet model can help managers and consultants design and carry out a focused, systematic, and productive process of organizational learning and knowledge dissemination. In this chapter, we illustrate the intervention process through in-depth case study of an organizational learning project carried out with the staff of the New Education Environment (NEE), a program aimed at helping secondary schools in Israel work more effectively with students at risk. Given the wide variety and complexity of organizations, learning processes need to be adapted to an organization's specific needs, characteristics, and circumstances. This chapter argues that there is no simple X-step formula that leads to organizational learning but that the multi-facet model does provide a useful framework for guiding this process of design. Each of the facets directs management attention to certain questions they must ask, certain factors they must take into account, and certain actions they need to take. This chapter shows how the multi-facet model can be used by managers and consultants to design and carry out focused, systematic, and productive process of knowledge creation and dissemination.

In Chapter 14, we conclude the book with a discussion of how the multi-facet model demystifies organizational learning and sets a future agenda for both researchers and practitioners.

❖ HOW TO READ THIS BOOK

This book is divided into three sections. The first section is this introductory chapter, which has provided a general but fairly comprehensive overview of what you are going to encounter in the rest of this book. It frames the problem of mystification that this book comes to address. The second section (Chapters 2–7) is a systematic in-depth presentation of the model, facet by facet. This section represents a "solution" to the problem, though not necessarily the only solution. The third section (Chapters 8–14) applies the model to analyze a wide variety of examples of organizational learning. It shows how the proposed solution can be used in actual practice.

The multi-facet model of organizational learning that we present is not intended to be a cookbook—more like the "Lonely Planet Guide to Organizational Learning." The multi-facet model (see Figure 1.1) provides a map for helping you see the lay of the land and locate yourself within it. If you are a deductive traveler who likes to acquire in-depth knowledge of the territory and a highly structured itinerary before setting out, your best bet would be to read systematically through the facets of the model that are presented in Chapters 2 through 7. If you are a more inductive traveler who likes to venture out into the field and learn through concrete experience, you might want to begin with one of the applied chapters, Chapters 8 through 13. If you choose this route, you may encounter unfamiliar terminology and concepts that may lead you to refer back to the second section for explanation. For such readers, a good place to start is Chapter 8, which looks at postflight reviews, because it describes an important exemplar of an OLM and a turning point in *our* inquiry about organizational learning.

❖ TO SUM UP

We believe that organizations learn and that people can, through their actions, promote or inhibit these learning processes. We believe that productive organizational learning matters for both organizations and for the quality of working life. We have written this book for managers, practitioners, and researchers who have an interest in organizational learning and want a realistic approach for putting these ideas into practice within the complexities of organizational life. We do not claim to have found the *one best way* to produce organizational learning, but we do want to share an approach that has worked for us.

In writing this book, we have attempted to avoid the tendency toward mystification described in this chapter. We present a model that we believe is both sophisticated and easily grasped. We take a middle path in both content and tone—being neither overly inspirational nor skeptical, neither too academic nor too simplistic. We illustrate our concepts and arguments with concrete examples. In the process of developing and refining the model, we have continually tested it out with our students, colleagues, and clients, who tell us that it helps them—finally—see how these inspirational ideas can be brought down to earth.

The multi-facet model presented in this book suggests that being a learning organization is not a distant vision but rather occurs within the context of everyday activities. The prosaic nature of organizational learning does not mean that it is easy to achieve. Productive learning is complex and difficult. It often involves complexity, uncertainty, conflict, and threat. For this very reason, we hope that the following chapters will help demystify the field, providing firmer ground for practitioners and researchers who wish to engage the challenge of promoting productive organizational learning.

PART II

The Multi-Facet Model

2

Organizational Learning Mechanisms

D espite its ready acceptance by researchers, consultants, and managers, the claim that organizations can learn is problematic because it implicitly attributes a human capacity, namely learning, to organizations, which are nonhuman entities. This problem or fallacy of anthropomorphism can be illustrated by comparing Figure 2.1A, which presents a slight adaptation of a well-known model of *how* individuals learn from experience (Kolb, 1984), with Figure 2.1B, which presents a model of organizational learning (Shaw & Perkins, 1992).

The two figures are virtually identical except for "dissemination," which does not fit into the star-shaped configuration, in that it depicts both individual and organizational learning as a sequence of information-processing operations. However, although it is clear how individuals can perform these operations owing to their central nervous system, it is not at all clear how organizations perform them. Furthermore, the awkward position of "dissemination" in Figure 2.1B indicates that nontrivial features of organizational learning may have no analogue in individual learning.

Figure 2.1   Organizational learning

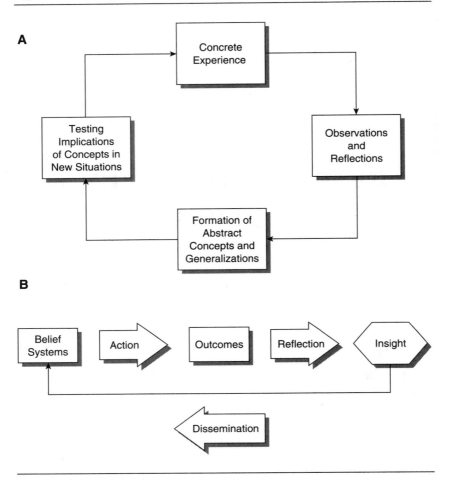

The comparison of Figure 2.1A and Figure 2.1B leads, therefore, to the conclusion that in order to learn, organizations must posses structures analogous to the central nervous system that enables their members (who can learn) to collect, analyze, disseminate, and apply information and knowledge. These structures are organizational learning mechanisms (OLMs), like after-action and postproject reviews, communities of practice, and benchmarking teams. In our approach, the study of organizational learning begins with the identification of organizational learning mechanisms and the exploration of their natures.

The concept of OLMs is useful for several reasons. First, it highlights the similarities and differences between individual and organizational learning. The two are similar inasmuch as they both involve the processing of information and knowledge (see Chapter 7 on dissemination). They are dissimilar inasmuch as both the nature of the systems with which information is processed and the nature of these processes in each one of them are different. In the individual case, information is processed by the central nervous system, which produces individual level output such as changes in mental models and individual behavior. In the organizational case, information is processed by groups of people interacting within organizational learning mechanisms, which produce organizational level output in the form of changes in shared mental models, formal procedures, and informal norms. As a corollary, while individual learning is a mental or cognitive process, organizational learning is primarily a social process.

The second contribution of OLMs is that they help to demystify organizational learning by providing a nonmetaphorical way of showing how organizations learn. Through the operations of OLMs, information and knowledge relevant to the organization's survival and prosperity are collected, analyzed, disseminated, and stored for future use. OLMs also provide a means of demonstrating how individual level learning becomes organizational level learning. Through the interactions in OLMs, individual knowledge and learning are transformed into changes in organizational routines, standard operating procedures, shared beliefs, and informal norms.

Organizational learning mechanisms have been discussed by other researchers without necessarily using this terminology (Baird et al., 1997; Carroll, 1995; Cheney, 1998; DiBella et al., 1996; Dodgson, 1993; Gulliver, 1987; Shani & Docherty, 2003; Shani & Mitki, 2000). The purpose of this chapter is to demonstrate the conceptual and practical usefulness of the concept of OLMs by presenting a basic typology that organizes every OLM we have encountered so far into one of five basic categories (Figure 2.1, Row 4). In doing so, we will illustrate typical OLMs and examples of best practice within each category. We hope to demonstrate the conceptual power of OLMs by their ability to integrate a large and fairly disparate literature within a single conceptual framework.

We also hope to illustrate the practical usefulness of the OLM concept in two ways. First, analyzing organizational learning in a particular organization can begin by identifying and characterizing the OLMs that it operates. Second, the first step in initiating organizational learning in a system is to design OLMs that are suitable for its particular circumstances. The basic typology and detailed specific examples presented in this chapter should be helpful in both respects. It may also be useful to refer back to Figure 2.1 at the beginning of each subsection to keep track of how the discussion proceeds as we move from one type of OLM to another.

❖ TYPES OF ORGANIZATIONAL LEARNING MECHANISMS

Given the wide variety of OLMs, it is useful to have a classification scheme that organizes them and highlights their essential characteristics. We propose a two-dimensional scheme for OLMs derived from two basic questions regarding the nature of learning: Who carries out the learning? When/Where does learning take place relative to the task itself? The first question regards the "agents" of learning; that is, who collects information about a particular task or problem, analyzes this information, draws conclusions, and disseminates the products of learning? Agency entails the extent that learning is carried out by the same people who perform the task. "Internal" agents of learning are those people who engage in both task performance and learning about task performance. "External" agents are people whose role is to engage and promote learning about tasks performed by others.

The second question regards the temporal and spatial relations between task performance and the act of learning. This question concerns itself with the extent to which learning about the task (collecting, analyzing, and disseminating information) takes place at the same time and place as the work itself. "Online" learning takes place in very close proximity to task performance itself; "off-line" learning takes place at a distinctly different time, and often a different place, than the work itself. These two characteristics yield four basic types of organizational learning mechanisms: online/internal agency, online/external agency, off-line/internal agency, off-line/external agency. This simple two-way classification is exhaustive: any organizational learning mechanism—and hence any type of systematic organizational learning activity—can be classified as one of these types. In the remainder of the chapter, we will discuss specific OLMs in each category based on their prominence in the literature:

- After-action reviews, postproject reviews, and communities of practice (off-line/internal OLMs)
- Online experimentation and online debriefing (online/internal OLMs)
- Postproject assessment units and scenario planning units (off-line/external OLMs)
- Coaching networks and peer assists (online/external OLMs)

The four basic OLM types formed by the two dimensions are primarily concerned with learning (knowledge creation) and to a lesser degree with knowledge dissemination. A fifth type of external organizational learning mechanism is specifically dedicated to knowledge dissemination. These mechanisms are discussed in Chapter 7 and included in Figure 2.1 only for the sake of closure.

❖ OFF-LINE/INTERNAL OLMs

After-Action Reviews (AAR) and Postproject Reviews

These OLMs, which are arguably the most thoroughly discussed in the literature, are predicated on two principles. The first principle is that organizations accumulate valuable knowledge that is directly relevant to their success in the course of their operation, so they benefit from critical reflection on past experience by their individual members, units, or the entire organization. The second principle is that reflection is best carried out by the same individuals who participated in the action or project because they are the ones responsible for its outcomes and for the implementation of lessons learned. There are potential dangers to this approach because individuals may be subject to pressures to cover up errors and shirk responsibility for failure. However, choosing this OLM assumes that the advantages outweigh the disadvantages.

After-action reviews are frequently practiced in the military following training exercises and combat operations. One best practice example of this OLM—postflight reviews in a combat squadron of the Israel Defense Force Air Force—is analyzed in detail in Chapter 8. Chapter 10 presents a general model of high-quality organizational learning that we developed by comparing successful and unsuccessful postaccident reviews in an elite combat unit of the Israel Defense Force. The U.S. Army provides another best practice example of systematic after-action reviews. Margaret Wheatley observed the U.S. Army's AARs, and her vivid description captures the difficult requirements for openness that require successful AARs to be embedded in a culture that promotes transparency, inquiry integrity, and issue orientation (see Chapters 3, 8, and 10 for further discussion of this point):

During an AAR soldiers and their commanders gather to probe in detail: "What went on . . ." "What actions occurred . . ." "What actions should have occurred . . ." Who did what . . ." Every participant in these AARs is under a microscope, being called to accountability by their colleagues for their decisions and actions during the time under review. Behaviors of the leader, individuals, and the group are all analyzed. They are equal, engaged in discovery learning. Soldiers describe these sessions as brutal, sweat inducing—and absolutely necessary for their learning. The process has become so ingrained that during the Gulf War AARs would be held spontaneously in the rear of a truck—called by anyone independent of rank. These AARs have fostered an expectation that behaviors and decisions will be reviewed, and that everyone will benefit from the learning, no matter how difficult it is to hear at the time. (Wheatley, 1994, p. 52)

Boston University's researcher Lloyd Baird and his associates identified the basic characteristics of AARs as *focused* on few critical issues; done *immediately after* the action; *inclusive* of all those who took part in the action; following a *structured* process; and *leading back to action* as soon as possible (Baird et al., 1997.) The purpose of focus is to enable participants to identify a few key factors that are important to improve performance in less than an hour and get back to action. Proximity to the event helps participants recall what happened most accurately. Finally, inclusiveness helps to gain all relevant perspectives on what happened (and, in our opinion, to maximize the understanding and commitment of all relevant parties to the implementation of their lessons learned).

Baird and his associates also proposed a simple five-step procedure for effective AARs, which we have slightly revised as follows:

1. Establish what was the intent or purpose of action.

2. Establish what happened exactly—why, how, and what were the results?—by asking participants to reconstruct what happened chronologically.

3. Determine lessons learned: What new facts emerged in the previous two steps, and what can be done on this basis to improve action next time around?

4. Identify which other parties should know the lessons learned and how they are going to be told in order to ensure their implementation and to improve the performance of other units in the organization.

5. Take action (lessons learned that do not lead to action do not matter).

Finally, Baird and his associates (1997) recommend that AAR facilitators should (a) "follow the rule of objectivity" by asking participants to report the facts of the events and to separate these facts from their interpretations; (b) "balance inquiry and advocacy" by asking participants to focus on other participants' factual reports and explanations as much as on their own explanations; (c) "climb the ladder of inference" by encouraging participants to proceed systematically from direct observation through their interpretation on the basis of past experience to final conclusions; and (d) "ready, fire, aim, aim"; that is, encourage participants to take action and complete their learning as they go, in the manner of the smart bomb that corrects its course by tracking its target as it goes.

Despite their ubiquity in the military, AARs and postproject reviews are not confined by any means to it. Microsoft, where postproject reviews are called "postmortems," provides another best practice example of how this OLM is carried out. In a high-tech environment, people's familiarity and comfort with electronic media allows the OLM to engage several layers of the organization in the process, conduct the reviews in a distributed rather than face-to-face fashion, and retain their effectiveness by holding on to norms of transparency, inquiry, integrity, and issue orientation (see Chapter 3 for a discussion of the cultural norms that generate productive learning):

Since the late 1980s, between half and two thirds of all Microsoft projects have written postmortem reports and most other projects have held postmortem discussion sessions. The postmortem documents are surprisingly candid in their self-criticism, especially because they are circulated to the highest levels of the company. . . . Groups generally take three to six months to put a postmortem document together. The documents have ranged from under 10 pages to more than 100 pages, and have tended to grow in length. . . . The most common format is to discuss what worked well in the last project, what did not work well, and what the group should do to improve in the next project. . . . The functional managers usually prepare an initial draft and then circulate this via e-mail to the team members, who send in their comments. The authors collate these and create the final draft, which then goes out to team members as well as senior executives and directors of product development, and testing. The functional groups, and sometimes an entire project, will then meet to discuss the postmortem findings. Some groups . . . have also gotten into the habit of holding postmortem meetings at every milestone to make midcourse corrections, review feature lists, and rebalance schedule. . . . The Excel team took the lead in finding solutions for relatively large projects. (Cusumano & Selby, 1995, pp. 331–332)

Communities of Practice

Communities of practice are groups whose members meet regularly to share knowledge and learn together in areas of joint concern (Lesser & Storck, 2001). Thus, communities of practice are similar to AARs and postproject reviews in that both are predicated on the assumption that organizations can benefit by sharing knowledge that accumulates "inside the heads" of their own members. Different from the latter, they are not tied to or focused on specific shared experiences but rather enable members with different levels of expertise to share information and knowledge and reflect on problems of common interest.

It is possible to get a sense of how communities of practice operate from the testimony of a member of Microsoft Excel's testing team:

> On the testing level, I speak quite frequently with the Word testing managers. . . . We have testers hooked up who are working on similar features across their groups, so they share ideas and information. We meet once a month right now for lunch for two hours—the test managers from Word, Excel and Project. We talk about "what are we facing?" "How did you solve this problem?" "I am thinking about this issue, what did you guys do?" . . . We meet monthly with all the test managers within the company, within the Worldwide Product Group. . . . We do a presentation, and we all share what our groups are doing. (Cusumano & Selby, 1995, p. 342)

Participation in a community of practice differs from both working within a team and from participation in training. Whereas communities of practice are voluntary and focus on improving professional skills, teams focus on performing job-related tasks and are assigned by the organization. And whereas training activities (workshops, conferences, and courses) typically last several days or weeks, communities of practice may last for several years. Most important, communities of practice and training differ in terms of the nature of the knowledge that their participants acquire. Courses and workshops provide explicit textbook-type knowledge that can be expressed verbally or numerically and that usually seek to apply across contexts and situations. The type of knowledge delivered by communities of practice is technically known as "tacit" and "situated."

Tacit knowledge refers to "the ability to do things without being able to explain them completely and also the inability to learn to do them from a theoretical understanding of the task" (Orr, 1990, p. 170.) For example, knowing how to talk, walk, or ride a bicycle is tacit knowledge.

It cannot be learned by reading an instruction manual but can be acquired by watching proficient performers and by receiving corrective feedback from them. *Situated knowledge* (Lave, 1991) is embedded in the particular context of practice in which it arises or applies. For example, it means not just knowing how to drive, but how to drive this or that vehicle, in this or that terrain, or for this or that purpose. Another example of situated knowledge is knowing the appropriate actions in specific situations that arise as part of fulfilling a particular job in a particular organization (see Chapter 7 for additional discussion of the differences between tacit and explicit knowledge and its importance for organizational learning).

Communities of practice are self-organized, which means that they cannot be mandated by the parent organization. What organizations can do, however, is encourage their formation and support their functioning. Specifically, organizations can provide communities with infrastructure such as official sponsors and support teams, which help them operate. Management can support them by assessing their value to the organization through nontraditional methods such as members' stories about how communities of practice contributed to learning and improvements (Orr, 1990). In addition, the parent organization can identify potential communities and help them to organize by assisting people who wish to start a community to reach prospective members.

British Petroleum, for example, uses a voluntary corporate Yellow Pages system, dubbed "Connect," as the platform for making networks visible. Connect serves as a directory to BP's knowledge workers and associated networks. Originally conceived as a way for technical staff to articulate their capabilities, BP's Connect system has grown to include the Web-based personal profiles of more than 18,000 knowledge workers and more than 250 networks. Knowledge workers use Connect to select networks they wish to join, to locate individuals with common skills and interests, and as an aid in matching people with needed skills and experience to particular project needs. Connect also provides a way for all of the networks in the corporation to be recognized and to operate transparently—in such a way that everybody can see what everybody is doing (Barrow, 2001; Prokesch, 1997).

❖ ONLINE/INTERNAL OLMs

Online/internal learning means that working and learning are fused together: Task performance becomes an organizational learning mechanism. This form of learning materializes when work is accompanied by certain practices that produce changes in organizational routines, standard operating procedures, or norms of behavior. Basically, it is the organizational level analog of "reflection-in-action," Donald Schön's term for the skill of proficient practitioners who combine action with critical reflection on that action (Schön, 1983). Reflection-in-action accounts for the artistry of professional performance in the short term and high levels of performance in the long term. Two practices of internal/online organizational learning are reported in the literature: online experimentation and online debriefing.

Online Experimentation

This form of internal/online organizational learning corresponds to "on-the-spot" experiments, Schön's term for testing hidden assumptions unearthed by reflection-in-action or for testing a new course of action generated this way. These experiments are usually carried out by acting on the assumptions or implementing the new courses of action and observing the compatibility of their outcomes with the practitioner's expectations. The organizational level analogue of on-the-spot experiments was developed in Chaparral Steel (see Chapter 11 for an in-depth analysis of online/internal learning) where responsibility for R & D and work improvement is assigned to line workers so that "many creative simulations are conducted right on the production line" by the production workers themselves (Leonard-Barton, 1992, p. 31).

Online Debriefing

Online debriefing is a form of deliberate practice that denotes the mindful way in which experts practice and constantly hone their skills. It was coined by Anders Ericsson to describe the key he and his colleagues discovered for achieving high-level performance (Ericsson, Krampe, & Tesch-Romer, 1993). Online debriefing is similar to on-the-spot experimentation in the requirement for mindfulness but differs in that it does not involve testing in any formal or informal sense. Rayner provided a vivid description of the online debriefing that emerged at Globe Metallurgical, Inc., a steel mill, when its unionized workers went on strike:

> As the union workers left the plant, about 35 salaried workers and 10 company managers stepped in to take over operation of two of the five furnaces. . . . I [the General Manager, Sims] was assigned to work on the maintenance crew, the dirtiest job in the whole

plant. I still don't know who made the assignments. . . . The strike was a time of great stress but also a time of great progress. We experimented with everything. . . . A few weeks after management took over operating the plant, output actually improved by 20%. . . . We were operating in a very fast, continuous improvement mode. Every day people would suggest ways to improve the operation of the furnaces or the additive process or the way we transported material around the plant. I kept a pocket notebook, and if I saw something I'd note it down and discuss it with the team over coffee or during meals. I filled a notebook every day. . . . As we made more changes and as we settled into the routine of running the plant, we didn't need first-line supervisors. We could produce the product more effectively if everyone just worked together cooperatively—welders, crane operators, furnace operators, forklift drivers, stokers, furnace tapers, and taper assistants. (Rayner, 1993, pp. 287–289)

The example of the emergence of online/internal learning at Globe Metallurgical highlights a conceptual problem that arises when the distinction between working and learning is blurred. It is fair to assume that people usually learn something when they work, most certainly if they engage in reflection-in-action. Does that mean that at all learning on the job is a form of organizational learning and that all work is essentially an online/internal agent OLM? We do not think so. Rather, we suggest that only reflection-in-action (e.g., online experimentation or deliberate practice) that leads to organizational or unit level changes constitute online/internal OLMs.

❖ OFF-LINE/EXTERNAL OLMs

The basic assumption that differentiates external from internal, off-line OLMs is that learning is best performed by experts. Usually, these experts are assigned to this task on a full-time basis, possess specialized analytic skills, and work in centralized units that serve as organizationwide repositories of knowledge and as knowledge dissemination centers. Three best practice OLMs that fall under this heading are the U.S. Army Center for Army Lessons Learned (CALL) (Baird et al., 1997), British Petroleum's Post-Project Assessment Unit (Gulliver, 1987), and Shell's Strategic Scenario Planning Unit (De Geus, 1988; van der Heijden, 1996).

Postproject Assessment Units

The Center for Army Lessons Learned, or CALL, was established in 1973 with a mandate to observe Army training activities and identify lessons learned for improving future training activities. In 1992–1993, this mandate was expanded to include lessons learned for future operational activities. CALL teams are assigned to observe operational activities such as the U.S. Army's peace missions in Ethiopia, Somalia, and Rwanda. Boston University researchers Baird and colleagues' (1997) description of CALL reveals that the center operates in three capacities: developing the Army's simple format of after-action reviews and training units in its implementation; observing training activities, collecting lessons learned, and transforming then into training materials such as combat scenarios; and collecting lessons learned from observation of actual operations and transforming these into training materials tailor-made for troops going into action. In short, CALL is both a collector and repository of lessons learned for the entire Army and a developer of forcewide capacity for the collection of lessons learned independently of its own activities:

> Observers from CALL were assigned to troops going into Haiti [in order to capture] lessons-learned as the troops deployed, quickly identifying critical knowledge and skills needed, and immediately imbedding them in the training program of troops to follow. An example of CALL's success is the transition of troops from the Schoenfeld Barracks in Hawaii to replace the 10th Mountain Division. Immediately upon receiving notification they would be the replacements, troops at Schoenfeld Barracks began training using 26 scenarios developed by CALL from observing the 10th Mountain Division. The 26 scenarios included situations faced by the first troops in and suggested best solutions, complete with video footage of the actual events, virtual simulations, and scripted responses. (Baird et al., 1997, p. 387)

Whereas CALL is designed to serve the entire U.S. Army with a strong focus on helping its operational units, British Petroleum's Post-Project Assessment (PPA) Unit is designed is to help the energy giant's corporate management (Gulliver, 1987.) The unit is located in the corporate headquarters of this conglomerate, which consists of 11 independent business units, each with its own board of directors and chief executive officer. The mission of the unit is to study selected projects, identify generally applicable mistakes and best practices, disseminate this knowledge, and help implement it throughout the corporation.

In 1987, the unit was staffed by a manager and four assistants, who reported directly to British Petroleum's board of directors. British Petroleum's board of directors approves the projects selected by PPA for investigation on the basis of potential interest for the entire organization. Each project is studied by a team of two or three PPA staff members from the time it was conceived through its various stages—proposal, construction, up to the first 2 years or so of operation. Six projects are appraised each year.

The duration of the appraisal of a large project is about 6 months. The team begins by spending 2 months or so studying project and corporate files (e.g., accounting, legal, or planning) to familiarize itself with the background information such as the economic climate at the time of the project's inception, its objectives and planned timetable, methods of operation, and identity of the contractors. Next, pairs of team members interview on average some 40 people involved in the project. In addition to factual material, the interviewers collect impressions regarding the psychology of the project members and managers. By piecing together the information collected from various sources, the team creates a broad integrative report regarding the important factors that contributed to the project's problems or its success. Before submitting reports to the board of directors, PPA allows the managers of the appraised project to inspect it and dispute its fairness and validity.

The fact that the PPA unit enjoys the cooperation of the appraised units and does not encounter their resistance is amazing, given that project managers have been reprimanded for problems unearthed by appraisals of their projects. This can be attributed to three factors. First, British Petroleum has gained the commitment of its managers and workers, who are genuinely interested in helping the organization correct mistakes and benefit from successes. Second, the postproject appraisals are perceived as a useful source of knowledge to which managers themselves can turn when seeking help in solving their own problems. Finally, the corporation has persuaded its members that it values learning by instituting a variety of OLMs in addition to the PPA and the communities of practice, which we reviewed earlier in this chapter.

Scenario-Planning Units

There was a time when planning, which is future oriented, was associated with forecasting rather than learning, and particularly learning from past experience. This perception has changed, thanks to the work of a group of scenario planners in another energy giant, Royal Dutch Shell. Both British Petroleum and Royal Dutch Shell attribute their long-term survival at the top of the world's oil industry to their ability to learn and adapt in a market that experiences unanticipated shortages followed by periods of glut. Within this common denominator, the two arch rivals adopted very different approaches to organizational learning. British Petroleum opted for learning from past experience, to which end it developed a wide array of OLMs such as the Post-Project Appraisal Unit, as well as a network of communities of practice supported by state-of-the-art information technologies.

In contrast, Royal Dutch Shell opted for learning by planning, a notion advanced by Arie de Geus, former head of planning for Royal Dutch Shell's group of companies (De Geus, 1988). De Geus defined institutional (organizational) learning as follows:

> The ability of a company's senior managers to absorb what is going on in the business environment and to act on that information with appropriate business moves. [This ability is achieved through a] process whereby management teams change their shared mental models of their company, their markets, and their competitors. For this reason we [Shell's department of corporate planning] think of planning as learning and of corporate planning as institutional learning. (De Geus, 1988, p. 70)

The notion of planning as learning is very different from the ordinary notion of planning, which is deciding on future courses of action. As we have already noted, planning is traditionally associated with forecasting—a plan's effectiveness is clearly contingent on accurate prediction of the future for which the plan is intended. During the 1950s and 1960s, corporations began to rely on sophisticated quantitative forecasting methodologies, which performed well in the relatively stable business environments of that period.

These methods lost their luster as the increased pace, competitiveness, and unexpected twists and turns of the following decades made prediction of the future by extrapolating from the past less and less viable. In response to this adversity, corporate planners in Shell and elsewhere replaced forecasting by *scenario building*, the principal tool for planning as learning. The purpose of scenario building is not to predict the future but to change manager's shared mental models (which De Geus calls "world views"), thereby sensitizing them to a variety of potential eventualities. This requires thorough information search and analysis by a group of specialists:

> In contrast to strategic plans which historically have been built on line and range forecasts associated with probabilities, scenarios present several starkly contrasting futures, none of which is

"right" or more likely than the next, and each of which is plausible. The theory . . . [of] scenario building is that, if executives are aware of and at least modestly prepared for several possible outcomes, they will be better prepared to adjust if the world takes an unusual turn.

[We at Shell's planning department see] our task as producing a documented view of the future business environment five or ten years ahead. Our real target [is] . . . to design scenarios so that managers would question their own model of reality and change it when necessary; so as to come up with strategic insights beyond their minds' previous reach.

But exposing and invalidating an obsolete worldview is not where scenario analysis stops. Constructing a new model is the most important job and is the responsibility of the managers themselves. The planners' job is to engage the decision makers' interest and participation in this reconstruction. We listen carefully to their needs and give them the highest quality materials in making decisions. The planners will succeed, however, only if they can securely link the new realities of the outside world—the unfolding business environment—to the managers' microcosm. Good scenarios supply this vital bridge; they must encompass both mangers' concerns and external reality. Otherwise no one will bother to cross the bridge. (Wack, 1985, pp. 80–87)

Numerous success stories (see Fahey & Randall, 1998; Schoemaker & Schuurmans, 2003) show that Shell's early success with scenario planning can be duplicated by other organizations. This is not to say that scenario planning is fail-safe, shielding users from nasty surprises. Shell itself learned this lesson the hard way twice in 1995. First, it insisted on dumping a redundant oil rig, Brent Spar, into the North Sea, only to retract 3 years later after a costly consumer boycott and occupation by a Green Peace team. Then later that year, the Nigerian poet and environmental activist Ken Saro-Wiwa and nine codefendants were hanged by the Nigerian government for protesting the destruction of native land by Shell and other oil companies, generating another international storm of protest and cries to boycott the company (Elkington & Trisoglio, 1996).

The common denominator of learning from after-action or post-project reviews and learning from projections of potential futures is twofold. First, in both cases, learners answer the same questions: How do I understand these events and what implications do they have for my own, my unit's, or my organization's future actions? Secondly, successful learning involves challenging current assumptions and beliefs about the world that drive decision making and action. This challenges results in the development of new more appropriate ways of thinking, which have been referred to as "theories of action" (Argyris & Schön, 1974) or "mental models" (Senge, 1990). The learning processes in post-project reviews and scenario planning are very similar, although one deals with reconstructed past events and the other with plausibly constructed future events.

❖ ONLINE/EXTERNAL OLMs

Online/external OLMs are designed to link organization members with persons with relevant knowledge or expertise who can help them learn or apply this knowledge online. They are exemplified by the extensive analytical staff employed by American football teams who, although not participating in the game itself (carrying out the central task), work with those who do (the players). These analysts actively observe the game and pass information and strategy to the head coach, who combines it with his own online analyses and then calls in plays to the team itself. Indeed, coaching is the quintessential online/external OLM and is often referred to as "coaching networks" or "peer assists."

Coaching Networks

"Coaching is working with others, in one-on-one relationships to help them achieve breakthroughs in knowledge, work, or thinking" (Bowerman & Collins, 1999, p. 203). These authors report that during the 1990s several Canadian organizations established coaching networks in which "individuals work with each other as coaches and performers to resolve problems that they define for themselves, and in which no immediate solution is readily visible or available" (p. 203).

Peer Assists

Talisayon (2001) described peer assists in the following way:

Horizontal face-to-face transfer of tacit knowledge across equals, . . . combining knowledge about what works or what works well, with the knowledge of the assistee about specific local conditions and needs. . . . The process works best as a horizontal (no pulling of rank) collaborative process that is based on mutual respect and associated "people skills." . . . The aim of peer assist is for the assistee to be enabled to perform an action better or to achieve a desired result. It is to bring collective knowledge to bear efficiently and effectively toward this end. . . . The peer assist process takes place during performance of an action, and learning takes place while assister and assistee perform the details of the task together. (pp. 1–2)

Coaching networks and peer assists are very similar in their method of operation and the assumption that organizations have within them useful resources of knowledge that can be called on to help members learn and tackle difficult problems. The difference between the two is that coaching networks assume that knowledge is found only in a select group of experts (who are called on to serve as coaches), whereas peer assists further assume that useful knowledge is distributed throughout the whole of the organization.

Dixon (1999) provided a detailed description of how peer assists work at British Petroleum:

The "assisters" are not corporate staff, nor are they in any hierarchical or reporting relationship to those who are asking for assistance. Rather, they are peers who, in the coming months, are themselves likely to be asking others to give them the same kind of assistance. These assisters travel to the site of the team that is requesting the assistance and work with that team on a specific issue the team is facing. They do not arrive with a "dog and pony" show; rather the focus of the day-long meeting is on the specific objectives that the team making the request has laid out. (p. 214)

Several aspects of coaching networks as exercised in British Petroleum are worth noting. First, the relationship between the person or group who does the coaching and the person or group who is being coached is determined ad hoc; that is, peer assists are predicated on the assumption that every organization member is potentially a source of valuable knowledge (a practice that is also consistent with the value of issue orientation). Secondly, peer assists will not work unless organization members will perceive coaching as equally important to doing their own work and without management's support, namely, performance evaluation and remuneration policies that are consistent with this perception.

❖ MECHANISMS, TECHNOLOGIES,
   AND CHOOSING THE "RIGHT" OLM

Having surveyed a representative sample of the variety of mechanisms that are discussed in the literature, it is important to draw a distinction between *organizational learning mechanisms* and organizational learning (and knowledge management) methodologies and technologies. *Organizational learning methodologies* include learning by joint ventures or the hiring of key personnel, training, reverse engineering, imitating inward investors, best practice transfer, and learning from customers and users. *Organizational learning technologies* include the intranet, internal yellow pages, and Lotus Notes groupware. Organizational learning methodologies and technologies are not themselves OLMs, but they are important for their smooth operation. A particular methodology or information technology (IT) qualifies as an *element* of an OLM once it is systematically employed by a team (or teams) of organizational members for the purpose of learning. Similar to organizational learning in general, OLMs are social entities, as distinct from pieces of hardware or software.

The distinction between OLMs and organizational learning methodologies and technologies is particularly important for selecting a strategy for introducing organizational learning into an organization. Here we just pointed to a relevant distinction between two strategies of knowledge strategies. The first is a *codification* strategy, where knowledge is carefully codified and stored in databases, and the second is a *personalization* strategy, in which knowledge is closely tied to the person who developed it and is shared mainly through person-to-person contacts. The same distinction has been drawn between an *IT* knowledge management track or focus, which "views knowledge as 'objects' to be documented, classified, stored, retrieved, analyzed and otherwise manipulated for useful applications," and a *people* knowledge management track or focus, which "views knowledge as primarily tacit, largely embodied in the skill of experts, embedded in processes intimately linked with people, and often difficult to codify" (Hansen, Nohria, & Tierny, 1999, p. 107).

Each of these strategies or approaches has its advantages and disadvantages. Some of these differences can be traced to the different capabilities that people and IT systems bring to organizational learning and knowledge management.

When we seek to understand knowledge, to interpret it within a broader context, to combine it with other types of information, or to synthesize various unstructured forms of knowledge, humans are the recommended tool. These are the types of knowledge tasks at which we excel, and we should be employed for these purposes. Computers and communications systems, on the other hand, are good at different types of things. For the capture, transformation, and distribution of highly structured knowledge that changes rapidly, computers are more capable than people. They are increasingly useful—though still a bit awkward—for performing these same tasks on less structured textual and visual knowledge. But it is still the case that most people don't turn to computers when they want a rich picture of what is going on in a particular knowledge domain. Given this mixture of skills, we need to construct hybrid knowledge management environments in which we use both humans and people in complementary ways (Talisayon, 2001, p. 1).

One of the disadvantages of the IT/codification approach is that it leads people to focus on organization learning technologies or practices instead of on OLMs and the other facets of organizational learning. Instituting organizational learning in a particular situation requires not merely the importation of the methodologies and technologies but setting up the mechanisms that enable members to use them as aids for reflection on behalf of the organization. Simply installing an IT system, or even starting an organizational learning or knowledge management initiative by installing one, is a misguided approach to organizational learning. Rather, organizational learning begins with setting up OLMs as well as instituting polices that foster a supportive psychological climate and cultural norms.

What guidelines are there for "choosing the right OLM for my organization?" Our own fundamental position on this subject can be summarized in terms of four principles:

1. OLMs can be both formal and informal organizational entities. Communities of practice, for example, are often informal, though managers who are cognizant of their usefulness can encourage and support their formation, as we have noted in the discussion of this OLM. The common denominator of both formal and informal OLMs is that they are enduring and, in that sense, institutionalized features of the organization.

2. There are no hard and fast rules that match OLM of type X with organizational contingency Y. Two ways to begin the design and systematic implementation of OLMs in a particular organization are the design approach and the replication approach. The design approach consists of considering the four generic types and specific best practice exemplars presented in this chapter and selecting the one—or some variant of one—that best suits the needs and circumstances of the particular organization. The replication approach consists of surveying the OLMs that are already in place in the organization and selecting those, or variants of those, that can be replicated in other units of the organization. For example, Collison and Parcell (1998) describe how

they started a knowledge management initiative in British Petroleum by "listening to what was already going on inside the organization and identifying successful examples 'and then spreading these success stories' around the company as implicit challenges to the way other businesses operated" (p. 32).

3. Because the crucial factor for productive organizational learning is engaging members' hearts and minds in the process (see Chapter 10), the "right" OLM is the one which they deem suitable for the specific circumstances, rather than the assertion of some "objective" guideline or classification scheme.

4. It is important to remember that descriptions of best practices, which abound in the literature (and are used in this chapter), pertain to mature systems that typically evolved into their present state through considerable trial and tribulation. The unique feature of organizational learning (and we think its beauty) is that "the process is the product." In other words, setting out to mindfully learn how to design and implement productive OLMs in one's own organization is already to engage in organizational learning. Thus, we wholeheartedly adopt Ralph Stayer's (1990) advice to managers who wish to transform their organizations:

> Just start. Don't wait until you have all the answers. When I set out to make these changes, I had no clear picture of how these new systems would interact with one another or with other company systems and procedures, but if I had waited until I had all the answers, I'd still be waiting. A grand plan was impossible; there were too many variables. I wasn't certain which systems to change; I just knew I had to change something in order to alter expectations and begin moving toward my goal. (pp. 74–75)

The concept of OLMs shows that "creating the learning organization" does not have to be framed as either a mystical quest or total transformation. Rather it can be seen, at heart, as a rather mundane process of supporting or creating OLMs. OLMs provide the structural basis for understanding, managing, and studying organizational learning, but they are not the entire story. The existence of OLMs does not ensure that learning will occur or that it will be productive. Therefore, the next step in demystifying organizational learning is to look at the "cultural facet," those norms that shape the thinking and behavior of organizational members interacting in the context of OLMs. The cultural facet and its impact on learning will be the subject of the next chapter.

3

The Cultural Facet

The Key to Productive Learning

Organizational learning mechanisms described in the preceding chapter can be viewed as the nonmetaphorical, directly observable social infrastructure that enables organizations to learn. The existence of organizational learning mechanisms (OLMs), however, does not guarantee that organizational learning will occur or that learning will be productive. Organizational culture has been widely recognized as having an important effect on organizational learning and knowledge management (Ford et al., 2000; McDermott & O'Dell, 2001; Schein, 1996; Tan & Heracleous, 2001). As Davenport and associates (1998) put it, "If the cultural soil isn't fertile for a knowledge project, no amount of technology, knowledge content, or good project management practice will make the effort successful" (p. 53).

AUTHORS' NOTE: The authors wish to thank Dr. Michal Razer, Boaz Warschawsky, and Estie Bar Sadeh of the New Education Environment, a program sponsored by the Youth and Education Division of the Joint Distribution Committee-Israel and the Shahar Division of the Israel Ministry of Education, for the use of their transcript data in this chapter.

Demystifying organizational learning requires clearly defining the "cultural soil" conducive to productive learning. In this chapter, we discuss five behavioral norms that we believe constitute such a culture: inquiry, transparency, integrity, issue orientation, and accountability. These values are rarely reflective of the dominant cultures of most organizations, raising the question of how learning is possible at all (Argyris & Schön, 1978, 1996; Schein, 1996). Therefore, before discussing the norms of a learning culture, we will address this question by clarifying our approach to organizational culture.

❖ CULTURAL ISLANDS OF LEARNING

Debate over the definition of *culture* has raged for several academic generations among sociologists and anthropologists (Swidler, 1986, p. 273). The management literature, however, has generally used the definition offered by Schein (1985, p. 9), who summarized culture as a pattern of basic assumptions—invented, discovered, or developed by a given group as it learns to cope with its problems of external adaptation and internal integration—that has worked well enough to be considered valid and, therefore, to be taught to new members as the correct way to perceive, think, and feel in relation to those problems.

Culture defined in this functional way is created by groups and manifests itself at three levels: deep tacit assumptions, values that often reflect a group ideal, and the products and behaviors that represent complex compromises between values and demands of the situation (Schein, 1996).

The literature on the relationship between organizational culture and organizational learning has largely focused on the ways in which organizational culture inhibits learning (e.g., De Long & Fahey, 2000; Ford et al., 2000; Schein 1996; Tan & Heracleous, 2001). Tan and Hercaleous (2001), for example, described organizational culture as a "highly conservative, self-legitimizing force that is inherently oppositional to double-loop learning" (p. 364). Schein (1996) argued that organizations are dominated by "executive" and "engineering" cultures that inhibit, or even punish, the learning-oriented tendencies of the "operational" culture. De Long and Fahey (2000) studied over 50 companies and concluded that "organizational culture is widely held to be the major barrier to creating and leveraging knowledge assets" (p. 113).

These studies all advise managers to analyze their organization's culture and try to fit it to the demands of organizational learning. However, changing organizational culture is a complex, difficult, and long-term process with only limited chances for success (Pettigrew, 1987). McDermott and O'Dell (2001) took the opposite approach, suggesting that organizations fit knowledge-sharing methods to the existing culture.

In the companies they studied, however, fit appeared to evolve naturally, so it is not clear what managers can do to make it happen. In fact, none of the studies mentioned in this chapter provides a method for achieving fit. Rather they offer sensible but abstract advice such as rewarding information sharing and encouraging open communication. Thus, the idea of fit, which appears to make good sense, also contributes to mystification.

An alternative approach defines *culture* as a "repertoire of capacities from which varying strategies of action may be constructed" (Swidler, 1986, p. 284). This approach sees organizational culture in more complex and dynamic terms than as a relatively fixed overarching set of values that shapes individual behavior. Rather, the values and norms of individuals and groups may be shaped by many cultures to which they have been exposed. As a consequence, people and groups can draw on different parts of their cultural repertoires to solve different kinds of problems (Friedman & Berthoin-Antal, 2004; Swidler, 1986).

This approach to culture helps explain how OLMs develop learning-oriented norms and values that are not necessarily characteristic of the organization as a whole (Redding & Catalanello, 1994). In other words, effective OLMs are "cultural islands of learning" within a "sea" of organizational culture and subcultures. Postflight reviews in the Israeli Air Force (see Chapter 12) provide an excellent example of a cultural island of learning. The deeply held values and norms that guide the behavior of pilots in these review processes are not characteristic of the Air Force or the Israel Defense Forces as a whole. Nonetheless, this OLM functions very effectively and has contributed enormously to knowledge creation and dissemination.

In order to be effective, an OLM must develop a cultural repertoire that facilitates learning in the context of a particular set of demands, problems, members, and constraints. The key, then, to demystifying organizational learning is to specify the features of this cultural repertoire. Given our definition of productive learning (see Chapter 1), the repertoire needs to include cultural norms that generate valid knowledge and lead people to act on this knowledge. In the multi-facet model, we suggest the following norms:

- *Inquiry*—persisting in investigation and suspending judgment until full understanding is achieved
- *Issue orientation*—sharply focusing learning on a specific issue or problem and considering the relevance of information regardless of the social standing or rank of the person giving or receiving this information
- *Transparency*—exposing one's thoughts and actions to the scrutiny of others

- *Integrity*—admitting errors in judgment or action when shown compelling evidence to that effect, even at the risk of incurring losses as a consequence
- *Accountability*—taking responsibility for learning and for the implementation of lessons learned

In order to make each of these cultural norms clearer and more easily understood, we will illustrate each one, using excerpts from discussions that took place in actual OLMs.

❖ THE NORMS OF A LEARNING CULTURE

The OLMs discussed in this chapter operate in Israeli high schools that serve a student population defined as "at risk." These schools are characterized by a high degree of academic failure as well as extreme social and behavioral problems (Friedman, 1997; Friedman, Razer, & Sykes, 2004). The OLMs, or "workshops," meet on a biweekly basis as part of a long-term intervention process intended to help the schools serve this population more effectively. They are off-line/internal agent OLMs that include the principal, the school counselor, a select group of teachers, and an outside facilitator. The goal of the workshops is to produce more effective action strategies for dealing with very difficult practice problems.

During these meetings, members orally present "cases," describing a problem or question that arose in their practice. With the help of the facilitator, group members analyze these cases and develop new strategies of action, which are then tested out in practice. The outcomes of these new action strategies are then reflected on in subsequent meetings. In this section, we will first define the cultural norms and then illustrate them with a vignette from the school workshops.

Inquiry

Inquiry reflects a determination to persist in investigation and to suspend judgment until full understanding is achieved. Davenport and associates (1998) include inquiry as an element of a "knowledge friendly culture" in which "people have a positive orientation to knowledge—employees are bright, intellectually curious, willing and free to explore, and executives who encourage their knowledge creation and use" (p. 52). Dewey (1938) provided an operational definition of inquiry as the "controlled or directed transformation of an indeterminate situation into one that is so determinate in its constituent distinctions and relations as to convert the elements of the original situation into a unified whole" (p. 108). Put more simply, the process of inquiry is like putting together a jigsaw puzzle without a picture on the cover of the box to guide us. The norm of inquiry reflects a determination to persist until the pieces of the puzzle fit together and a new, more coherent understanding of the situation is achieved.

Inquiry is illustrated in the following vignette in which the teachers were discussing the problem of students who are present in school but do not show up for class. One of the teachers insisted that her colleagues find the students and round them up. Another teacher rejected this suggestion on the grounds that it would be making a fool of himself. Rather, he insisted that "there has to be law and order around here" and that "students need to know to go to class as soon as the bell rings." The facilitator then suggested that the problem was not just a lack of law and order but that enforcing the rules is a demeaning experience.

The OLM Discussion	Commentary
Facilitator: Let's take a look at what happens in the schoolyard when you try to get the students to come to class. **Teacher B:** What happens? I call him and he shouts back at me: "Hey, who are you?"	*The facilitator initiates an inquiry process to help the group get a better understanding of the problem and what prevents the teachers from solving it. She begins by trying to get a more detailed picture of the problem situation.*
Facilitator: Why is that demeaning to you? **Teacher C:** When I tell the student to come into class, I want him to come into class and not to play games with me.	*The facilitator questions the teacher's emotional reaction, raising doubts about what seems "obvious."*
Facilitator: That's clear, but it's still not clear why you feel demeaned when the student says that to you. **Teacher B:** Because he's not "giving me the time of day!" He's undermining my authority. He has absolutely no respect and no ability to follow rules. . . .	*The facilitator persists in "questioning the obvious." She is trying to get at the reasoning underlying the teacher's reaction.*
Facilitator: Can you tell me something about this child? **Teacher C:** (Describes the student)	*The facilitator generates more information about the problem situation.*
Facilitator: You're telling me about a student with a horrendous background, a child who really needs you. If he were able to follow rules, he probably wouldn't be your student.	*The facilitator organizes the information and creates a new interpretation of the problem situation.*

Inquiry was called for in this situation because none of the participants in this OLM knew how to get the students into class. By insisting that everyone round up the students, the first teacher asked her colleagues to do something they really did not know how to do. By insisting that the students need to know how to follow rules, the second teacher advocated a solution that simply could not be implemented. Rather than argue over two solutions that were not working, the facilitator initiated an inquiry process that might lead to a new understanding of the problem situation itself.

Inquiry is clearly necessary when organizational members do not fully understand a situation, but it may be equally important when people think they understand a situation all too well. As illustrated in this vignette, inquiry often involves questioning the obvious. It constitutes an effort not to accept things at face value and not to jump to conclusions. Genuine inquiry can only take place if there is some degree of doubt, uncertainty, ambiguity, or confusion. It requires *not* knowing so as to open the way for new ways of perceiving a situation and for the formation of new ideas (Friedman & Rothman, 2001). Nevertheless, one of the challenges of inquiry is creating doubt and suspending judgment, which can be quite difficult, as will be seen in our discussion of the psychological facet (see Chapter 4).

One of the most difficult challenges in generating inquiry is framing a question that is truly puzzling to people so that they can learn something new. When organizational members tell us what they have "learned" from a particular experience, one of the questions we ask them is "Didn't you know that already?" Quite frequently the answer is "Well, yes, we knew that!" In other words, when people say they have learned something, they often mean that their experience has simply confirmed what they already know.

As illustrated in this vignette, which represents only a fragment of the entire discussion in the OLM, inquiry does not necessarily end with a concrete solution. At the very least, however, it fosters productive learning by increasing the likelihood that members of an OLM will arrive at a more complete, more accurate, and less distorted perception of the reality of a situation. In other words, it generates valid information on which to base choices about what should be done. In addition, it provides a better basis for learning from experience. Finally, by generating fuller and more nuanced views of a situation, inquiry may also lead to the discovery of new and more fruitful options for action. When people are feeling stuck, inquiry may actually be the most effective way of getting moving again.

Issue Orientation

The norm of *issue orientation* carries two different but interconnected meanings. The first meaning relates to the importance of focusing the learning on a specific issue or problem. Issue orientation is essential for organizational learning because productive learning is not a skill or activity that is carried out for its own sake. Rather it always operates on some specific organizational task or problem. As Seymour Papert (1980) states, "You can't think seriously about thinking without thinking about something" (p. 42). The importance of issue orientation is implicit in McDermott and O'Dell's (2001) finding that best practice companies regard sharing knowledge as a practical way to solve business problems and that knowledge management tools and initiatives need to be tied to a clear business purpose in order to take hold.

The following vignette illustrates issue orientation:

The OLM Discussion	Commentary
Teacher A: I want to say that I am very disappointed and angry. Yesterday a student in my class threw a chair and nothing was done about him. I expect the administration to get tougher and to punish that kind of behavior.	*Teacher A identifies an incident that occurred in her class.* *Teacher A blames the problem on the administration's weakness and expresses her negative feelings.*
Teacher B: I think that the Ministry of Education doesn't give us the "teeth" to handle these situations. The childrens' rights laws really hurt us. The most we can do is suspend a child for three days. . . . We don't have any power over these kids. . . . These new laws have taken away our authority.	*Teacher B blames the problem on the Ministry of Education and on legal constraint to their ability to punish students.*
Facilitator: You may really feel that you don't have enough power, but it's not clear to me how that is connected to the childrens' rights laws. **Teacher B:** If it weren't for laws that limit our power, then we would have more.	*The facilitator acknowledges the problem and frames it as a lack of power. Her rhetorical question casts doubt on the claim that the law is the cause of the problem.*
Facilitator: Let's not get into the issue of the law since there is no way we can repeal it. But is there a way you can give yourselves more power?	*The facilitator shifts the focus from blame to the problematic issue itself—the teachers' lack of power. She frames the problem in a way*

(Continued)

(Continued)

The OLM Discussion	Commentary
Teacher C: How?	that emphasizes the teachers' responsibility for solving the problem.
Facilitator: That's the question. What are your sources of power? Is it only possible to be strong if you are allowed to give strong punishments?	The facilitator now engages in inquiry.

One of the most commonly cited barriers to learning is a "blame and shame" culture. In this vignette, the discussion began with the teachers blaming the administration, the ministry, and the laws. If the discussion had continued in that vein, there would have been little chance of generating any productive learning. The facilitator employed issue orientation to make a shift from blaming to framing the problem itself. In this case, it meant focusing on how the teachers could strengthen their own power base without necessarily punishing the students. Issue orientation is not a strategy for avoiding disagreement and conflict but rather a way of using conflict to stimulate inquiry.

Rather than focus on individual failings or even on the nature of the relationships between people, issue orientation keeps inquiry focused on the real needs for knowledge that have to be met in order to improve organizational performance. The teachers may have been quite right about the failings of the administration and the legal constraints, but these accusations obscured the real causes of the problem and how they themselves might be able to solve it (Razer, Warschawsky, & Bar Sadeh, 2005). In this way, issue orientation sets the stage for the norm of accountability to be discussed later in this chapter (Paul, 1997).

Issue orientation also keeps OLMs from becoming support, encounter, or training groups. In their work, these teachers experienced intense emotional distress and even physical danger. The discussion among them could easily have ended with the teachers agreeing that they themselves are victims of an impossible situation. By the same token, it could have become a kind of interpersonal encounter in which teachers simply vented their feelings about the situation. However, neither emotional support nor catharsis would have generated valid information that could enable these teachers to act more effectively. Emotions were expressed and taken seriously, but inquiry went beyond expression and acceptance to look at the causes and effects of the emotions.

The first question to ask when setting up and managing an OLM ought to be "learning about *what?*" (Overmeer, 1998). When working with an organization, we help managers define the "learning questions" that will guide the creation and networking of OLMs as well as the collection of information to be used in the learning. Similarly, we work with participants of an OLM to clarify the questions that will guide their inquiry, focus their efforts, and keep them on track. Issue orientation, as expressed through clearly defined learning questions, provides the members of an OLM with criteria for monitoring their effectiveness and determining when they have completed their task.

The second meaning of issue orientation is a willingness to consider the relevance of information regardless of the social standing or rank of the person giving or receiving this information. We first recognized the importance of this value in the postflight reviews in the Israel Defense Forces Air Force (see Chapter 12). During postflight reviews, as one high-ranking officer put it, "rank does not count and everybody feels free to comment on the pilot's performance." As illustrated in Chapter 12, this statement was born out by our observations of this OLM, in which lower-ranking pilots freely questioned and criticized their superiors.

In developing the cultural facet, at first we thought of this value more generally as "egalitarianism," or the willingness to treat all organizational members as equal. On deeper analysis, however, we realized that we were not dealing with a general commitment to equality and lowering status differences. There is nothing egalitarian about the military, as well as many other organizations that engage in serious learning. In fact, rank and status are deeply held and zealously guarded values. However, postflight reviews are so effective precisely because rank and authority are not applied as criteria for determining the validity of information. In other words, issue orientation is a rejection of the logic that the boss is right just because she *is* the boss. Information is evaluated on its own terms or in terms of the trustworthiness of the source—but not in terms of status. Issue orientation maximizes the potential for generating useful information and minimizes the triggering of defenses by messages perceived as disrespectful or offensive.

Transparency

Transparency refers to the willingness to expose one's actions and thoughts to the scrutiny of others. Pagano and Pagano (2003, p. 4) have described transparency as a "what-you-see-is-what-you-get" code of conduct, which shows respect and concern both for the individual and for the common good. At the behavioral level, transparency simply means saying what you really think and feel. Transparency is critical for productive learning to the extent that peoples' observations about the organization, its environment, and each other constitute an important source of information. Without transparency, information inputs from others would be limited or flawed.

Transparency can be illustrated through the following discussion in the school's OLM. The issue discussed was how to react when students act violently, a common occurrence in this school. The specific case was an incident in which students acted aggressively toward a teacher, who unintentionally ended up on the floor wrestling with one of them.

The OLM Discussion	Commentary
Principal: Above all, it's clear to me that we cannot permit a situation in which teachers are involved in physical violence with students. The students claim that the teacher pushed them first. I don't want to be a judge, but that kind of behavior is in no way acceptable. And, in fact, I told Teacher A that in these situations he has to act differently.	*The principal makes her thinking absolutely clear, giving unequivocal feedback to the teacher and all the staff.*
Teacher B: How do you want us to respond when [students attack us]? I think that in the next violent incident, I'll just disappear from the scene. Why take a risk? Teacher A, they [attacked you] and *you* get accused of being violent towards the students. That's ridiculous! (Everyone speaking at once)	*Teacher B makes her own thinking transparent. She openly shares her negative judgment of the principal's stance. She openly shares her fears and concerns. She also describes how the principal's stance will lead her to avoid problems rather than deal with them.*
Facilitator: Teacher A, what bothers you about this case? **Teacher A:** Now? Nothing. I'm finished with it.	*The facilitator attempts to focus inquiry, which requires making Teacher A's thoughts and feelings more transparent. Teacher A refrains from revealing any more information.*
Principal: Teacher A, we gave you full backing and we didn't blame you. But it's also important to look at how you might have handled it differently.	*The principal attempts to establish norms of transparency and accountability.*
Teacher A: I understand what the other possibilities were. You've already told me. I should have ignored the particular incident and then spoken with the student later.	*Teacher A still refrains from making his deeper thoughts and feelings about this situation transparent.*

Teacher C: It happens all the time. They're stronger than we are. Even in much simpler cases, such as when a student walks out in the middle of a lesson. I let him go. What am I going to do, fight with him? I don't have the strength for that!

Teacher C reveals her way of dealing with this kind of situation, which is also avoidance. She also reveals her feelings of weakness relative to the students.

Facilitator: Then what happens?

The facilitator drives the inquiry deeper.

Teacher C: Everyone sees what happens, that there is lack of limits, and then a student lets himself [act violently with] a teacher. But it doesn't begin there. It begins with the little things that people don't do.

Teacher C continues her line of thinking and admits to the negative consequences of her avoidance strategy.

Principal: Yes, I really think that we don't really know how to set limits.

The principal is open about the inability of the school staff to set limits.

Teacher A exhibited transparency by presenting his case to the group and opening himself to inquiry from others. However, he was a newcomer to the school and to this OLM. He believed that it was sufficient to simply admit his mistake and to say that he learned his lesson. He saw no reason to go any further with the case. However, this attitude ran counter to the group's norms of transparency and accountability (discussed later).

Both the principal and Teacher C were inducting Teacher A into the norms necessary for organizational learning. The principal modeled transparency in a number of ways. First, she made her judgments and expectations of the teachers absolutely clear. At the same time, she was willing to openly admit that she, and the school staff in general, did not know how to set limits. She also insisted to Teacher A that simply admitting a mistake was not enough. Rather he needed to use this incident as a learning opportunity—for himself and for the other teachers as well. When Teacher A was unable to do this, Teacher C modeled transparency. She openly shared her difficulties in handling a similar situation, which helped focus the inquiry and keep it moving.

Transparency is challenging because it requires a relatively high degree of self-awareness and the courage to share information that could upset others or reflect badly on oneself. Information and knowledge are typically considered to be sources of organizational power to be carefully hoarded. Giving away information is often seen as working against one's own self-interest, especially if it is liable to upset others or make one look bad. Transparency requires more than openness to sharing. As Argyris and Schön (1974) illustrated, much of human behavior is almost automatic. People may be largely unaware of the thoughts and feelings driving their actions. One of the goals of inquiry is to interrupt these automatic processes and generate reflection, enabling underlying reasoning and emotions to come into consciousness and be openly discussed.

One of the problems with transparency is that it is often associated with an unrestrained "let-it-all-hang-out" or "dumping" kind of behavior. This approach to transparency was greatly encouraged by the "T-group" and "encounter group" movements that became popular in the 1960s and 1970s and which still linger in organizations today. Giving free reign to one's thoughts and feelings was often cathartic but rarely led to any significant learning or lasting change. In our work, we constantly encounter managers who refrain from transparency, and inhibit learning, because they rightfully fear what might happen if they actually said everything they think.

Transparency, however, is not a bipolar, either-or choice between withholding information or dumping one's thoughts and feelings onto someone else. In being transparent, people need to make judgments about what is relevant and necessary for *learning* and what is superfluous or gratuitously harmful. In this regard, transparency is bounded somewhat by issue orientation. Furthermore, the degree to which people reveal their actions and thoughts to the scrutiny of others depends largely on the psychological climate of an OLM (see Chapter 4).

The norm of transparency in an OLM does not develop overnight but rather emerges as group members gradually open themselves up and see what happens as a result. In order to facilitate this process, managers should first let OLM members know that they control the information they share. Rather than begin with declarations about the importance of openness and information sharing, managers can encourage OLM participants to consciously consider and choose the degree of transparency appropriate for any given situation. At the same time, managers should look for opportunities to positively reinforce transparent behaviors and to moderate reactions that work against them.

Integrity

Integrity refers to conscious, self-critical effort aimed at determining which interpretations of a situation make the most sense given the information at hand and the implications for action. In particular, it means admitting errors in judgment or action when shown compelling evidence to that effect, even if there is a risk of incurring some costs as a consequence. The norm of integrity comes into play when members of an OLM find themselves in disagreement in the learning process. Disagreements may involve the existence of a problem, the definition of the problem situation, its causes, the proper actions to be taken, or the evaluation of actions that have already been taken.

Integrity is often mentioned in discussions of leadership and organizational theory, but it is not clearly defined and understood (Parry & Proctor-Thomson, 2002). Generally, it refers to an active commitment to a set of moral principles and values (e.g., Becker, 1998) or to consistently truthful and ethical behavior (e.g., Craig & Gustavson, 1998). Our finely tuned definition of integrity focuses not on the personal attributes of individuals but on the ways in which they deal with ideas and opinions that differ from their own. As a cultural norm in an OLM, integrity means that people not only remain open to changing their minds but actually seek information and feedback that might lead them to see things differently.

The following vignette illustrates the norm of integrity in an OLM. The learning in this particular case focused on an incident in which a student, who had been suspended for 4 days, suddenly burst into the teachers' room and began cursing the school. The members of the OLM engaged in a process of inquiry into this incident and what might be learned form it. The facilitator suggested that they first get a more comprehensive picture of the incident and the student himself, who was known for regularly skipping school for days at a time. At that point the following interchange ensued:

The OLM Discussion	Commentary
Facilitator: It appears that this incident was only a small part of the story. . . . This kind is hardly in school at all. . . . Does anyone know why he doesn't show up? (Long silence)	*The facilitator inquires in order to get a fuller understanding of what is going on with this student.*
Teacher C: What kid of question is that? He doesn't come to school because he doesn't want to come to school. Who are we? The police?	*If teachers don't know why the student doesn't show up, it implies that they are not doing their jobs sufficiently. Teacher C became defensive.*
Facilitator: You are not the police, but you have to deal with him, don't you?	*The facilitator does not respond defensively. Rather she models issue orientation, keeping the focus on the problem situation.*

(Continued)

(Continued)

The OLM Discussion	Commentary
(**Teacher D** gives more details about the student's behavior, with whom he hangs around, and the lack of contact with his parents.)	
Facilitator: Explain to me why you decided to suspend this kid.	*The facilitator inquires into the reasoning behind their decision.*
Teacher A: Your questions are really unpleasant—as if we're the ones who are wrong.	*Teacher A responds defensively but openly, modeling transparency.*
Teacher B: Well, it does seem rather funny to suspend a kid for not attending school.	*Teacher B exhibits integrity. She openly admits that their reasoning might not have made sense.*
Facilitator: Maybe I don't understand, which is why I am asking. What was the reasoning behind your decision to suspend him?	*The facilitator continues to inquire into the reasoning behind the decision.*
Principal: I thought it would shake him up. Suspension is a pretty drastic step and it might wake him up.	
Facilitator: Isn't that what happened? You suspended him and he woke up. His bursting into the teachers' room was a way of saying, "Don't kick me out!" You actually achieved what you wanted? Do I understand correctly?	*The facilitator provides an alternative interpretation of the student's behavior. The behavior they saw as incorrigible is now interpreted as a sign of progress.*
Teacher B: I hadn't thought about it that way, but you are right.	*Teacher B admits error, saying that the facilitator's interpretation makes sense.*

Through the facilitator's inquiry process, the participants in the OLM began to see that their decision to suspend the student did not make much sense. The norm of integrity played an important role in keeping inquiry on track despite the growing discomfort and feelings of defensiveness. Eventually the participants were able to admit that their decision to suspend this student was not a very logical way of dealing with the problem. They were also able to accept a very different interpretation of the incident that triggered this discussion. They could see that they were wrong in considering this student incorrigible, even if it was still not clear exactly how to deal with him more effectively.

Integrity is particularly important because people can exercise considerable control over the realities they construct. In our work, we have found that people can be made aware of the implicit choices that they make in selecting and interpreting information (Friedman, 2000, 2002; Friedman & Lipshitz, 1992, 1994; Friedman et al., 2004). Once people see perception as a matter of choice, at least in part, they become aware of the multiple, reasonable interpretations of any situation. They also become more open to the possibility that the interpretations of others might be more reasonable than their own.

When organizational members face a difficult situation or conflict, we encourage them to think of what they "know" not as "facts" but as "hypotheses" to be tested through action. This strategy links the values of inquiry, transparency, and integrity. Inquiry means experiencing doubt and suspending judgment in order to understand a situation more fully and accurately. Integrity means applying the same standards of doubt and uncertainty to one's own thoughts and feelings. Transparency coupled with integrity means that feedback should always be accompanied with a question mark and a willingness to change one's own judgments or perceptions on the basis of new information or more reasonable interpretations.

Integrity is critical for enabling people and groups to overcome cognitive, emotional, and social barriers to the flow of full and accurate information. However, integrity should not be interpreted as meaning that people should never become defensive or make others defensive. Some defensiveness is inevitable, and sometimes people become defensive for good reasons, as when others are distorting or mistakenly portraying their views. As this vignette illustrates, integrity reflects an appreciation of defensiveness as an opportunity for learning rather than a threat. When regarded in this way, defensiveness serves as a stimulus to inquiry rather than as something to be overcome or avoided. Integrity, coupled with inquiry and issue orientation, enables people to deal with their own defensiveness—and that of others—by eliciting information that may reveal errors or misinterpretations.

OLMs with a norm of integrity persist in learning, despite the threats involved, because the organization's members would rather risk losing face than an opportunity to learn and improve. It is manifested in the assertion of an Israeli Air Force pilot that "the first principle in debriefing yourself and others is to be able to say honestly 'here I made an error' or 'here you made an error.'" This kind of integrity involves a high degree of self-interest. Because even slight errors can prove fatal, these pilots know that their lives depend on learning (see Chapter 6). The norm of integrity stems, at least in part, from the belief that the best "defense" is the most accurate and undistorted view of reality that can be obtained.

Accountability

Accountability is the willingness to assume responsibility for learning and for the implementation of lessons learned. Insight and understanding are necessary, but not sufficient, for productive organizational learning. Rather, members of an OLM must feel accountable for producing insights and knowledge that enable them to take new and more effective actions—and then take them.

In notes taken during our own work in a hospital (Lipshitz & Popper, 2000), we found the following quote in an interview with the head surgeon of one of its surgery wards that illustrates accountability for both learning and implementation:

> I believe that if a patient dies or fails to heal it is our [the staff's] fault. This is a healthy attitude, even if factually it may not be true. One can always rationalize that the patient was 80 years old, that his heart was weak, that his wife nagged him to death, and so on and so forth. There are an infinite number of excuses that one can find to CYA [cover your ass]. For me, this attitude is unacceptable. If the basic premise is that we are at fault, it follows that we should find out what went wrong so that next time we will avoid this error. In my opinion, that's the key to constantly learning and improving.

As this quote illustrates, there is a difference between *learning* and coming up with reasonable *explanations* based on the facts. For the head of surgery, genuine learning only occurred when insights enabled his staff to act more effectively in similar future situations.

In order to illustrate the norm of accountability in action, we return to the case of the teacher who reacted inappropriately to student violence. In that discussion, the teacher admitted that his reaction was inappropriate. However, this led one of the teachers to suggest that it was easier to turn a blind eye to the problem than deal with it. The facilitator then suggested that the principal's reaction to Teacher A might unintentionally communicate the message that it is better not to take responsibility so as to avoid making a mistake. The principal then responded:

The OLM Discussion	Commentary
Principal: I want to be clear. Everyone will get my backing, but I cannot promise that I won't criticize a teacher's work. I know that a teacher might get into trouble, which is why I asked Teacher A to bring the case to this group, so that he can learn how to respond differently next time. . . . I am not angry at you [Teacher A] and don't blame you, but I do want you to learn additional skills—and not just you. You are just an example. All of us need to learn again and again how to deal effectively with violence. I don't accept what Teacher A said about calling me or the school counselor next time. You can call me, but you also have to learn how to handle it yourself.	*The principal makes her thoughts and feelings transparent. The principal demands accountability from the teachers. She makes it clear that the teachers bear personal responsibility for implementing the learning.*
Teacher A: I accept that. You're right. So what could I have done so as not to get into trouble? (OLM members raised different ideas about what a teacher could do in such a situation. They also focused on the feelings that lead teachers to freeze up. In order to discover and test out more effective ways of acting, the group engaged in a series role plays.)	*Teacher A shows integrity.*

As this case illustrates, a shared norm of accountability is essential because it is easy to confuse insight and understanding with learning. Teacher A seemed to be quite aware of what he did wrong and what he should do differently next time. In fact, Teacher A's admission of error was also an implicit attempt to put responsibility for dealing with the problem onto him. The principal's response was extremely important because it expressed both a willingness to "back" the teachers and at the same time keep them personally accountable both for learning and for their performance in these difficult situations.

Even honest intentions to act differently may be insufficient for putting lessons learned into practice. One of the central concepts in the organizational learning literature, first noted by Argyris and Schön (1978), is the gap between the "espoused theory"—what people say or intend to do—and their "theory-in-use" that is implicit in their actions. This gap is caused, at least in part, by the fact that people's behavior is largely "automatic" or highly "skilled." People can perform complex actions—from driving a car to handling a group of violent students to making decisions—with little conscious thought about what they are doing. Highly skilled behavior is extremely useful because it enables people to react quickly and effectively in a wide variety of situations. However, this very same skill can be the source of difficulty when people want to change their deeply rooted patterns of behavior. When having to react quickly and under pressure, people often fall back on old routines, even when they know they should be doing something different.

This vignette illustrates the difference between knowing what *not* to do and knowing how to act more effectively. No one had a proven method for handling this kind of situation, which is why the principal suggested that Teacher A bring the case to the OLM. Later in the discussion, the school counselor advised the teacher not to get into a "power struggle" with the student. This advice made good sense, but it did not really help Teacher A to know what to do next time. Furthermore, the teachers realized that any new action strategy would have to include a way of dealing with their fears, which could cause them run away or freeze up. Therefore, the facilitator suggested using role playing as a way of translating this general advice into specific and, it is hoped, effective actions.

Clearly, the best way for managers to foster accountability, as well as the other learning norms, is to model it. However, organizations need to formally and informally reinforce accountability. Beer and Spector (1993) pointed both to the importance of accountability and to ways of establishing it:

> Organizations must hold managers accountable for engaging in [a process] if that process is to become an on-going, institutionalized part of the organization's life. Such accountability should occur when a significant part of a manager's performance evaluation is based on ability and willingness to undertake [this process] within her or his unit and among peers and subordinates. (p. 648)

As this quote indicates, the products of learning will become embedded in culture only if managers are held accountable for implementing them on an ongoing basis. In order for this to occur, organizations need to embed the products of learning in the broader systems of management. The role of the organization in creating conditions for accountability will be addressed more thoroughly in the chapter on the policy facet (see Chapter 5).

❖ DEMYSTIFYING CULTURE AND ORGANIZATIONAL LEARNING

Productive organizational learning is contingent on the existence of a learning culture because of the social nature of organizational learning. In organizational contexts, valid knowledge requires the cooperation of others to provide undistorted information and for the interpretation of this information from multiple perspectives. The five norms described previously—inquiry, transparency, integrity, issue orientation, and accountability—provide a comprehensive but parsimonious model for capturing the key features of such a culture. Although we have treated each value separately, we have also shown that they are highly interdependent and mutually reinforcing.

In focusing on these five norms, we are not claiming to have discovered some ultimate truth about organizational learning. There may be other important norms that we have overlooked or ways of generating productive learning with fewer norms. However, we have been guided by a pragmatic approach aimed at cutting through the mystification unintentionally created by overarching treatments of organizational culture and by vague concepts such as "fit."

The rationale for selecting these five norms is because they support understanding (the generation of valid knowledge) and action, the two necessary ingredients for productive learning. Inquiry, transparency, issue orientation, and integrity, support understanding, whereas accountability supports both understanding and action. All these norms imply a willingness to incur costs in order to achieve productive learning. Assuming that organizational learning involves tackling nontrivial, ill-defined problems in complex and dynamic situations, understanding requires inquiry, that is, dogged, persistent investigation in spite of difficulties. Inquiry, of course, is also required from the physicist who might single-handedly solve a problem in advanced quantum mechanics. In social contexts, it requires the collaboration of others and transparency, without which input from others will necessarily be limited or flawed. Transparency is risky owing to the potential exposure of one's failures and faults. The ensuing anxiety induces defensive routines, which can block inquiry or subvert its integrity:

"When [sensitive] information . . . is made public . . . [it is] apt to make participants uncomfortable. . . . They may call for closure, rarely in the name of being anxious, but rather in the name of getting on with the task" (Argyris & Schön, 1996, p. 57).

Integrity and issue orientation help people proceed with inquiry despite the threat that it involves. Integrity means that a person prefers the loss of face and other costs incurred by public exposure to the loss of an opportunity to learn and improve. Issue orientation prevents the triggering of defensive behavior by messages that are perceived as disrespectful or offensive. The benefits of issue orientation to the detection and correction of error were observed by a shop floor worker interviewed by Edmondson (1996):

> Lets' say I just did a part and got drips on it. Now, if they [those next in the production process] told me I got drips on the edge, I say "thanks"—and then I'm glad I can get these drips off. Where it used to be, when that happened, we'd just try to find something wrong that person did—we'd keep an eye out for it! It wasn't to be helpful, it was to bring them down to your level, or something like that. . . . Now we think nothing of it. We just fix it.
>
> I think that the reason we are now so open to that kind of thing is because we feel that the people who are telling us are not telling us because they want to pull us down and say we are doing a bad job but because they want us to do a good job—to do the product good—so they want to work together to make the product better. (p. 28)

Fostering an organizational culture conducive to learning is clearly much more difficult than establishing organizational learning mechanisms. Organizational members with whom we work frequently raise the follow puzzle: "We know that organizational learning will not take off without a learning culture. But how can we change the culture without organizational learning?" As Dixon (2000) has rightly noted,

> It is a kind of chicken-or-egg issue: Which comes first, the learning culture or the exchange of knowledge? Given many organizations' rather abysmal success rate at changing their culture, I would put my money on having the exchange impact the culture rather than waiting for the culture to change. (pp. 5–6)

We agree with Dixon about the improbability of creating overall cultural change as a prerequisite to organizational learning. Furthermore, we believe that the "chicken and egg" problem can be addressed by shifting the focus from the overall organizational culture to the cultural norms promoted within specific OLMs.

We have chosen to focus on behavioral norms rather than on values or underlying assumptions because behaviors are more easily observable. Another reason for focusing on behavioral norms is that they are the place to begin in changing culture and instilling values. By specifying and illustrating these norms in specific behaviors, we aim at providing a framework that can guide action. Rather than focus on the barriers to learning or on vague recommendations, these five norms provide organizations with clear targets to aim for in establishing and managing OLMs. Every OLM will manifest them in a different way and to a different degree, depending on factors such as on the nature of the learning task, the culture repertoires people bring to an OLM, and their past experience working together.

Putting these learning-oriented norms into practice also depends on the abilities and personalities of the people involved in an OLM. Some of these norms mean acquiring special skills and even a kind of artistry (Friedman & Sykes, 2001; Schön, 1987). Inquiry, for instance, involves much more than simply asking questions. Skillful inquirers see gaps, contradictions, and other openings to learning in situations that often seem quite closed to most people. Issue orientation involves skill in the process of framing and reframing problems. Transparency requires an ability to communicate one's thoughts and feelings in ways that can be clearly understood. The speed and extent to which integrity and accountability will be exercised depends on the personalities of the individuals involved.

In the foregoing vignettes, which involved the relatively early stages of an intervention process, these skills were modeled mainly by a professional facilitator. In other cases, such as the postflight reviews in the Israeli Air Force (see Chapter 10), learning-oriented norms develop naturally without outside intervention. Either way, they become embedded in the culture of effective OLMs and can be enacted by employees at all levels, as illustrated by the case of Hewlett-Packard (Chapter 11) and Chaparral Steel (Chapter 12).

Probably the best way to make learning and knowledge sharing *values* of the organization is to make sure that these behaviors actually occur and produce positive outcomes for organizational members. To the extent that participants in an OLM exhibit these behaviors, especially when it entails considerable risk and threat, learning and knowledge sharing will have been internalized as values. To the extent that OLMs are seen by organization members to be contributing to their work, the cultural norms and values are likely to be exported to the organization at large, along with the substantive knowledge.

Rather than aim at an overall transformation of organizational culture, the change strategy implied in this chapter focuses on OLMs as "cultural islands" of organizational learning. The role of management is to make sure that values of a learning culture are promoted and supported within these frameworks. Over time, these cultural islands engage in "trade" relations—sharing and disseminating knowledge among themselves and among other units in the organization. The greater the number of effective OLMs with strong learning cultures—and the more extensive the links with the organization as a whole—the more the organization is likely to learn.

4

The Psychological Basis of Productive Learning

T his chapter presents the psychological facet of organizational learning and asks, "What are the psychological conditions under which people are likely to take the risks involved in learning?" Two major arguments are presented to answer this question. The first argument is that a feeling of psychological safety is a main precondition for organizational learning. People who feel insecure tend to avoid risks, minimize their exposure, and bypass potentially confusing situations. To the extent that people experience a sense of psychological safety in the organization, they are more likely to enact the cultural norms described in the previous chapter.

The second argument is that people may be motivated to learn on an individual level out of personal self-interest but not necessarily to put themselves out for the learning of others. Thus, psychological safety will not necessarily be transformed into organizational learning unless individuals have strong positive feelings for their organizational unit. In other words, organizational commitment is a psychological precondition for learning to become organizational. This chapter takes an in-depth look at the relationship between organizational learning, psychological safety, and organizational commitment.

❖ PSYCHOLOGICAL THREAT AND PSYCHOLOGICAL SAFETY

Psychological threat and psychological safety are two sides of the same coin. Almost all modern schools of psychology address these two factors in some way. Freud (1957) made a critical distinction between the objective physical threats and psychological threats. Psychological threats are feelings that may be generated and not only linger long after the real threats have disappeared but may themselves be a reaction to fantasies or imaginary threats to the ego that have no basis in reality. To a large extent, Freud's theory of personality is based on the intricate and powerful mental and emotional defenses that people develop to manage psychological threat.

Maslow's (1970) theory of motivation posited that all human beings have a need for a safe, orderly, and stable world. This need is essentially a response to the threat of disease, accident, physical violence, and loss of livelihood. Here too, however, there is a distinction between physiological safety that deals with external threats and psychological safety that deals with internal threats (Poduska, 1992). Psychological safety is really an attempt to free oneself from anxieties about things that might happen. In fact, anything that might prevent the fulfillment of any of the needs in Maslow's hierarchy—physiological, safety, belonging, esteem, or self-actualization—can be a source of psychological threat.

B. F. Skinner (1989), one of the founding fathers of behavioral learning theories, showed that the threat of punishment is a powerful source of psychological threat. People who expect punishment do not really learn the target behavior but rather how to avoid any action that can lead to punishment. This discovery led Skinner to conclude early on that positive reinforcement substantially raises the probability that the reinforced behaviors will be repeated.

Cognitive psychology does not relate directly to psychological safety. However, it posits that human beings strive to maintain a sense of balance and rationality in their perceptions of the world—and of themselves. According to these theories, for example, people have a need to maintain a belief in a just world, in equity, and in the consistency of their own thoughts and actions. Threats to this cognitive balance lead to discomfort and drive people to regain balance or consistency. Research has shown that if they cannot achieve this balance by influencing objective reality, they will simply change their perceptions, even if it involves distorting reality (Abelson et al., 1968).

The common denominator of all of these approaches is that human behavior is strongly motivated or shaped by the need for psychological safety. In many cases, psychological safety is more the result of a person's own internalized thoughts and feelings than the physical reality around them. Finally, the ways in which people attempt to maintain a sense of psychological safety often involve distortions of reality or counterproductive behavior.

❖ ORGANIZATIONAL LEARNING AS A SOURCE OF PSYCHOLOGICAL THREAT

The issue of psychological safety is one of the key differences between learning at the individual and organizational levels. The threatening nature of organizational learning, as it transpires in organizational learning mechanisms (OLMs), stems primarily from the fact that it is fundamentally a discussion process among people (Argyris & Schön, 1978; Edmondson, 1999; Senge, 1990). Kahn (1990) defined psychological safety in the workplace as "feeling able to show and employ one's self without fear of negative consequences to self-image, status, or career" (p. 708). This definition points to a source of threat that Turnley and Bolino (2001) called "image risk." Organizational members are formally evaluated by others who enjoy higher status and have power over them. They are also evaluated, either formally or informally, by their peers and subordinates. Thus people rightly fear being seen by others or even themselves in negative ways.

Edmondson (1999, 2003), who has extensively studied the concept of psychological safety with regard to organizational learning, defined safety as a shared belief that the team is safe for interpersonal risk taking (1999, p. 354). Edmondson posited four specific risks to image that people face in the learning process. The first risk is being seen as ignorant. This risk causes people to avoid asking questions or pretend they know things they don't. The second risk is being seen as incompetent, which causes people to be afraid of experimenting or admitting mistakes. The third risk involves being seen as negative, especially when critically reflecting on the performance of others or even one's own team. This risk often stops people from delivering critical assessments, limiting the thoroughness and accuracy of reflection processes. Moreover, as Edmondson (2003) and Argyris (1991, 1996) claimed, the tendency of people to save face—both their own and that of others—inhibits sharing negative feedback. The fourth risk is being seen as disruptive. This risk leads people to avoid imposing on the time and goodwill of others by seeking feedback, information, or help.

Another source of psychological threat is the feeling of losing control over the task environment. The loss of control is related to the idea that organizational members perceive reality and act on the basis of relatively fixed mental models of the world (Senge, 1990). Mental models make the world seem familiar, predictable, and relatively stable. Mental models may change gradually over time, but they are considered to be one of the major barriers to learning that involves significant new ways of thinking and acting. For organizational learning to occur, organizational members need to collectively "unlearn" (Hedberg, 1981) their mental models, that is, discard old worldviews and behaviors to make way for new ones.

Viewed in this way, organizational learning is not a matter of adding or sharing information as if it were like simply passing books or computer diskettes. Rather, it is a bit more like a group of people trying to switch gears in an automobile with a standard transmission. First, they need to know where they are going. Second, they need to experience and recognize the need to switch gears in order to get there. Third, they need to disengage from the current gear. Once they depress the clutch, however, the vehicle is in neutral and literally *out of control*. When the learning is relatively unproblematic, organizations smoothly switch into the new gear, and the moment of being out of control passes unnoticed. However, when things go wrong, either because of a high level of uncertainty or a lack of agreement, the learning process itself can be highly threatening.

Individual learning also involves a loss of control, as is well known to anyone who has ever learned to ride a bicycle, ski, or solve differential equations. At the group or organizational level, however, the psychological threat of losing control is greatly magnified and more difficult to manage. The degree of this threat is also influenced by the nature of the problem or situation that calls for learning. When problems are relatively technical, organizational members agree that a problem exists. In addition, they agree on the problem definition, its causes, and the desired outcome of any solution. Solutions exist, but the challenge is finding the most appropriate one and applying it correctly (Schön, 1983).

When problems are highly nontechnical, or "wicked" (Rittel & Webber, 1973), just the opposite is true. There is disagreement about the very existence of a problem, its definition, causes, and desired outcomes. Known solutions do not exist and must be invented through experimentation. In addition, solutions often create new problems or are regarded by some of the parties involved as worse than the original problem itself. Wicked problems usually involve fundamental conflicts, dilemmas, and paradoxes that face the organization in its work.

Most of the problems that people in organizations face are relatively technical. They are by no means trivial and may require a great investment in learning. However, they involve less psychological threat than wicked problems because it is easier to control the task environment. As problems become less technical and increasingly wicked, feelings of losing control over the situation become stronger. Feelings of psychological threat are magnified ever further when the problem situation involves image risk. People who perceive their work environments as risky or threatening in these ways "learn" how to avoid taking risks and the feelings of threat, usually at the expense of productive learning. Furthermore, they may cling to old mental models, even if they are clearly ineffective, because they provide a *sense* of security and control.

The teachers in the schools described in Chapter 3, for example, faced what appeared to be a nearly impossible task. They faced not only a constant risk of failure but also very real threats of physical violence. The problems they faced were enormously complex, and no one had ready solutions. Under these conditions, it was natural for many teachers and administrators to retreat from the objective problem and withdraw into their own feelings of being victims. In trying to assuage their own fears and feelings of failure, they could blame the students, the parents, the system, or each other. These ways of thinking and behaving provided temporary relief from uncertainty but were counterproductive to learning. They prevented the teachers from engaging the objective reality in a way that might hold some hope for actually changing things. In addition, blaming and rejecting the students made the objective problem even worse. Finally, these ways of thinking robbed the teachers of a source of positive mutual support that might enable them to face the real challenges more effectively.

❖ DEFENSIVENESS AND DEFENSIVE ROUTINES

Psychological threat is not itself an obstacle to learning. In fact, feelings of threat can be a highly motivating force to engage in learning. The problem arises when individuals and groups invest their energies in defending themselves from the *feelings* of threat rather than in addressing its causes. Freud's concept of defense mechanisms focused on the systematic ways in which people protect themselves from anxiety and threats to the ego by distorting reality. By their very nature, these distortions prevent the free flow of valid information that is essential for productive learning. Defensiveness has come to be seen as a major obstacle to organizational learning (Argyris, 1982; Argyris & Schön, 1978). At the group and organizational level, individual defense mechanisms become mobilized as powerful social defenses (Bion, 1959; Hirschhorn, 1990) that focus energy on containing anxieties rather than addressing the issues that create these anxieties. Social defenses are at work when groups in organizations see each other as *the* problem, when they stereotype or scapegoat individuals or other units, when they undermine each other, or when they become overly dependent on or dismissive of leaders.

The members of the top executive branch of a large governmental organization with whom we worked saw the Treasury Department as a major obstacle to their effectiveness. They complained that Treasury did not recognize the real needs of the organization and continually tried to micromanage them. When they began to analyze specific examples of the conflict with Treasury, however, the executives began to realize that Treasury *did* understand their needs. The problem, however, was that the executives themselves were in a bind. They wanted to encourage initiatives from their subordinates, although they knew that there simply was not funding for every good idea. Rather than make tough decisions themselves, which involved conflicts with their subordinates, they preferred to push the problem up to Treasury, which then invited micromanagement.

Janis's (1972) well-known concept of groupthink represents a common social defense in which cohesive groups facing real dangers adopt norms aimed at maintaining a positive feeling and atmosphere. This defense mechanism prevents members from providing information that might upset the false sense of security, leading to a distorted view of reality and disastrous results. Senge (1990), for example, described the demise of a firm that was an outstanding success story for several years until its situation began to change for the worse. The situation deteriorated over a long period and was well known in the company. Nevertheless, nobody lifted a finger to stop the downward slide. The steps that were finally taken came too late and were drastic, including dismissal of the company president. The retrospective analysis of the case revealed that the department managers had seen many problems with the company and the president but said nothing. They hesitated to express their doubts for fear that they would be perceived as questioning the authority of the company president or damaging his image. The president revealed a similar behavior pattern. He was a young, new president who wanted very much not to disappoint his colleagues. Therefore, he avoided expressing doubts or lack of confidence. He admitted, in retrospect, that he had made a mistake in not asking his more experienced colleagues for advice.

Argyris (1982) coined the term *defensive routines* to describe the kinds of behavior organizational members use to avoid psychological threat and embarrassment. Defensive routines lead people to omit precisely the kind of valid information needed for learning. This tendency was

The Psychological Basis of Productive Learning   73

powerfully illustrated by Argyris and Schön (1974, 1978) when they asked managers to write personal case studies describing their performance in dealing with difficult situations using a "two-column format." In one column, they were asked to record the words or actions they took. In the other, parallel column, they were asked to record the unspoken thoughts and feelings they recalled having at the time. Managers were shocked when the consultants pointed out gaps and contradictions between their thoughts and their words. In many cases, they said just the opposite of what they really meant or so carefully camouflaged their real meaning that the listener could understand anything he wanted.

Defensive routines are responses to problems that leave the problems unsolved, or even worse. In the case of organizational learning, the problem is the gap between what one knows and what one needs to know. For example, David, the manager of a factory in an Israeli kibbutz, was faced with a problem of younger workers who threatened to quit because one of the elderly factory veterans, Kalman, kept interfering with their work, telling them how to maintain their machinery. Kalman, whose wife had recently passed away, was currently on a trip abroad, and the production manager insisted that he be transferred out of the department on his return. David said that he would not make a decision until Kalman returned, at which point the following discussion occurred:

David's Thoughts and Feelings	The Conversation
I'll start by creating a positive atmosphere. I'm sure he isn't even aware that there is a problem.	**David:** Hello, Kalman! How was your trip? Are you feeling better now?
	Kalman: It was a wonderful trip, but the truth is that I really missed work. At work I forget all of my troubles. When I go home, I'm alone again and all of the problems come back to me.
Oy! My conscience is bothering me even before I've gotten to the point. His work is his lifesaver.	**David:** I'd like to take this opportunity to hear your views about the integration of younger members into the Production Department and the state of the department in general.
	Kalman: Listen, David, I have to work hard to teach these kids.

(Continued)

(Continued)

David's Thoughts and Feelings	The Conversation
	They have no respect for machinery. It costs the kibbutz a fortune and they think maintenance is a joke.
I'll try to channel him into the issue indirectly.	**David:** Listen, Kalman. I greatly appreciate your dedication to the issue of maintaining the machinery, but we have a problem. Production is structured in such a way that each department is dependent upon the other. If your department hasn't finished its production run, it causes delays to other departments. . . . We have to be flexible, even if it means putting off maintenance.
He's sees it as his sacred mission! He doesn't understand the younger workers or the real needs of the department.	**Kalman:** It's not worth it. If a machine breaks down, then all of production stops. I worked for years in an auto shop, and I know what it means when a machine breaks down.
I'll bring the issue up directly and try to explain the problem to him.	**David:** Listen, Kalman. I've called you in to offer you a new position in the factory. Because I really value your dedication and because you've toiled over the machines for 15 years, I think the time has come for you to take on a management job. I want to offer you the management of the Raw Materials Department.
He's getting entrenched in his position. He'll never understand what industry is really about. All his ideas are based on old ways of doing things. I'll present him with my offer in a nonthreatening way, without connecting it with the problem. He doesn't realize that he is the problem.	**Kalman:** That's really nice of you, but I think that it would be a shame to leave production now. I could contribute a lot more by training the younger workers.

This excerpt illustrates a number of features of defensive routines. First, they are not necessarily motivated by bad intentions. David liked Kalman, and he wanted to solve the problem without hurting his feelings. Second, defensive routines are not the result of poor communication skills but rather the result of communication that skillfully avoids raising threatening issues, what Argyris (1996) called "skilled incompetence." David spoke in vague double messages and often said exactly the opposite of what he was thinking. Third, people are unaware of the contradiction between their thoughts and actions and of the fact that they are engaged in a defensive routine. In fact, the more this defensive routine got David into trouble, the more he saw Kalman as the problem. Finally, defensive routines may solve problems in ways that block learning. In this case, David was unsuccessful in achieving his goal, but many defensive routines are effective. However, even if David had convinced Kalman to accept the new job, neither of them would have learned anything from the problem situation. David acted as if the claims against Kalman were valid and there were no problems with maintenance. Kalman never received the information that would enable him to discover his errors or to honestly defend himself. However, if Kalman was right, David missed an opportunity to help the younger workers learn about how to maintain the machines.

❖ PSYCHOLOGICAL SAFETY AND TRUST

Genuine psychological safety enables people in organizations to deal with these threats in ways that promote rather than inhibit productive learning. It means creating conditions in which people feel comfortable taking the risks that are essential for learning because they do not expect to be punished and because they believe that doing so is likely to lead to a positive outcome. In an empirical study of 47 midsized German companies, Baer and Frese (2003) found that a climate of psychological safety in which employees are safe to speak up without being rejected or punished was positively related to innovations that led to improved business performance.

Edmondson (1999) described psychological safety in teams as a feeling of being respected and valued by other team members. It blends mutual respect, caring for each other as people, and trust. People feel that the benefits of speaking up outweigh the potential costs and that errors will not be held against them. The degree of psychological safety is determined by perceptions of relations with supervisors, relations with coworkers, and by the strength of behavioral norms (May, Gilson, & Harter, 2004; McAllister, 1995; Whitener, Brodt, Korsgaard, & Werner, 1998). The belief that supervisors and coworkers act in ways that are supportive and trustworthy produces feelings of safety at work.

Trust is clearly central to psychological safety. Although interpersonal trust alone does not necessarily produce psychological safety, trust is considered to be a critical ingredient (Edmondson, 1999; Moingeon & Edmondson, 1998). Trust has been defined as the expectation that others' future actions will be favorable to one's interests, such that one is willing to be vulnerable to those actions (Edmondson, 1999; Mayer, Davis, & Schoorman, 1995). In her research on trust, Lapidot-Raz (2002) found four dimensions of behavioral intentions that express trust: willingness to be open, willingness to cooperate, willingness to learn, and willingness to take risks.

What are the sources of trust? Studies conducted in recent years reveal that the factors and processes that build trust are not necessarily identical to those that erode trust (Kramer & Tyler, 1996). Certain behaviors that do not necessarily build trust constitute a kind of line that, when crossed, destroy trust. For example, a recent study found that support was the main factor in building trust but that a lack of integrity was the main factor in destroying it (Lapidot-Raz, 2002).

There is still a need to create additional psychological conditions that will enhance the level of trust to the extent necessary for effective organizational learning. This view maintains that trust is derived from formal and informal organizational practices and procedures that instill confidence in the rules, perceived fairness, and its supportive atmosphere (Baer & Frese, 2003). For example, the number of Japanese who say that their managers take care of them personally is 87% higher than the number of Americans who say the same thing (O'Reilly & Pfeffer, 2000). Indeed, Japanese corporations are often described as trustworthy systems in the eyes of their workers, and much of their achievement is attributable to this aspect (Fukuyama, 1990).

The story of the New United Motor Manufacturing (NUMMI) automotive plant illustrates the building of trust and its influence on the organization. In 1963, a General Motors production plant was opened in Fremont, California, to meet the growth of the automobile market on the west coast. In 1978, the plant employed 7,200 workers, but the relationship between the unionized workers and management was characterized by conflict and an atmosphere of extreme suspicion (O'Reilly & Pfeffer, 2000). Everything had to be signed and documented. Every gain by management or workers was achieved by aggressive confrontations. In the face of strikes and confrontations and with countless production problems, GM decided to close the plant down in 1982. One year later, in 1983, the factory was reopened under the joint ownership of Toyota and GM headed by a Japanese management team. In 1988, the plant won the national prize for excellence. The Fremont plant became GM's most efficient factory.

Cynics may argue that closing and reopening the plant were enough to create pressure for improvement. However, a similar plant in Van Nuys, California, was closed down and reopened in almost identical circumstances but not under Japanese management. It failed to function properly and was shut down again after a short time (Brown & Reich, 1989).

At NUMMI, the atmosphere of trust and psychological safety that was created affected fundamental processes underlying effective organizational learning. During the year after the change, 86% of the staff made improvement proposals, an average of 3.2 improvement proposals per worker, of which 81% were adopted. This is an unmistakable sign of involvement and motivation to learn and improve work processes.

The interesting and unique point in this case is that the employees were the same people who had worked in the plant in its previous incarnation. They were not offered a more generous pay package. They were still unionized. In fact, nothing in the structural sense had changed substantially. All this could not have happened without feelings of psychological safety and trust, which were most likely induced by the new approach.

What had changed, and dramatically so, was the way the people were managed. The company shifted from a policy of threats and intimidation to a policy of creating trust and psychological safety. For example, it was made clear in advance that firing would not be used as a weapon or threat. In addition, considerable effort was devoted to provide professional and psychological support through coaching, training, and development of the workers. Toyota brought 400 instructors from Japan and sent 600 employees to Japan to learn Japanese techniques. All the employees received training in which they thoroughly internalized an underlying management philosophy based on trust and respect, as well as production methods.

The value of trust for system functioning has been recognized by the Nobel Prize—winning economist Kenneth Arrow (1974):

> Trust has immense practical value. Trust is one of the most important lubricants in every social system. . . . Trust and similar values such as loyalty and integrity are examples of what economists call "external influence." In terms of merchandise, they are commodities with real practical economic value, they raise the effectiveness

of the entire system, they allow you to produce a larger quantity of goods or of anything else that is important to you, but they are not goods that can be traded in the open market in a technical or even meaningful sense. (p. 15)

In recent years, economic and organizational success has become closely associated with trust (Fukuyama, 1990). Concepts that include psychological and social elements such as "social capital" (Coleman, 1988) are now widely used and understood by economists, managers, scholars, and leaders in a wide range of industries and occupations.

The works of Banfield (1958) and Putnam (1993) empirically demonstrate the practical meaning of social capital. In studies comparing southern and northern Italy, they found that the south straggled far behind the north because it had a lower level of social capital. Banfield, who lived for a long period in Monterano in the south of Italy, observed that the people there were incapable of organizing to establish a school, a hospital, businesses, charitable institutions, or any other community activity. Consequently, the initiative for any kind of organized life in the town depended on two external and centralized sources of authority: the church and the government. Putnam, on the other hand, showed such a lack of trust did not exist in the northern areas that he investigated (Lombardy). He found civil communities whose high social capital was reflected in the flourishing of literary guilds, sports clubs, and trade unions. As expressed by Putnam, "Civil communitarianism cannot be predicted by the economic situation, but civil communitarianism predicts the nature of the economic activity more than the economic factors themselves" (Putnam, 1993, pp. 156–157).

The element of trust essential in creating social capital is relevant to organizational learning as well. Organizational learning is, as a collective phenomenon, based on social interactions. The quality of relationships and a general atmosphere of trust provide conditions in which individuals feel freer to take risks and are less apt to engage in defensive routines. This atmosphere also contributes to the willingness to deviate from familiar routines and try new things.

❖ CREATING PSYCHOLOGICAL SAFETY

Acknowledging the critical role of trust as an ingredient to psychological safety does address the fundamental problem of how to build trust. After all, the initial level and nature of trust among people is a given. If levels of trust and psychological safety are so low that there is little risk taking in the service of learning, then managers must somehow raise the level of trust. Building trust, however, is most likely a long and complex process rooted in interpersonal relations that are not within management control. If managers have to build trust as a precondition to learning, they are likely not to get there in the near future.

Another difficulty in creating psychological safety is the fact that trust can be understood very differently from the ways discussed in this chapter. In our work in schools, we have often encountered principals and teachers who praised their staff's team spirit, mutual respect, and trust in each other. However, as we began to work with the school, we discovered that the real meaning of caring, respect, and trust is that people stay out of each other's business. Teachers knew that when they closed the classroom door, no one would question what they were doing or suggest changes unless something went very wrong. The meaning of trust in these schools, and in many other organizations we have encountered, is a pact of mutual protection in which people keep threatening issues covered up and come to each other's defense when questioned or criticized. This kind of trust does produce psychological safety because people in such organizations live in a highly predictable and protected environment. However, it is a kind of psychological safety that is antithetical to learning.

For these reasons, our starting point for building psychological safety is not building trust in others or in the group. Rather our assumption is that psychological safety can be fostered, at least in part, by enhancing the ability of organizational members to construct collective views of reality that are more accurate and provide a better basis for positive action. This ability requires fostering certain insights about thinking and behaving that enable people to experience greater control and choice in threatening situations (Friedman & Lipshitz, 1992).

The first insight is that the "realities" that people experience are at least partially reality images or mental models that people construct both individually and collectively. It has long been known that selective perception causes managers to see the very same situation quite differently, leading them to attend to different information and to frame problems in different ways (Dearborn & Simon, 1958; Friedman, 2001a; Friedman & Lipshitz, 1994). The act of organizing is essentially the process of constructing a shared reality among a group of people who then impose this image on the environment through their actions (Weick, 1979).

The second insight is that people can become aware of the implicit choices that they make in selecting and interpreting information in the process of reality construction (Friedman, 2000; Friedman &

Berthoin-Antal, 2004; Friedman & Lipshitz, 1992, 1994; Friedman et al., 2004). Once people see perception as a matter of choice, at least in part, they become aware of the multiple, reasonable interpretations of any situation. They also become more open to the possibility that the interpretations of others might be more reasonable than their own. When organizational members face a difficult situation or conflict, we encourage them to think of what they know not as facts but as hypotheses to be tested through action.

The third insight is that people's own actions often reinforce, if not create, the very threats they experience as imposed on them from outside. In almost every organization with which we have worked, one of the most significant steps in creating conditions for learning was when members of an OLM discovered ways in which they unintentionally contributed to what they saw as the lack of openness of others. These moments are evident in almost every example given in this chapter so far. The implication of this insight is that the way to reduce psychological threat is not necessarily through the building of interpersonal relations but through changing one's own thinking and actions.

The fourth insight is that defensiveness is not necessarily a bad thing. The desire to defend one's self is a natural, often healthy, human response to challenges and threats. There are real threats in the world, and people need to know how to defend themselves. After all, people might be defensive for good reasons, such as when others are distorting or mistakenly portraying reality. Therefore, the advice we give is *not* "Don't get defensive!" or "Don't make others defensive!" Rather, we suggest that managers appreciate defensiveness as an opportunity for discovering errors, both their own and those of others. In his discussion with Kalman, for instance, the factory manager had taken Kalman's response as an indication that there might be more to the problem than he originally thought.

This approach to psychological safety is based on the belief that the best defense in a threatening environment is to obtain the most valid and undistorted view possible of the situation. This meaning of psychological safety is closely associated with the five norms of a learning culture (see Chapter 3): inquiry, issue orientation, transparency, integrity, and accountability. In fact, these norms and psychological safety reinforce each other in a kind of virtuous cycle. They lead people to deal with uncertainty and threat by engaging in inquiry. Transparency encourages people to freely share information as a means of protecting themselves. Issue orientation ensures that everyone's point of view will be regarded equally and that inquiry will be focused on learning rather than blaming. Integrity means that people believe that they and others will change their minds or admit error when presented with compelling evidence. Finally, accountability means that people can depend on each other to act in ways that are consistent with their insights.

❖ COMMITMENT TO THE ORGANIZATION

Although psychological safety and trust are necessary conditions, they alone do not guarantee that organizational learning will happen. Organizational learning requires cooperation, openness to others, and collective factors that go beyond personal learning. To ensure organizational learning, individuals have to possess a high level of commitment to the organization. When individuals say that they are committed to the organization, it can mean many things. It might be identification with an idea the organization represents in the eyes of its members. It might be identification with a tradition that appeals to the individual, such as in religious or cultural organizations. It might reflect a desire to be associated with a certain group of people or with individuals in the organization. It might be identification with messages inspired by leadership or the feelings of obligation and responsibility people have toward their families. Whatever the reason, people who experience these feelings are committed to a cause greater than their own short-term instrumental needs (Allen & Meyer, 1990).

In a study comparing two metal plants, the workers did exactly the same work, but one plant produced components for consumer goods and the other produced components for national security needs. It was found that the organizational commitment in the security plant was much higher than in the commercial plant. Workers there felt that they were making a more important and meaningful product. They felt they were doing something important for the country. Commitment was expressed in the level of cooperation and in the willingness to implement organizational learning processes (Vardi, Wiener, & Popper, 1989).

One of the most salient negative examples of organizational commitment is academia as it operates in most Western countries. This example stands out because the aim of universities is to create and transfer knowledge. The heart of the university is research, teaching, and learning. Nevertheless, it is well known that universities are among the more conservative institutions. Their form of organization, their teaching methods, and their hiring and promotion procedures have changed very little over hundreds of years. Only relatively recent competitive threats from corporate initiatives like Motorola University (see Chapter 9), or technological developments such as distance learning, have brought about some gradual shifts at these levels.

How can we explain this contradiction between an organization whose aims and resources are directed toward learning and knowledge creation and the inability of such an organization to learn in order to improve it own functioning? Anyone familiar with the university scene knows only too well that commitment of most academics is first of all to advancing their personal career, especially through research and publication. In many cases, the organization is simply a setting or platform for their career advancement. Committee work and academic management are usually perceived as unavoidable burdens rather than opportunities to contribute to and develop the organization. Many academics do not even know what is happening in the university because their attention is focused on knowledge generated in other places in their professional contexts.

In order for people to invest their personal resources into organizational and not just personal learning, they have to feel that the organization, or some organizational unit, is an integral part of their personal identities. They have to see their unit's achievements as their own. In demonstrating the link between organizational commitment and organizational learning, the Japanese provide most outstanding examples. A considerable part of the ongoing process of improvement in Japanese industrial organizations comes from the work of "quality groups" that were established in large numbers and aimed at improving work processes in the organization (Abegglen & Stalk, 1985). In order to give workers a forum in which to freely express their opinions, these groups meet after working hours in an open atmosphere distinct from the official atmosphere prevalent during working hours. The groups also provide professional guidance for workers to make correct use of statistical methods for analysis of problems in order to aid the process of inference from data. It is now well known that these learning activities provided key leverage for the constant improvement of Japan's industries throughout the years. However, these improvements could not have occurred if the workers had not been deeply committed to their organizations (Fukayama, 1990).

Researchers have found strong positive correlations between emotional commitment to the organization and the importance ascribed by the workers to organizational learning and to values underlying the cultural norms described in Chapter 3. Because the fundamental process in organizational learning is creating collective learning, most organizational learning occurs in teams and through "dynamic interaction" (Nonaka & Takeuchi, 1995) rooted in dialogue and communication. These interactions facilitate the development of social relationships that are the basis for knowledge sharing and knowledge creation. In order to maintain such processes of sharing information, people must feel that they are committed to entities that are beyond their immediate personal interest.

Each component discussed in this chapter—psychological safety, trust, and organizational commitment—is important for learning to occur in organizations. The lack of one component cannot be compensated for by another. The extent and strength of all these components determines the existence of the psychological conditions necessary for transforming individual learning into organizational learning.

5

The Context of Organizational Learning

The structural, cultural, psychological, and leadership and policy facets of the multi-facet model provide a basic set of tools for analyzing and instituting organizational learning. Managers can promote productive learning by instituting organizational learning mechanisms (OLMs), by nurturing the five norms of a learning culture, and by enhancing organizational commitment and psychological safety among their subordinates. Such actions, however, do not take place in a vacuum. Rather they are conditioned by the context in which they occur. The context includes characteristics of the organization and its environment. It determines to a great extent the likelihood that organizational learning will take root and be productive. Contextual factors are largely beyond management's control. Nevertheless, recognizing them is useful for assessing the likelihood that organizational learning efforts will succeed and for taking appropriate actions to increase their likelihood of success.

The specific contexts of different organizations vary infinitely. In this chapter, we focus on six contextual factors that research has shown to influence organizational learning. These factors include environmental uncertainty, task uncertainty, error criticality, task structure, proximity to the core mission of the organization, and the organization's structure.

❖ ENVIRONMENTAL UNCERTAINTY

We define uncertainty as a sense of doubt that blocks or delays action (Lipshitz & Strauss, 1997). Although uncertainty is affected by objective conditions such as the rate at which environmental conditions change or the novelty and complexity of the task to be performed, we define uncertainty as a subjective feeling. Different persons, experts as compared to novices for example, may experience different degrees of uncertainty in the same situation. People's actions, including the proclivity to learn, are influenced by perceived uncertainty rather than the uncertainty that can be measured by objective indicators.

The claim that uncertainty affects learning is based on the observation that people have little motivation to learn unless they experience doubt: Why spend time and effort on gathering and analyzing information when operations run smoothly or when problems that arise can be solved effectively by well-rehearsed solutions? Following Dewey (1933), who posited that reflection (and hence learning) begins with doubt, Srikantia and Pasmore (1996) suggest that organizational learning begins with individual doubt and ends with "collective consensus."

> Learning must begin with individuals who are willing to express doubt, and to examine alternative interpretations of reality. Once they have done so, for learning to become organizational in nature, these same individuals must be able to communicate their interpretations to others so that they may be adopted for consideration by others. (p. 44)

Organizations are open systems that import raw materials and other resources from the environment to which they also export their products or services. The ability to do this may be affected by environmental trends such as market changes, new technologies, economic shifts, political upheavals, and social transformations. Consequently, it is customary to attribute the objective uncertainty in which they operate to three attributes of the environment: its complexity (the number of elements that must be taken into account in determining the organization's strategy and the extent to which their behavior is well understood); the rate in which these elements change (for example, the rate at which new products are introduced into the market); and the intensity of the competition the organization faces.

The relationship between environmental uncertainty and organizational learning is widely accepted by theoreticians and researchers (Dodgson, 1993; Ellis & Shpielberg, 2003; Fiol & Lyles, 1985; Garvin, 1993; Goh, 1998). This is because organizations must provide products or services that are valuable to some people at a price and quality that are superior to the competition. If the environment changes (e.g., people change their tastes or the competition acquires a new technology), the organization must adapt, which means that it must learn. That is why there are relatively few examples of organizational learning in the public sector (in which organizations rarely face competition), and many examples of organizational learning in high-tech organizations, which operate in dynamic and competitive environments.

The perception of environmental uncertainty and potential strategic threats is a particularly important stimulus for learning (Stopford, 2001). For most managers, however, planning has been the traditional response to uncertainty. Many planning approaches aim at reducing uncertainty through forecasting and risk analysis. These approaches assume that future trends can be predicted, usually on the basis of past behavior, and that solutions to foreseeable problems are already at hand. Paradoxically, these approaches are unlikely to stimulate learning precisely because they reduce perceived uncertainty. Management is unlikely to invest time and resources in learning if it does not experience uncertainty about how the environment is going to behave and about how potential changes will affect their organizations. An investment in learning, on the other hand, is likely to happen when management realizes that past experience is not necessarily a good predictor of the future and that the future will demand novel responses.

Scenario planning was developed by the planning department of Royal Dutch Shell (an external OLM) specifically to align senior managers' perceived environmental uncertainty with actual conditions (Kleiner, 1996; see also Chapter 2). During the 1960s, planning departments in large corporations, including Royal Dutch Shell, used sophisticated forecasting techniques to predict the future price of oil and to guide their investments in exploration, production, and transportation. These methods worked well as long as the environment was relatively stable: Demand for oil rose steadily at roughly predictable rates, and the oil producing countries collaborated with the large oil corporations to meet occasional fluctuations that did occur in demand.

Toward the end of that decade, it became evident that this stability was about to change. Continued economic growth in the Western world and the Far East would drive demand beyond the capacity of known reserves outside the Middle East to meet the increases in demand. In addition, Middle East oil producing countries would use the situation to increase their revenues by hiking the price of their oil to undreamed of levels. By 1972 and the advent of OPEC, this change was clear to the managing directors of Royal Dutch Shell. Nevertheless, they did not make the required changes in the corporation's policies. Ted Newland and Pierre Wack of the Royal Dutch Shell Group Planning Department conjectured that the directors could not comprehend—and adapt to—the new environment. To change their basic worldview, which Wack called "microcosms," the future implications of the new environment had to be made tangible to them. To this end, Newland and Wack decided to adapt the scenario's method originally developed by futurologist Hermann Kahn as a tool for "thinking about the unthinkable."

Wack and some 20 members of the Group Planning Department who specialized in this method developed six alternative scenarios. Each scenario represented a version of how the future might unfold based on the trends in oil demand and changed political realities in the Middle East that were already in place. Five of the scenarios did not require a change in the directors' current worldviews: They told five stories in which the *certain* impending gaps between oil demand and oil supply would be met by different countermeasures such as controlling demand by increased oil prices, voluntary energy savings by the public, and effective collaboration among the governments of consumer states. As he presented these scenarios to groups of managers, Wack showed them to be "miracle stories" owing to the implausible assumptions on which they were based. For example, the "high-supply" scenario that some oil executives particularly favored suggested that increased demand would be met by aggressive exploration and development of new oil fields. This scenario, however, was based on a number of assumptions. First, companies would have to find and develop new fields at incredible speed in areas that were either unprepared for or closed to exploration. Second, OPEC would have to collaborate in meeting new demands with no financial incentive for acting this way. Finally, no sharp increase in demand could occur because of a war or an extra cold winter.

As they worked through the implausibility of the assumptions underlying all five scenarios, Wack's audience realized that their worldviews had to change to accommodate the sixth scenario: an energy crisis with a fivefold jump in the price of oil. They also became acutely aware that their current policies were not designed to respond to such a scenario. As the scenario group continued to disseminate this message throughout Royal Dutch Shell, it slowly began to take effect. Refineries were designed to handle different kinds of crude oil or to be converted to chemical plants. When the crisis following the 1973 war between Israel and Egypt and Syria came, Royal Dutch Shell was better prepared and reacted more swiftly than the other large oil companies and the scenario method was introduced in numerous corporations in addition to Royal Dutch Shell.

In conclusion, scenario planning represents a form of organizational learning aimed at generating knowledge about the potential behavior of an organization's environment in the future. As a result of its experience in the 1970s, Shell made the use of scenarios a permanent part of its planning processes. The group planning unit at Shell represents an off-line/external agent OLM because most of the research and scenario development is carried out by experts especially assigned to this function. However, scenarios can also be developed by the same managers who make and execute strategy. Indeed, other organizations have adopted the scenario method and applied it through various mechanisms for the purpose of organizational learning.

❖ TASK UNCERTAINTY

The complexity and novelty of the tasks that the organization's members have to perform constitute a second major source of uncertainty that may promote organizational learning. One example of this relationship is reported in the memoirs of the general who commanded Israel Defense Force units in the Gaza Strip during the Palestinian uprising there in the 1970s. When he realized that the Palestinians presented him "with a new kind of war with which he and his subordinates were not familiar," the commander initiated a vigorous process of organizational learning in which "the commanders were open to any useful idea or suggestion. . . . Every operation was thoroughly debriefed soon after its conclusion and the lessons learned were disseminated and quickly implemented by other units" (Maimon, 1993, p. 97).

The development of the IBM 360 family of computers provides an example of the effects of environmental and task uncertainties on organizational learning (Quinn, 1988a). In the early 1960s, IBM dominated the computer industry. Nevertheless, its top leadership felt that the company had to undergo a major change in direction in order to stay ahead when the industry would move, as was expected, into a new generation of computers. The change was fraught with task uncertainty because its exact nature was initially unknown and because it required the use of new technologies with which there was no prior experience, either in IBM or in other organizations and research institutions.

The search, and later on implementation, of IBM's new direction was managed by Vincent Learson, the head of the company's computer development and production operations. He and IBM's CEO Watson began by conducting a series of conversations with their top management team to identify a new strategy. When these conversations led nowhere, Learson appointed a committee composed of representatives from the various divisions and functions of the company to develop policy guidelines for determining the new direction. Based on an analysis of the company's current state and the current and future state of the market, the committee proposed a basic concept for a totally new line of computers, the 360 system, which was to replace all of IBM's existing lines of computers. This ad hoc task force constituted a temporary OLM that used IBM's available expertise to analyze the company and its environment in order to produce a new concept, not just for the 360 but for the company as a whole.

IBM emerged from the 360 development process as a very different company from the company that went into it. Learson convened other committees to decide on the 360 operating system and on the use of a new hybrid integrated-circuit technology. These committees can also be regarded as temporary OLMs because they relied very heavily on the experience that was garnered in previous development projects of large systems that failed.

There are obvious differences between the Gaza Strip and IBM examples. Nevertheless, they suggest a common strategy for dealing with the uncertainty that is produced by complex, ill-defined, and novel tasks: Divide the task into discrete subtasks and design OLMs to develop the knowledge that is required to perform them effectively, either from relevant experience that exists already in the organization or from experience that is produced by tackling the subtasks experimentally.

Error criticality refers to the severity of the costs of potential error. The more severe the consequences of error, the more effort will be invested in learning how to prevent it. This proposition is based on empirical findings that people are more likely to engage in learning after failure. Two social psychologists (Wong & Wiener, 1981) asked people to describe situations in which they ask themselves why events happened the way they did. The researchers found that failure rather than success induced a stronger tendency to look for causal explanations

(Wong & Weiner, 1981). Another study asked managers to rate the need for initiating a learning process when presented with vignettes that had either a positive or a negative outcome. These managers were also asked what kind of learning should take place for each vignette. The findings showed that the more negative the outcome, the greater the likelihood of a recommendation for learning *and* the more extensive the follow-up measures to ensure implementation of recommendations.

These empirical findings are consistent with the fact that many examples of organizational learning come from organizations that face potentially catastrophic, life-threatening errors. Such critical-error organizations include nuclear power plants (Carrol, 1995; Carrol, Rudolph, & Hatakenaka, 2003; DiBella et al., 1996; Weick, Sutcliffe, & Obstfeld, 1999), hospitals (Carrol & Edmondson, 2002; Popper & Lipshitz, 1998; Tucker & Edmondson, 2003), and airplane combat units (Ron, Lipshitz, & Popper, in press). A study that tested the relationship between error criticality and organizational learning (Ellis, Caridi, Lipshitz, & Popper, 1999) found that persons working in organizations with relatively high costs of error (air traffic controllers and managers in high-tech organizations) produced higher mean scores on a questionnaire measuring the values of integrity, transparency, accountability, and issue orientation than did persons working in organizations with relatively low costs of error (teachers, psychiatrists and physicians in a mental hospital).

The aftermath of the notorious *Exxon Valdez* accident provides a good illustration of the relationship between error criticality and organizational learning. In 1989, the tanker *Exxon Valdez* collided with a reef and spilled some 11 million gallons of oil into the Prince William Sound in Alaska. The immense environmental damage prompted the oil corporations that operated in the sound and the various state and federal authorities that regulate their operations to cooperate in the institution of two OLMs in an effort to prevent future disasters. The first OLM was the Regional Council Advisory Council (RCAC), which oversees the environmental management of the marine oil trade in the sound. The second OLM is the Best Available Technology review (BAT), which compares the safeguards employed in the sound to those employed in similar systems anywhere in the world. The RCAC initiates, funds, and organizes studies and symposia to develop proposals for enhancing safety in the sound and implements some of the proposals in collaboration with various public and business interests. For example, RCAC conducted a computer simulation and experimental study of the tanker escort and navigation system in the sound in collaboration with the oil industry, the Alaska Department of Environmental Conservation, and the Coast Guard. Based on the results of this study, RCAC proposed that the oil industry use new types of tractor tugs. The industry contested the necessity of these changes but acquiesced after a second collaborative risk assessment study and a BAT review demonstrated the superiority of the new tugs (Busby, 1999).

❖ TASK STRUCTURE

In addition to the complexity and novelty of tasks, the way in which the activities that are required for their performance are organized affects organizational learning in two ways. It determines the ease with which people can obtain valid feedback on their work, and it influences their motivation to cooperate and share information with others. The feasibility of valid feedback is determined by the extent to which the task is standardized and the delay that occurs between its completion and the reception of feedback. Adler and Cole (1993) compared the work systems in two auto plants: Volvo's plant in Uddevalla, Sweden, and Toyota-GM plant in Fremont, California. Workers in both plants were encouraged to suggest improvements and received feedback on their task performance at the conclusion of each work cycle. At New United Motor Manufacturing (NUMMI, the Toyota-GM plant), the work cycle was about 60 seconds, and work was rigidly standardized. At Uddevalla, the cycle was approximately 2 hours long, and workers were given freedom to introduce changes in how they perform the tasks. The results showed that the shorter cycle facilitated the detection of problems and that standardization facilitated both the diagnoses of their causes and the diffusion of changes among different production units.

Tasks that are well bounded in time or divided into clear phases also facilitate learning. The completion of each phase and of the complete task presents a natural unit for conducting after-action or midcourse reviews, and the availability of specific objectives facilitates the determination of success or failure. This is exemplified by Boeing, where an OLM called "project homework" was devised to capture lessons learned on the development of its 707, 727, 737, and 747 models to speed up the development of the 757 and 767 models (Barrow, 2001).

Task structure can also influence the motivation to share information through the degree of interdependence that it imposes on the persons who perform it. One of the pilots in our study of postflight reviews (Chapter 8) testified that he and his fellow pilots were intensely competitive and strove to become "Number 1" in everything they did. When asked why this intense competitiveness did not prevent pilots from disclosing their errors in public and helping others to improve, the pilot's answer was that "since we fly in duos and quartets, my chances of survival depend on their skills as much as on my own." This somewhat dramatic example, which illustrates the influence of error criticality as well as of task structure, confirms the simple rule that people will cooperate out of self-interest.

❖ PROXIMITY TO THE ORGANIZATION'S CORE MISSION

An organization's core mission is what the organization is designed to deliver. Some tasks that organization members perform are directly related to its core mission; others are in support roles. Tasks that are related to the organization's core mission are important for its survival. Naturally, they receive more attention and resources than other tasks. This means that the organization feels more compelled to improve on these tasks through learning and that OLMs that are related to the core task are more likely to receive necessary resources. In a study that we conducted in a university-affiliated hospital, we identified 14 different OLMs. All were associated with the hospital's core mission, the delivery of treatment and training of interns and students (Lipshitz & Popper, 2000). The influence of proximity to core mission can be tied to error criticality, as errors related to core mission are likely to be more costly to the organization than errors in the performance of noncore missions.

One way to ensure that learning receives attention and resources is to turn it into a core task of the organization. This is what happened at Chaparral Steel (Chapter 12), which set the dual mission for its production workers of producing cutting-edge products and continuously improving the production process. As a result, Chaparral Steel workers instituted online OLMs, such as online experimentation that produced continuous improvements, helping it to compete successfully with steel mills in developing countries that benefit from much lower labor costs than those possible in the United States.

❖ ORGANIZATIONAL STRUCTURE

Organizational learning requires the free flow of information and knowledge throughout the organization. To the extent that the organization's structure—the division of labor among different units and persons—erects barriers to this flow, it inhibits both learning and the dissemination of information and knowledge (Englehardt & Simmons, 2002; Miller & Mintzberg, 1983; Tan & Heracleous, 2001). Two other structural factors that inhibit organizational learning in the same way are size and geographical separation. Division of labor, size, and geographical separation inhibit organizational learning in three ways. First, they constrain the amount of time that people in different units spend together, particularly in large organizations, depriving them of opportunities to exchange information. Second, different units have different goals, different responsibilities, and different specializations. Consequently, people in different units have different learning needs and develop different kinds of knowledge. Thus, knowledge relevant to people in one unit may be irrelevant to people in other units. (Note, however, that diversity is, at the same time, a positive source of knowledge, albeit one that is not easy to harness, owing to the differences in experience, language, assumptions, and interests.) Third, people develop loyalties to their particular units that may lower their motivation to share information with people in different units, particularly when the two are competing for the same scarce resources.

Two methods can be used to counteract the difficulties that division of labor, size, and geographical separation put in the way of organizational learning. The first method is creating centralized OLMs that serve as hubs in which knowledge that is accumulated in different parts of the organization is collected, stored, and disseminated back to operations that it can help. This method is illustrated by the U.S. Army Center for Lessons Learned (CALL; Baird et al., 1997) and BP's Post-Project Assessment Unit (Gulliver, 1987). As discussed in Chapter 2, CALL sends teams of observers to study and conduct after-action reviews of major training exercises and actual combat operations (e.g., the invasion of Granada) and generates lessons learned that can be of interest to other elements of the Army. These observations and lessons are used to develop training exercises that prepare units for similar future operations and that are made available to the Army at large through the Internet. BP's Post-Project Appraisal Unit performs a similar function, evaluating a selected number of projects of general interest each year. Although the unit works primarily for the corporation's head office, the lessons that it accumulates are also available on request to managers who think that they can be helped by them.

The second method for counteracting size and geographic dispersion is developing a thick network of OLMs that facilitates the direct transfer of knowledge among different units. BP Global also employs this method. Since 1995, the corporation, which literally spans the globe, has invested a great deal of resources into improving its ability to transfer knowledge among its diverse units. John Brown, the CEO, championed this effort because he held two assumptions. The first was that because of the size of its operations, BP has more experience to draw on than smaller companies. The second assumption was that disseminating this experience effectively should be a key factor for its success in the increasingly competitive energy environment. The number of OLMs and dissemination mechanisms that BP employs, particularly in its project-based exploration and production business unit, is truly impressive and includes many of the OLMs that are discussed in Chapter 2 (survey of OLMs) and Chapter 7 (dissemination) (Barrow, 2001; Berzins, Podolny, & Roberts, 1998; Gulliver, 1987; Prokesch, 1997).

The OLMs developed by BP Amoco include the following:

- *Communities of practice.* Different business units that are engaged in similar tasks (onshore oil production) are formally integrated into networks (called peer groups) that cut across BP's business unit divisional structure. Peer groups collaborate in managing the capital allocated to the activities that form their common denominator and share know-how relevant to their common technological and strategic issues. Leaders of business units that belong to the same peer group function as communities of practice when they meet regularly to manage their capital program, review performance, and share knowledge. Other BP workers are also members of communities of practice (see the Connect system below).

- *Peer assists.* In addition, their subordinates spend between 3% to and 10% of their time working in a different business unit on problems about which they have acquired expertise. Peer groups and peer assists are lateral communication channels for sharing know-how directly and more efficiently than the alternative method of disseminating knowledge through corporate functional units.

- *Computerized knowledge dissemination technologies.* BP operates a Web-based corporate yellow pages system called Connect through which people publicize their personal profiles of skills and experience. The system serves to connect people who wish to form or join communities of practice. It allows every manager or member to find the knowledge or expertise she or he requires within the organization. A computer-supported visualization technology called HIVE (highly immersive visualization environment) allows teams of experts to examine physical systems (e.g., geological structures) from thousands of miles away, from different angles, and at different resolution levels. This enables highly specialized experts to advise a team in the field in real time without having to leave their offices. In one celebrated example, HIVE allowed a team of geologists, geophysicists, reservoir engineers, pipeline engineers, and drilling and facilities engineers to save more than 10% of the development cost of a new offshore field in the Gulf of Mexico.

Another example of using computerized knowledge dissemination technology to circumvent structural barriers to knowledge sharing is the K'Netix system developed for Buckman Labs. This system includes seven Web-based forums in which Buckman employees can post questions and receive answers from other Buckman employees who happen to have the relevant knowledge. According to Carol Willett of Applied Knowledge Group, Inc., K'Netix essentially flattened Buckman Lab's rigid hierarchical structure that impeded knowledge sharing prior to K'Nerix's installation (Willett, n.d.).

In conclusion, four of the contextual factors that we discuss in this chapter—environmental uncertainty, task uncertainty, error criticality, and proximity to the core task of the organization—drive organizational learning. Task structure and organizational structure can either drive or restrain organizational learning, depending on their particular configuration. The four driving factors do not ensure the success of organizational learning; they just increase its probability of success. The two restraining factors do not preclude its feasibility; they just make success more difficult and require that the design of the OLMs overcomes the difficulties that they create.

Although the six factors that we discuss present a very partial list of the diverse factors that influence knowledge dissemination, they present a useful set with which to begin to analyze the particular context in which organizational learning is to be initiated, or improved. Our aim was not to develop an exhaustive model but a conceptual framework that strikes a balance between exhaustiveness and parsimony—a useful tool in practice.

6

Organizational Learning and Managerial Channels of Influence

L eadership scholars agree that leadership is distinct from management (Kotter, 1988, 1990; Mintzberg, 1973; Zaleznik, 1992). At the same time, managers at every level of the organization have leadership functions (Mintzberg, 1973). The key terms that describe management functions are *allocating resources* and *solving problems* (Mintzberg, 1973). The key terms that describe leadership functions are *inspiring, building trust and commitment* (Kotter & Heskett, 1992), *creating esprit de corps* (Kotter, 1988), and *forming a vision* (Zaleznik, 1992). Thus, managers exercise leadership when they influence the hearts and minds of their subordinates.

Promoting productive learning is part of managers' leadership function because it requires persuading subordinates—literally influencing their hearts and minds—that learning and the implementation of lessons learned is essential for their own performance and well-being as well as the performance and well-being of the organization. In this chapter, we describe how managers can exercise their leadership to promote organization learning by employing the channels of influence, through which they affect the attention, goals, and priorities of their subordinates. These channels include the enactment of both learning-oriented policies and behaviors that support them. Policies that support learning express a tolerance for failure and the organization's commitment to learning and knowledge sharing. These policies, together with the appropriate leadership behaviors, promote both the psychological conditions (see Chapter 4) and the cultural norms conducive to learning.

Several scholars emphasized the role of leaders in organizational learning and knowledge management (Crossan & Hulland, 2002; Vera & Crossan, 2004). For example, Senge (1990) asserted that the learning organization "will remain a distant vision until leadership capabilities they demand are developed" (p. 22). In their study of knowledge management at Buckham Laboratories, Pan and Scarbrough (1999) concluded that management's leadership is crucial for the success of any knowledge management program. In addition, there is evidence that leadership style influences the incidence or quality of organizational learning (Amitay, Popper, & Lipshitz, 2005; Chew, Bresnaham, & Clark, 1986; Johnson, 2002; Levinson, 1998; Politis, 2001). For example, Amitay et al. (2005) studied the relationship between leadership style and organizational learning in 44 community health clinics. They found that transformational leadership, which broadens and elevates the interests and aspirations of employees, was associated with more intensive organizational learning activity and with a stronger learning-facilitative culture than transactional leadership, which operates within existing employee interests and aspirations. In addition, case descriptions of learning organizations emphasize the role of their visionary CEO, for example, Chaparral Steel's Gordon Forward (Chapter 10) and Johnsonville Foods' Ralph Stayer (Chapter 9).

The association of successful exemplars of organizational learning with the visionary CEOs contributes to the mystification of organizational learning by implying that success requires unusual leadership at the top of the organization. The fact that we ourselves have used many such figures in our examples and illustrations reflects the tendency of the literature to focus on heroic leadership. Our own position is quite different. Without downplaying the achievements of the Gordon Forwards and Ralph Stayers in the world, we believe that managers at all levels in the organization can take the lead in instituting learning in their areas of responsibility. The preceding three chapters on the culture, psychological climate, and context of organizational learning make it clear that leadership is not necessarily the most important factor in determining the feasibility and quality of organizational learning in every circumstance. Leadership is not required for high-quality organizational learning in the combat squadrons of the Israel Defense Force Air Force. In these units, which are responsible for the Air Force's core task, the costs of potential error are high, a learning culture is well established, and the nature and design of the task make the latter particularly amenable to inquiry through postflight reviews (see Chapter 12). Leadership is crucial for organizational learning when contextual conditions are not favorable for it. Bad leadership, on the other hand, can subvert learning, even under favorable contextual conditions (see Chapter 13).

❖ INSTITUTING OLMs

During his graduate studies, one of the authors was assigned to interview the manager of a high-tech plant. Near the manager's office, there was an open space with hot and cold beverage and sandwich vending machines. Throughout the 2-hour interview, employees could be seen standing and chatting around the machines. When the author wondered if it would not be better to minimize the time that employees spent away from work by serving them food and drinks in their offices, the manager had this response:

> One of the wisest things that I have done since my appointment was to install these drink and snack machines. Before that our engineers sat in their cubicles staring at their computer screens all day long. They barely spoke to one another and certainly did not know what their colleagues were doing. Now that they talk to one another, you will never guess how many ideas, collaborations, and integrative projects were hatched in the seemingly idle conversations around those vending machines.

The manager in this episode unwittingly created an informal organizational learning mechanism (OLMs), thereby allowing his engineers to exchange useful information—and learn. Pillsbury Corporation provides an example of a deliberate creation of an OLM by a manager. Having lagged behind its archrival General Mills in the 1970s, Pillsbury forged ahead in the 1980s (Quinn, 1988). The turning point in Pillsbury's history began when new CEO William Spoor created a temporary OLM (a project-like OLM, usually associated with change efforts; see Chapter 8) consisting of a team of managers who met regularly for a year to diagnose the causes of Pillsbury's lukewarm performance. The team developed a strategy that turned Pillsbury around and allowed it to surge ahead of General Mills.

In the next section, we turn to the discussion how managers can encourage learning by instituting policies of tolerance for failure and commitment to the workforce.

❖ TOLERANCE FOR FAILURE

Experimenting with new methods, practices, and skills is likely to produce failure. Failure may discourage further experimentation because it reduces psychological safety, either because negative feelings are aroused or because the person who experimented is penalized. Thus, a policy of tolerance for failure is a prerequisite for promoting psychological safety and sustaining organizational learning.

"A study of more than 150 products concluded that knowledge gained from failure [was] often instrumental in achieving subsequent success. . . . In simplest terms, failure is the ultimate teacher" (Garvin, 1993, p. 80). Consistent with this conclusion, IBM's Thomas Watson Sr. purportedly suggested that "the fastest way to succeed is to double your failure rate" (Farson & Keyes, 2002, p. 64). At 3M, the adhesive used in the now ubiquitous Post-it Notes was the botched version of another product development project (Brand, 1998). The motto of product design firm IDEO is "Fail often, so you will succeed sooner" (Katz, 2001, p. 61). Similarly, Cannon and Edmondson (2001) describe a ritual of "mistake of the month" in a public relations firm in which meetings are opened with a review of mistakes—a light-hearted way to acknowledge the learning value in mistakes and build a sense of a learning community.

Managers have an important role in effective enactment of a policy of tolerance for failure. Elaborating on what managers can actually do to engender tolerance for failure, Farson and Keyes (2002) draw a portrait of failure-tolerant leaders who encourage intelligent risk taking by reducing the fear of failure. Managers who lead learning distinguish between excusable mistakes, such as those of a novice, and inexcusable mistakes, such as those attributable to negligence or sloppy preparation. They approach both success and failure nonjudgmentally, preferring doing an analysis in order to generate deeper understanding to simply praising or penalizing. Such managers discourage internal competition, which draws attention away from learning in favor of short-term winning and reduces both transparency and issue orientation. Finally, they focus on increasing the intellectual capital of their organizations through learning and staying closely engaged with their subordinates.

❖ COMMITMENT TO THE WORKFORCE

The policy of commitment to the workforce is required for encouraging members' commitment to the organization. The underlying rationale is the norm of reciprocity, a basic principle that regulates social behavior:

> The norm of reciprocity is truly a ubiquitous rule of behavior. It means that favors are returned and social obligations are repaid. It is difficult to think of situations, at least in healthy, adult relationships, in which one side is committed and the other is not. (Pfeffer, 1998, p. 181)

Von Krogh (1998, p. 133) suggests that "effective creation of new knowledge, especially tacit social knowledge, hinges on strong caring among organization members." Commitment to the work force is the organization's way of showing that it cares about its employees so that they reciprocate by caring about the organization.

BP CEO John Brown takes a step beyond reciprocity when discussing the partnership between businesses:

> You can't create an enduring business by viewing relationships as a bazaar activity—in which I try to get the best of you and you of me—or in which you pass off as much risk as you can to the other guy. Rather, we must view relationships as a coming together that allows us to do something no other two parties could do— something that makes the pie bigger and is to your advantage and to my advantage. (Prokesch, 1997, p. 152)

Brown's words are equally applicable to the relationships between an organization and its members. According to this view, commitment is not simply a matter of give and take but of interdependence. In this kind of relationship, neither employees nor organizations can fully achieve their goals or realize their potential without the other.

Ouchi (1981) traces the effectiveness of Japanese-style management, or Theory Z, to Japanese companies' success in generating organizational commitment *from* the workforce by organizational commitment *to* the workforce:

> [Ouchi] claims that in the Theory Z organization, as well as in many Japanese firms, people are so convinced that the organization has a "holistic concern" for them, or is concerned about them as a whole person, that they are willing to give their intense

loyalty to the firm. These firms select people whose values and assumptions are similar enough to those of the firm that acculturation is easily achieved. They also encourage long-term employment. This gives employees reason to feel a part of the organization and to learn the firm's culture. (Wilkins & Patterson, 1985, p. 273)

Commitment to the workforce is shown through employment security, investment in training, empowerment, stock ownership, profit- or gain-sharing programs, and fair treatment of their needs and grievances. Employment security is particularly important for organizational learning. Downsizing and outsourcing damage organizational learning because they reduce psychological safety. When people are focused on survival, they are less likely to risk failure through experimentation or to speak their minds freely. In addition, people who are let go take with them valuable information and knowledge because they disrupt the social networks on which the creation and dissemination of knowledge depend and because they demoralize the workforce that is retained and decrease its organizational commitment (Fisher & White, 2000; Ley & Hitt, 1995).

❖ MANAGERS' BEHAVIORAL CHANNELS OF INFLUENCE

Beyond providing a necessary structure, the creation of OLMs promotes organizational learning by sending a message that learning has high priority in the manager's agenda. Symbolic behavior is a behavioral "channel of influence" through which managers affect the behavior of their subordinates and steer the organization in their chosen direction. Tom Peters (1978, p. 10) pointed out that "symbols are the very stuff of management." Pfeffer (1981) similarly argued that managers use symbolic language, settings, and ceremonies to invoke powerful emotions. And Johnson (1990) identified the various ways in which symbolic acts can galvanize change process.

Managers can employ five behavioral channels of influence in order to support the policies of tolerance for failure and organizational commitment and the norms of a learning culture specified by the cultural and psychological facets. These channels are agenda setting, allocating time and attention, selling and telling, walking the talk, exploiting moments of truth, providing support, coaching, and dispensing rewards and recognition. Each of these has a role in organizational learning.

Agenda Setting

For organizational learning to take hold, managers must make it an activity of central, strategic importance in the organization's agenda. One way of achieving this goal is instituting OLMs and appropriating the necessary resources for their proper operation. Another way is using rhetoric that emphasizes the importance of organizational learning. Consider, for example, how BP's CEO John Brown describes his belief in the role of organizational learning:

> Learning is at the heart of a company's ability to adapt to a rapidly changing environment. It is the key to being able both to identify opportunities that others might not see and to exploit those opportunities rapidly and fully. . . . In order to generate extraordinary value for shareholders, a company has to learn better than its competitors and apply that knowledge throughout its business faster and more widely than they do. . . . Anyone in the organization who is not directly accountable for making a profit should be involved in creating and distributing knowledge that the company can use to make profit. (Prokesch, 1997, p. 148)

Allocating Time and Attention

Time and attention are scarce valuable resources in organizations. In field visits, we are often told that "in our work the urgent displaces the important." In other words, meeting deadlines and "putting out fires" leaves little time for centrally important issues such as long-term planning. Managers' time is therefore at a premium. In his classic study of how managers actually work, Mintzberg (1973) found that the managers that he observed dealt every day with a wide range of issues to which they attended only briefly. Managing, he concluded, is the art of being superficial. As a consequence, the time and attention that managers allocate to different subjects signals to their subordinates what is important for them. Pillsbury CEO Spoor insisted on taking part in the various learning activities that engineered his organization's turnaround, and in a study of four managers classified as leaders of learning organizations, Johnson (2002) emphasized the importance of this managerial province.

> All four leaders related the importance of their own attention to both the learning organization initiative and their own personal learning. One leader typified this best when he indicated that he

attended as many of the dialogue meetings as possible in order to demonstrate the importance that he personally placed on the initiative. (p. 246)

Selling and Telling

Johnson (2002) also found that managers insist that others pay attention to learning. Robert Shapiro of Monsanto worked hard to convince his employees to view every project and product as experiments by repeatedly reminding them that deliberate, well-thought-out efforts that failed were not only excusable but desirable (Farson & Keyes, 2002). Smith and McKeen (2003) suggest that managers can persuade subordinates by appealing to their self interest, invoking potential benefits to the organization, and telling success stories. These authors suggest a "knowledge-sharing cue card" with specific instructions of how to promote knowledge-sharing behaviors by making it a habit to address subordinates with questions such questions as, "Who have you shared this with?" or "Who else can make use of this information?" (Smith & McKeen, 2003).

Walking the Talk

Selling and telling is doomed to fail unless managers back it by acting in a way consistent with the behaviors that they expect others to follow. As BP's CEO Brown noted, "Leaders have to demonstrate that they are active participants in the learning process. You can't say 'go do it' without participating" (Prokesch, 1997, p. 160). Leaders are aware of the importance of walking the talk and use it to their advantage. Consider the following example, which involves the owner and CEO of Johnsonville Foods, Ralph Stayer:

I discovered that people watched my every action to see if it supported or undermined our vision. They wanted to see if I practiced what I preached. From the outset I did simple things to demonstrate my sincerity. I made a sign for my desk that said THE QUESTION IS THE ANSWER, and when people came to me with questions, I asked myself if they were questions I should answer. Invariably, they weren't. Invariably, people were asking me to make decisions for them. Instead of giving answers, I turned the tables and asked the questions myself, trying to make them repossess their own problems. Owning problems was an important part of the end state I'd envisioned. I wasn't about to let people give theirs to me.

I also discovered that in meetings people waited to hear my opinion before offering their own. In the beginning, I insisted they say what they thought, unaware that I showed my own preferences in subtle ways—my tone of voice, the questions I asked—which, nevertheless, anyone could read and interpret expertly. When I realized what was happening, I began to stay silent to avoid giving any clue to where I stood. The result was that people flatly refused to commit themselves to any decision at all. Some of those meetings would have gone on for days if I hadn't forced people to speak out before they'd read my mind. In the end, I began scheduling myself out of many meetings, forcing others to make their decisions without me. (Stayer, 1990, p. 80)

Modeling behaviors has the additional benefit of encouraging others to follow suit. A former Lockheed executive recalled an episode in which CEO Dan Haughton gathered his manufacturing managers to discuss his own errors. One notable mistake, Haughton recounted, was when Howard Hughes once called to tell him that Douglas Aircraft was in trouble and that he should act promptly and buy it "before Jimmy McDonnell." Failing to follow Hughes's advice, Haughton said, was the biggest blunder he had made in his business career. Had he bought Douglass Aircraft, Lockheed would have avoided costly future moves. Haughton's willingness to admit his mistake modeled the norms of transparency and integrity and reinforced psychological safety by sending a message that "if Dan Haughton can make mistakes, I guess I can make one too"—that is, that making mistakes is part of the game. The meeting increased the manufacturing managers' respect for him and strengthened their willingness to take risks (Farson & Keyes, 2002, p. 68).

Exploiting Moments of Truth

Moments of truth are episodes that test the manager's commitment to his or her espoused goal or vision (Carlzon, 1989). As the episode in Carlzon shows, passing these tests successfully sends particularly potent messages regarding the manager's sincerity and commitment that frequently turn into organizational legends and shape the organization's tradition and culture. A famous IBM legend tells of a young manager who was called into the office of IBM's legendary founder Thomas Watson after losing $10 million in a risky venture.

The young man, thoroughly intimidated, began by saying, "I guess you want my resignation."

Watson replied, "You can't be serious. We just spent $10 million educating you" (Garvin, 1993).

This legend sent a strong message to all IBM employees that failures are occasions for learning and that valuable employees will not necessarily be let go if they fail.

Providing Support

When costly errors occur, persons who may be held accountable are likely to behave defensively and hold back or distort information that is vital for learning how to prevent future recurrence of these errors. As Chapter 13 recounts in detail, on such occasions it is essential that managers support their subordinates both by reassuring them that learning (in the form of after-action reviews) will be fair—that is, issue and not blame oriented—and by modeling integrity by taking responsibility for what has occurred.

Coaching

Coaching and mentoring have become a hot topic among executives and in the organizational literature:

Recently there has been a resurgence of interest [in the managerial functions of mentoring and coaching], because the learning organization literature has depicted managers and leaders as being primarily responsible for nurturing, developing, and measuring the knowledge capital of the organization. (Ellinger & Bostrom, 1999, p. 752)

Coaching systems are either online or off-line OLMs, depending on the time when coaching is performed (Waldroop & Butler, 1996; Watkins & Marsick, 1996). Coaching speaks to "individualized consideration," a component of transformational leadership, one of the most widely studied and discussed leadership styles in the literature (Bass, 1985). Individualized consideration is manifested in leaders' developmental approach. Such leaders help their workers to develop their strong sides and spend a lot of time guiding and training their people. In addition, leaders high in individualized consideration do not take success for granted and are ready to learn both from successes and failures.

Coaching requires managers to allocate time and attention to their subordinates' developmental needs. A nurse in an operating room described the head surgeon leading her very successful team as "very accessible. He is in his office, always just two seconds away. He can always take five minutes to explain something and he never makes you feel stupid" (Edmondson, Bohmer, & Pisano, 2000, p. 33). In striking contrast, the head surgeon leading a less successful team requested that nonphysician team members go through his residents (junior physicians who are still in training) rather than speak to him directly. Through their allocation of time, these two surgeons conveyed very different messages to their teams. The first surgeon increased the likelihood that people would come to him with questions or problems and speak up openly in the operating room with questions and observations, whereas the other surgeon made this more difficult (Edmondson, Bohmer, & Pisano, 2000).

Managers tend to see coaching as separate from managing (Ellinger & Bostrom, 2002) and thus have to be educated on its importance for learning. One way to become a manager-coach is to study how managers who exercise this function effectively do it. Ellinger and Bostrom (1999, p. 759) studied twelve managers who were recommended as exemplary coaches and identified 13 behaviors in which they engaged, dividing them into empowering and facilitating clusters.

The *empowerment cluster* includes behaviors such as framing questions, being a resource, removing obstacles, encouraging employees to own the problem, and refraining from providing answers. The first behavior—framing questions that stimulate employees to think things through for themselves—is clearly designed to encourage the cultural norm of inquiry (see Chapter 3). It is related to "intellectual stimulation," a component of transformational leadership related to organizational learning (Amitay et al., 2005). Managers model intellectual stimulation by subjecting the status quo to critical examination and rejecting it as an immutable fact. Managers who display intellectual stimulation cause their subordinates to consider old problems in new ways, encourage them to think differently, legitimize creativity and innovation, and test the viability of extant assumptions.

The *facilitating cluster* includes providing employees with various kinds of feedback, asking employees to give their own self-assessments, and coming up with options or action plans through group deliberation. These behaviors require the skill of active listening, which means thinking about what one is hearing and showing interest in it, for example, by asking questions to clarify its meaning. Through active listening, managers model learning, create involvement, and strengthen commitment (McGill & Slocum, 1998). Additional facilitation behaviors include creating a learning environment (creating OLMs); setting and communicating expectations; broadening employees' perspectives; engaging others to facilitate learning; and using analogs, scenarios, exemplars, and role playing.

Dispensing Rewards and Recognition

This is most common channel of influence in organizations. It includes monetary inducements (e.g., bonuses), verbal and written expressions of appreciation, promotion, and assignment to coveted positions. As we know from learning theory and research, positive reinforcement increases the probability that the same behavior will be repeated (Skinner, 1989). One of the best examples of linking rewards to learning is the policy of Johnsonville Sausages (Chapter 9), which awards pay raises only on the basis of acquiring new work-related knowledge or skills.

In conclusion, managers can promote organizational learning *directly* by announcing it as an important part of their agendas, instituting OLMs, and enacting supporting policies and *indirectly* by using the channels that are available to them for influencing their subordinates through their own leadership behavior every day.

7

The Dissemination of Knowledge

Organizational learning is the synthesis of two processes: learning and dissemination. The former refers to the creation of knowledge, the latter to the distribution of knowledge throughout the organization. In Chapter 1, we argued that this synthesis is a defining characteristic of organizational learning. Dissemination sets organizational learning apart from individual learning because transmitting knowledge among individuals or from one organizational unit to another is irrelevant or marginal to individual learning. In contrast, dissemination is a central task of organizational learning. It is also the source of some of the more difficult problems that organizations must solve in order to benefit from what members learn "on their behalf."

Much of the literature that we draw on goes under the rubric of "knowledge management" rather than of "organizational learning." This distinction is a prime example of the conceptual proliferation that results in mystification, owing to the fact that members of different disciplines studying the same phenomena use different terminologies. The interchangeability of the terms *organizational learning* and *knowledge management* is manifest in Carla O'Dell and Jackson Grayson's

(1998) suggestion that "internal benchmarking and transfer of best practices is one of the most tangible manifestation of knowledge management—the process of identifying, capturing, and leveraging knowledge to help the company compete" and that sharing and transfer are "tangible evidence of a learning organization—one that can analyze, reflect, learn, and change based on experience" (p. 154).

Knowledge dissemination involves the transfer of knowledge from one person or unit to other persons or units. Knowledge creation within organizational learning mechanisms (OLMs) also involves transfer of knowledge. When members of a community of practice share stories or when participants in a postflight review critique the performance of other participants, knowledge is clearly being transferred. In order to draw a sharp distinction between *knowledge creation* and *knowledge dissemination,* we use the latter term to refer to instances in which knowledge is transferred across boundaries in organizations. Transfer may occur as a follow-up to OLM operations, such as the distribution of lessons learned garnered by one unit to all relevant units in the organization. It might also occur without an explicit connection to OLM operation, such as one unit's adoption of a best practice invented by another. The distinction between knowledge creation and dissemination highlights a set of problems that is not addressed by focusing uniquely on knowledge creation.

❖ THE PROBLEM OF DISSEMINATION

Internal benchmarking—identifying and advertising existing "best practices" within the organization to promote their widespread implementation throughout the organization—is a quintessential activity of knowledge dissemination. Despite compelling evidence of its enormous payoff, successful dissemination of best practices is both difficult and rare. As O'Dell and Grayson (1998) note:

> You would think that . . . better practices would spread like wildfire to the entire organization. They don't. . . . [As] one Baldridge winner told us, "We can have two plants right across the street from one another, and it's the damnedest thing to get them to transfer best practices." . . . [Furthermore] even in the best of firms, in-house best practices took an average of 27 *months* [italics in the original] to wind their way from one part of the organization to another. (p. 155)

The fact that dissemination is a very difficult undertaking surprised researchers who tended to treat it as costless. The notion that knowledge is inherently resistant to transfer, or "sticky," has only recently come into good currency, and research on the subject is still sparse, though picking up pace (Szulanski, 2003).

Knowledge is sticky because the number of obstacles that can frustrate dissemination is fairly daunting. Dissemination takes place through numerous acts of transfer between knowledge sources and knowledge recipients within the organization. In order to put knowledge into practice, its recipient must be able to "absorb" it; that is, the recipient must comprehend what this knowledge means in terms of action. As Figure 7.1 shows, knowledge can be transferred directly through face-to-face interaction between sources and recipients or by the use of technological means such as e-mail and teleconferencing. The figure also shows that transfer can occur indirectly, through the mediation of a knowledge repository (e.g., internal publications or databases) to which the source contributes his or her knowledge for the benefit of potential recipients who can access the repository. Finally, Figure 7.1 indicates that dissemination involves six basic elements: (1) the source, (2) the recipient, (3) the relationship between them, (4) the knowledge to be transferred, (5) the method of transfer, and (6) the organizational context within which transfer occurs. Each of the six sources is associated with a corresponding obstacle to dissemination. These obstacles vary with relevance to direct and indirect dissemination (Szulanski, 2003). Each of these elements and the corresponding obstacles will be discussed in depth.

Figure 7.1   Direct and Indirect Dissemination of Information and Knowledge

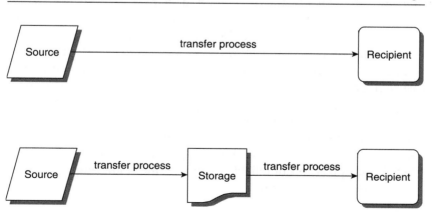

❖ THE SOURCE OF KNOWLEDGE

Successful dissemination hinges on the *motivation* of people to share their knowledge and the credibility that they enjoy among potential recipients. The motivation of the source is clearly influenced by self-interest. After all, dissemination involves costs to the source. To the extent that knowledge is seen as power, people who share knowledge give away a potentially valuable asset. Depending on the precise mode that sharing knowledge takes, they may also have to divert time and energy from their own work in order to document their knowledge, explain it to others, or coach them in its implementation. Thus, people who are sources have to believe that they will benefit—or at least not be hurt—from sharing knowledge. Knowledge sharing can be rewarded formally; some organizations evaluate and reward their members on the basis sharing knowledge. It can also be rewarded informally by enhancing one's status and self-esteem as an expert and a cooperative colleague.

Another factor that influences knowledge sharing is the source's belief regarding the ownership of work-related knowledge. Research shows that people who believe that their knowledge belongs to the organization—and hence should be shared—are more willing to respond favorably to a request for information from a coworker, even when the coworker has refused their similar request in the past (Constant, Kiesler, & Sproul, 2001). The motivation to share knowledge is also affected by organizational commitment, which blurs the distinction between the source's self-interest and the interests of the organization. Commitment increases knowledge sharing by fostering a sense of common purpose among the organization's members (Barrow, 2001). Finally, the motivation to share is strengthened by the sources' belief in their ability to access knowledge that is possessed by others should the need arise (O'Dell & Grayson, 1998).

Research on persuasion shows that the extent to which knowledge actually changes opinions and behaviors is partly determined by the *credibility* of its source (Hovland & Weiss, 1951). These findings can be easily extrapolated to the credibility of the source in the dissemination process. Potential recipients tend to seek or trust knowledge donated by sources who are experts or have extensive experience. Furthermore, they will more easily receive knowledge from sources that can be trusted not to pass on unreliable or misleading knowledge, owing to carelessness or other reasons.

❖ THE RECIPIENT OF KNOWLEDGE

In order to look for knowledge and successfully apply it, recipients must acknowledge that they require knowledge (motivation), must know where to obtain it (transactive knowledge), and must be able to understand and act on it (absorptive capacity). Looking for, asking for, and accepting knowledge involve costs. Therefore, knowledge recipients must also be motivated to receive knowledge by self-interest, just as sources must be motivated to share it on the basis of self-interest. At the very least, they have to admit that they lack important knowledge, which can create a real or imagined loss of face. Recipients must believe that looking for knowledge and putting it to use is worth the effort. Motivation to receive knowledge can be generated by fear, such as losing to a competitor (Wegner & Erber, 1991), or by the belief that the required knowledge is accessible in the organization (Argote, 1999). In addition, recipients need to avoid the "not invented here (NIH) syndrome," a norm that dictates rejection of practices and solutions imported from the outside. The NIH syndrome can be considered as the group or unit level analogue to the loss of face, which prevents individuals from seeking or accepting the help of others. To the extent that the values of inquiry, transparency, and integrity counter the loss of face by legitimating the search for knowledge (see Chapter 3), these values should counter this syndrome as well.

Transactive knowledge is a somewhat awkward but important term taken from Moreland and Argote (2003) and Wegner and Erber (1991). Possessing transactive knowledge means knowing who in the organization has knowledge about specific issues (who knows what). Transactive knowledge is critically important for finding what one needs to know, but it is surprisingly limited in many organizations. One survey of the barriers to internal transfer of best practices found the following:

> The biggest barrier to transfer was *ignorance. . . .* At most companies, particularly large ones, neither the "source" nor the "recipient" *knew someone else had knowledge they required or would be interested in knowledge they had* [italics original]. The most common response from employees was either "I did not know that you needed this" or "I did not know that you had it." (Szukanski, 1994, quoted in O'Dell & Grayson, 1998, p. 155)

Although we discuss transactive knowledge as an attribute of recipients, dissemination is contingent on the transactive knowledge of sources as well.

Absorptive capacity (see Chapter 1) refers to the readiness of the recipient to comprehend and apply new knowledge (Lane et al., 2002). A basic principle of knowledge acquisition is that new knowledge and skills build on existing prerequisites such as lower-level knowledge and skills. Consider, for example, what happened to the large quantities of sophisticated weapon systems and material for civilian purposes that were imported by Iran during the late Shah's attempt to modernize the country (artifacts such as gadgets and machines actually represent packages of knowledge). Many of these expensive systems were never put into use, and some were, in fact, left to rust at their port of entry. Iran simply lacked the technical capabilities (professional personnel and maintenance infrastructure) to cope with large quantities of advanced technology.

Three aspects of absorptive capacity are relevant to successful implementation of disseminated knowledge. First, it is dependent upon the availability of members within the recipient unit who have the conceptual knowledge to understand the nature of the acquired knowledge. For example, they must understand what a new technology or best practice can and cannot do, as well as the scope of application and its limitations. Second, absorptive capacity depends on the availability of organizational members with the basic skills required to begin implementing the new knowledge at a rudimentary level. Third, the recipient unit must have the necessary resources, including managerial skills and organizational arrangements, for putting the new knowledge in place and for long-term successful implementation.

❖ THE RELATIONSHIP BETWEEN SOURCE AND RECIPIENT

Dissemination is essentially a chain of interactions between recipients and sources in which knowledge is transferred. When transfer occurs directly, such as when one unit assists another unit in implementing a best practice, the nature of their relationship becomes an important factor in determining the success of dissemination. Three attributes of the relationship between source and recipient facilitate, or obstruct, the process of dissemination.

The first attribute is *frequency of contact*. The more two units are in contact with one another, the greater the likelihood that they will be familiar with what knowledge they can offer each other (transactive knowledge). In addition, frequent contacts also increase the number of opportunities for the initiation of transfer of knowledge and its ease of execution, owing to the experience that the two units gain in interacting with one another. For this reason, "networks for sharing knowledge build on existing networks that people use in their daily work" (McDermott & O'Dell, 2001, p. 79).

The second attribute is the *quality of the relationship*. The quality of the relationship between two units is manifested by the smoothness of the communication between them. Smoothness depends on trust, on the degree to which the source is willing to give knowledge, and on the degree to which the source and recipient find it easy to understand each other. The quality of the relationship is often influenced by a history of failed interactions or conflict. As can be seen, relationship quality is a function of several attributes: source and recipient motivation, the recipient's absorptive capacity, and the organization's culture.

The third attribute, *proximity* of a source and a recipient, has two aspects. The first is *proximity in physical space*: Are they situated in the same or in different cities or buildings? The second is their *proximity in organizational space*, as measured by the number of boundaries that separate them: Are they located in the same divisions, plants, or functional units? Spatial proximity influences dissemination through its effect on the frequency of contacts. Smaller distances increase the likelihood of unplanned contacts, which can serve the transfer of knowledge (e.g., chance encounters near the water cooler or the mail room). It also facilitates planned transfers of knowledge, such as visiting the source's site to observe firsthand his or her operations or traveling to the recipient when the nature of the disseminated knowledge requires direct transfer.

Psychological proximity refers to the extent to which source and recipient share similar goals as well as similar professional outlooks and vocabularies (the way they perceive and discuss problems and their methods for solving them). Dissimilar outlooks and vocabularies hamper recipients' ability to absorb the new knowledge and obstruct the source's attempts to overcome this deficiency in absorptive capacity through instruction and coaching. Similarity in outlook and vocabularies is obviously enhanced by the extent to which source and recipients perform similar tasks using the same methods. Similarity increases the likelihood that the source's knowledge will be relevant to the recipient and that its transfer from one system to the other will require small adjustments. Thus, Adler and Cole (1993) described how New United Motor Manufacturing, Inc. (NUMMI) the General Motors–Toyota joint venture in Fremont, California, facilitated knowledge dissemination through the standardization of work processes and their careful documentation (Adler & Cole, 1993, quoted in Argote, 1999, p. 18).

Dissimilar, to say nothing of competing, goals between individuals or units reduces the trust between them and their motivation to cooperate. Oft-repeated difficulties owing to spatial and psychological distances will decrease the motivation of both source and recipient to engage in dissemination. Spatial and psychological proximity and goal congruence account for the fact that knowledge transfers better between units within the same organization and between affiliated organizations than between independent organizations (Argote, 1999).

❖ UNDERSTANDING KNOWLEDGE

Understanding organizational learning draws attention to the *nature of learning*: How do organizations learn nonmetaphorically, and in what ways is their learning different from the learning of their individual members? Understanding dissemination draws attention to the *nature of knowledge*: What gets transferred from one unit of the organization to another in the process of dissemination? Normally people do not pause to reflect about the meaning of *knowledge* and *knowing* because these terms do not present them with problems in the course of daily life. In contrast, philosophers fail to agree on the nature of knowledge even after struggling with this question for ages, leading researchers to agree that knowledge is a slippery concept that defies simple straightforward definition.

The following definitions of knowledge capture both its slippery nature and the disagreements researchers regarding this nature:

> Knowledge is a product of human reflection and experience. Dependent on context, knowledge is a resource that is always located in an individual or a collective, or embedded in a routine or a process. Embodied in language, stories, concepts, rules, and tools, knowledge results in an increased capacity for decision making and action to achieve some purpose. (De Long & Fahey, 2000, p. 113)

> Knowledge is a fluid mix of framed experience, values, contextual information, and expert insight that provides a framework for evaluating and incorporating new experiences and information. It originates and is applied in the minds of knowers. In organizations, it often becomes embedded not only in documents or repositories but also in organizational routines, processes, practices, and norms. (Davenport & Prusak, 1998, p. 5)

Complex definitions and definitional disagreements are bound to produce mystification. Rather than try to produce yet another definition, we will draw attention to some distinctions between data, information, and knowledge and between different types of knowledge, which are directly relevant to the issue of dissemination.

Data is sometimes used interchangeably with *information* and *information* is sometimes used interchangeably with *knowledge*. Yet, if the purpose of learning is to result in improved performance (action), as we assume in this book, it is important to distinguish between them. The difference between data and information is fairly straightforward: Data are facts expressed pictorially, verbally, or numerically in regard to people, cases, events, actions, transactions, outcomes, and so forth. Facts do not convey, in themselves, any additional meaning such as causes (why did the event take place?), intentions (what was the purpose of the transaction?), significance (how did the outcomes of the transaction affect the balance of the company or the careers of the parties involved?), or their place in the larger scheme of things (what was the significance of the event for the history of the company and its future prospects?).

Information, in contrast, is data *plus* interpretation or, in Peter Drucker's apt words, "data endowed with relevance and purpose" (Drucker, quoted in Davenport & Prusak, 1998, p. 2). The following vignette, reported by the philosopher of science Pierre Duhem, illustrates the difference between data and information (and, incidentally, the importance of absorptive capacity for learning):

Enter a laboratory; approach the table crowded with an assortment of apparatus, an electric cell, silk-covered copper wire, small cups of mercury, a mirror mounted on an iron bar; the experimenter is inserting into small openings the metal ends of ebony-headed pins; the iron oscillates and the mirror attached to it throws a luminous band upon a celluloid scale; the forward-backward motion of this spot enables the physicist to observe the minute oscillations of the iron bar. But ask him what he is doing. Will he answer, "I am studying the oscillations of an iron bar which carries a mirror?" No, he will say that he is measuring the electrical resistance of the spools. If you are astonished, if you ask him what his words mean, what relation they have with the phenomenon he has been observing and which you have noted at the same time, and he will answer that your question requires a long explanation and that you should take a course in electricity. (Duhem, quoted in Hanson, 1964, p. 6)

Duhem begins by providing a factual description (data) of the actions of a physicist performing an experiment. Though indisputably correct, this description is uninformative (meaningless) because it does not provide the reader with the purpose of the experiment or the reasons why the experimenter goes through this particular sequence of actions in order to achieve this purpose. The physicist endows the data with meaning—transforms the data into information—by simply explaining that the purpose of his or her actions is to measure the electrical resistance of the spool. He or she then goes on to explain to the still puzzled observer that full understanding of the meaning of those actions requires background knowledge (improved absorptive capacity).

Although the difference between data and information is fairly straightforward, the difference between information and knowledge is more difficult to pin down. This can be seen by comparing Drucker's definition of information with the definitions of knowledge quoted on the previous pages. The latter enumerate the various ways in which data can be endowed by "relevance and purpose," such as incorporating the data within a story or relating (or even demonstrating) its application to action in a particular context. We will not attempt to elucidate information from knowledge on some theoretical basis. Instead, adopting a pragmatic approach, and consistent with the definitions of knowledge quoted previously, we will use the term *knowledge* to refer to information that enables the recipient to act in a way that is intended to improve performance. Whereas information is data that is endowed with meaning, knowledge is information that can be acted upon. This simple (and even simplistic) distinction makes sense for our purposes, because the approach presented in this book assumes that productive organizational learning produces knowledge that results in changes in norms, practices, and routines, which benefit the organization and its members.

Cognitive psychologists and researchers of knowledge management suggest numerous distinctions between different types of knowledge. Because such multiplicity can produce mystification, we will focus only on those distinctions which have clear implications for successful dissemination. These are the distinctions between knowing-what, knowing-why, and knowing-how; tacit and explicit knowledge; validated and unvalidated knowledge; and ambiguous knowledge versus unambiguous knowledge.

Knowing-what, knowing-why, and knowing-how designate distinctions about what knowledge is about. *Knowing-what* signifies mastery of facts or opinions, such as the resources and processes required to manufacture a certain product or obtain a certain result. *Knowing-why* signifies causal understanding, such as why particular resources and processes result in a certain outcome. *Knowing-how* signifies the ability to actually carry out the actions that are required in order to achieve a certain effect. Knowing *what* needs to be done does not qualify as knowing *how* to do it—as every novice who learns to swim by reading a book quickly finds out upon jumping into the water.

A study by Laprè and Van Wassenhove (2002) showed how different mixes of knowing-why and knowing-how obtained from a source determine the usefulness of dissemination. High levels of knowing-why and knowing-how lead to successful dissemination by reducing causal ambiguity, one of the obstacles to knowledge transfer. High levels of knowing-why coupled with low levels of knowing-how may supply a persuasive explanation for why things break down or work, but lacks evidence that the solutions they suggest actually work. High levels of knowing-how coupled with low levels of knowing-why produces practical knowledge that works for solving specific problems but cannot be transferred or adapted effectively to different situations. Finally, low levels of both knowing-why and knowing-how produce "firefighting behavior"—ad hoc local improvements that deal mostly with the observed symptoms of problems and do not prevent the problems from recurring somewhere else in the organization, or even in the same location.

In an extensive study of the effectiveness of improvement projects in steel wire plants, Laprè and Van Wassenhove (2002) found that the four combinations of knowledge that they identified had a significant impact on the effectiveness of knowledge dissemination:

> The real benefit of a process improvement project, we found, is not in its local impact on the few machines where it is implemented, but in the transfer of knowledge to other areas of the plant or other products.
>
> We found that only the operationally validated theories delivered a positive bottom-line impact. . . . Un-validated theories . . . were widely adopted, even without proof that they worked. As a result, un-validated theories slowed the global rate of quality improvement. . . . Fire fighting efforts, which are common in nearly every work setting, [were] largely ignored beyond the team dealing with the immediate problem [and] had no impact on global rate pf quality improvement. . . . Artisan skills . . . yielded solutions that worked for the problem at hand . . . [but] since nobody knew if [they] were transferable to other parts of the plant, . . . there was no attempt to duplicate [them] elsewhere. (p. 110)

Laprè and Van Wassenhove's findings show that the two aspects of organizational learning, knowledge creation and knowledge dissemination, are linked intimately. To ensure that knowledge transferred from a source to a recipient will have a positive effect on the latter's bottom-line results, the learning process of the source should produce both knowing-how (the precise sequence of actions that yields the desired results) and knowing-why (the factors that make the solution effective and under what circumstances they are expected to work). Knowing-why improves the applicability of knowing-how to different situations because it informs the adjustments and improvisations that are inevitably required when knowledge gained in one place or time is transferred to another.

Knowing-how is of primary importance for organizational learning, with knowing-why and, to a lesser extent, knowing-what playing supportive roles in the success of knowledge dissemination. Unfortunately, as the philosopher Michael Polanyi observed, people often know more than they can tell. Polanyi's observation is based on the distinction that he drew between *explicit knowledge* and *tacit knowledge*, a distinction that has profound implications for knowledge dissemination:

> Tacit knowledge is subconsciously understood and applied, difficult to articulate, developed from direct experience and action and usually shared through highly interactive conversation, storytelling, and shared experience. In contrast, explicit knowledge is more precisely and formally articulated, although removed from the original context of creation or use (e.g., an abstract mathematical formula derived from physical experiments or a training manual describing how to close a sale). (Zack, 1999, p. 46)

Conceptual knowledge (knowing-what and knowing-why) is largely explicit. It can be expressed in formulas or words and, as a result, is easy to disseminate in the form of documents that can be transferred either directly or by being stored in a library or an electronic database.

In contrast, knowing-how is largely tacit. As a person becomes more proficient in performing a task, his or her performance demands less and less conscious awareness. Finally, it becomes completely automated, defying attempts to describe it accurately. Thus, we can walk, talk, recognize faces, and drive cars with great ease but find it increasingly difficult to explain how we are able to achieve these feats smoothly and effortlessly.

The difficulty of providing an explicit description that does justice to skillful behavior was vividly demonstrated when we asked a colleague to send us a videotape of an interviewing technique that the latter developed. We wanted to make sure that we understood the technique correctly from its description in published articles but were amazed at how many details were missing from the verbal descriptions. Although the tapes fully presented the interviewer's know-how, the papers provided only an abridged, abstract description that did not allow faithful (and effective) replication. Reason (1990), who studies human error, claims that instructions are always underspecified, a fact that explains why novices can use manuals much less effectively than experts, whose larger absorptive capacity helps them to add the missing details.

In order to bridge the gap between knowing-what and knowing-how, Argyris (1993) proposed the concept of "actionable" knowledge. Actionable knowledge enables people to produce desired outcomes in specific practice situations (Argyris, 1993, pp. 2–3). It contains causal claims, or if-then propositions, which can be stored in actors' minds and retrieved under conditions of everyday life. Actionable knowledge is based on the concept of mental "theories of action" underlying behavior at the individual, group, and organizational level (Argyris & Schön, 1974, 1978; Friedman, 2002). A simple theory of action includes a description of the situation, an implicit goal, and an action strategy for achieving that goal under the given conditions. A somewhat more complex theory of action includes the assumptions underlying behavior and the underlying values that inform goals.

Theories of action provide a useful conceptual and analytical tool for capturing individual and organizational knowledge. This knowledge can be represented as a set of interrelated theories of action for task performance and problem solving. Theories of action facilitate both knowledge creation and knowledge dissemination. First, they provide a basis for systematic inquiry. Learning can focus on the action strategies: What did we do wrong or right? How can we do it better? It can focus on the situation: How did we perceive the situation we were dealing with? How did we misinterpret, misunderstand, or simply miss key signals or factors? How might we perceive or interpret the situation differently? It can focus on the goals of action themselves: What were we really trying to accomplish? Are those our real goals? Are they the "right" goals? What do we really want to achieve in this situation? Finally, it can lead learners to inquire into the assumptions underlying behavior and the deeper values that inform their goals. As we understand it, "single-loop" learning deals primarily with inquiry into action strategies whereas "double-loop" learning involves changes in the perceptions of reality, assumptions, goals, and values that generate these strategies (Argyris & Schön, 1974; Friedman, 2001b).

Theories of action package knowledge in a way that generates coherent and comprehensive displays of very complex individual and organizational practice. They link action strategies (the actions that need to be taken) to the goals to be achieved by those actions. They also place action into the context of the conditions that both require a response and influence effective execution. Structuring knowledge in this way and packaging it into clear causal theories facilitate relatively easy transfer among individuals and between organizational units (see Chapter 7).

One of the main obstacles in making knowledge "actionable" (transforming knowing-what into knowing-how) is the automatic behavior described in this chapter coupled with the fact that people frequently develop highly inaccurate theories about how they actually behave. This discovery led Argyris and Schön (1974) to draw the now famous distinction between people's "espoused" theories of action (how they intend to or think they act in a particular situation) and their "theories-in-use" (which actually guide their behavior). People are not only frequently unaware of their theories-in-use, but they are also unaware of inconsistencies and contradictions in their behavior that are easily observable to everyone around them (Argyris & Schön, 1974). From this perspective, organizational learning involves making tacit theories of action explicit so that people can become aware of, critically examine, and change them. The use of this analytical tool facilitates accountability by increasing self-awareness and enhancing the ability to exercise conscious choice and intention.

❖ DISSEMINATION MECHANISMS

The discussion of the differences between tacit and explicit knowledge points to the fundamental problem of knowledge dissemination. Whereas explicit knowledge can be captured (or codified) in documents that can be transferred readily, tacit knowledge is transferred most effectively through face-to-face interaction (Davenport & Prusak, 1998). The implications for knowledge dissemination are fairly obvious. Direct dissemination is far superior to indirect dissemination for the transfer of knowledge that is considered useful by organization members:

When a technology transfer manager was asked to describe how Semantech transferred knowledge, she commented: "We have document databases, an intranet Web, groupware, you name it. But the assignees [people who are assigned temporarily from one unit to another for the purpose of transferring knowledge between them] and the face-to-face meetings we have are by far the most important channels for transferring knowledge to the member firms. (Thomas, Sussman, & Henderson, 2001, p. 341)

Direct dissemination is superior to indirect dissemination, not only because it is more suitable for transferring knowing-how but also because it allows for two-way communication. Through face-to-face interaction, the source and the recipient can make sure that the knowledge that is transferred is suitable for the latter's specific needs and circumstances. Face-to-face interaction also allows recipients to test their understanding with the source, and it allows the source to clarify or explain until the recipient understands adequately.

The limitations of indirect dissemination can be relaxed by the use of such "rich media" as videotapes. Several organizations have, in fact, adopted such means. For example, the U.S. Army Center for Lessons Learned (CALL), which is responsible for capturing, collecting, and disseminating knowledge that can be learned from large-scale exercises and actual operations, provides customized videos tailored to meet the needs of clients (Zander & Kogut, 1995).

In short, written communication cannot replace face-to-face communication in transferring knowing-how, even if it is supported by highly sophisticated information technology. The following example, which preceded the advent of these high-powered systems, is nevertheless instructive:

Another computer consulting firm, Bain, learned a hard lesson about relying on documents. In the 1980s . . . managers at Bain developed a large paper-based document center at its Boston headquarters; it stored slide books containing disguised presentations, analyses, and information on various industries. The library's purpose was to help consultants learn from work done in the past *without having to contact the teams that did the work* [our italics]. But as one partner commented, "The center offered a picture of a cake without giving out the recipe." The documents could not convey the richness of the knowledge or the logic that had been applied to reach solutions—that understanding had to be communicated from one person to another. (Dixon, 2000, p. 217)

❖ ATTRIBUTES OF THE ORGANIZATIONAL CONTEXT

Since dissemination takes place within the context of the organization, its effectiveness depends, naturally, on the extent to which this context facilitates dissemination of knowledge. The multi-facet model of organizational learning provides a framework for capturing the attributes of the organizational context that influence dissemination. Organizations vary in the successful implementation of identical dissemination methods according to the extent that they have structural mechanisms, cultural norms, members' attitudes, leadership, and policies that promote knowledge sharing. Dissemination will also be influenced by the extent to which environmental pressures push them to learn.

One of the basic tenets of our approach is that organizational learning (knowledge creation) requires the existence of OLMs. The same logic applies to knowledge dissemination. Knowledge created or obtained (e.g., through recruitment) by one organizational unit will not migrate to other parts of the organization without *structural mechanisms for knowledge dissemination*. Some of the OLMs discussed in Chapter 2 double as both OLMs and dissemination mechanisms. In particular, communities of practice and peer assists are designed to help organization members and organization units transfer knowledge to other members and units across internal organizational boundaries. Other OLMs, however, need to be complemented by other specific dissemination mechanisms in order to spread the knowledge that they produce throughout the organization.

The headquarters of the Israel Defense Force Air Force, for example, includes a special unit responsible for collecting the lessons learned in the various after-action reviews conducted in its operational (flight) units and disseminating them to other units to which they are relevant. The Air Force has a standard operating procedure requiring all pilots to review the lessons learned sent to their flight squadrons. The Post-Project Assessment Unit, which is responsible for collecting lessons learned in British Petroleum, and the Center for Lessons Leaned, which is responsible for conducting and mentoring lessons learned in the U.S. Army, also serve as mechanisms for disseminating both the lessons created by themselves and those created by units they supervise. In this section, we intend to review other mechanisms that are specifically designed for knowledge dissemination.

Dissemination mechanisms basically fulfill two functions. First, they allow the organization to know *what* knowledge it possesses (generating transactive knowledge), thus assisting recipients to locate sources of the knowledge that they require. Second, they facilitate the transfer of knowledge from a source (or sources) to a recipient (or recipients). Some dissemination mechanisms are similar to OLMs in that they consist of a group of organizational members working together on a regular basis. Other dissemination mechanisms differ from OLMs because they consist of a computerized net-based infrastructure that performs the two basic dissemination functions identified above.

The process of *knowledge mapping* and its product, knowledge maps, illustrate this difference. Knowledge mapping is a method for identifying, organizing, and locating knowledge that exists in the organization. It is particularly useful for launching knowledge management programs (Vaill, 1999, 2000a). A knowledge map is a visual representation of the knowledge available in the organization, which can be presented on a computer screen and provides access to a database, helping potential recipients find relevant sources in the same way that a search engine directs users to information that they need on the Internet. Creating a knowledge map is in itself a knowledge creation process because it requires the organization to identify its knowledge needs, identify the extent to which these needs can be effectively met internally, and identify the needs that cannot be met effectively and require further development at the time of mapping. Although knowledge mapping can be performed periodically, it is typically a one-time affair. The resulting map should be updated continuously, provided it is maintained by a person or a team who is designated for this function. The next two dissemination mechanisms can contribute to the creation and updating of knowledge maps.

Best Practice Teams and Benchmarking

Best practice teams are responsible for assessing the current state of the organization, identifying shortcomings and gaps in work processes and performance, and finding outstanding practices—either within the organization or in other, typically competing, organizations—that can be adapted and adopted to remedy these gaps and shortcomings.

> These teams are usually led by functional experts (at Chevron they are called "process masters") who act as internal consultants assisting with transfer. Best practice teams also often provide guidelines on what constitutes a "best practice" in their function. Teams usually meet at least quarterly face to face to share practices and issues, and they continue to communicate via e-mail and electronic conferences to provide ongoing coaching and advice. (O'Dell & Grayson, 1998, p. 160)

Although best practice teams have a short life span, they perform the same task regularly and are chartered with facilitating the implementation of best practices within the organization. Benchmarking can also be used to create a sense of urgency in the organization by signaling the need to learn so as to improve performance and show what can be done.

Internal Audits

Internal audits are performed by technical organizations to assess their operations. Such activities can also be used to identify best practices that exist in some units of the organization and can be duplicated in other units to improve the overall performance of the organization (Davenport & Prusak, 1998).

Member Assignment

One well-known method of reinvigorating organizations is to recruit new members to influential positions from which they will be able to inject new perspectives and ideas into the organization. This process can be mimicked by systematically assigning members temporarily to different units within the organization or by attaching them to different organizations. These members learn useful practices and know-how that can be brought back with them to their parent unit or organization (Davenport & Prusak, 1998).

Knowledge Fairs and Talk Rooms

Knowledge fairs are virtual or actual events in which units and individuals are invited to present best practices in order to allow other members or units to discover useful knowledge and to facilitate interaction across organizational boundaries. "Talk rooms" are spaces set up in Japanese firms where members interact informally so as to facilitate "creative blending and exchanges" (Greco, 1999, p. 20). Any arrangement or occasion that encourages informal interaction among organizational members, such as on-site dining rooms and organizational picnics, can fulfill the same function.

Knowledge Officers

Compared with programs of organizational learning, knowledge management programs rely more on information technology to retain and transfer data, information, and knowledge. As a consequence, they also tend to spawn a host of related organizational roles to support this technology. A recent emerging role that is relevant to our discussion is that of the chief knowledge officer, or CKO. CKOs differ from chief information officers (CIOs) in that their responsibilities go beyond providing purely technical support, and they differ from chief learning officers (CLOs) in that the latter have "a very strong interest in the dimension of human capital" (Greco, 1999, p. 20). The very slight distinction between the CKO and the CLO reflects what we believe to be the subtle, and nonessential, differences between the two fields of activity. According to one estimate, there are no more than 100 practicing CKOs, typically in large centralized corporations (Greco, 1999, p. 20). Owing to its novelty and low incidence, there is no single agreed-upon definition of what CKOs actually do. Thus, the role's definition varies from the very abstract (and not too useful) to the very concrete. One way of defining the CKO's role is in terms of what it can do for people. "They understand it when you can say, 'This expertise locator can identify our go-to person for cross merger issues in Milan or Paris, or this database can identify the securitization work we have done with distressed bank loans.' When they see that, they say, 'Oh, now I get it'" (Dixon, 2000, p. 176).

In conclusion, the CKO role is an OLM that both creates and stores knowledge. This knowledge involves the learning and knowledge needs of the organization and how they can be satisfied internally or externally. It is also a human infrastructure responsible for promoting and maintaining organizational learning and knowledge dissemination efforts. The CKO advises management about the desirability and status of OLMs and dissemination mechanisms. The CKO is also responsible for shaping the cultural and psychological conditions as well as the policies conducive to the creation and dissemination of knowledge. One particular function of knowledge officers is to warn management against the common error of centering knowledge management efforts on information technology—an approach which has repeatedly failed. The two critical factors for successful technology-aided knowledge management in general, and knowledge dissemination in particular, are (1) the selection of appropriate dissemination methods, given the organization members' needs and the type of knowledge to be transferred, and (2) the promotion of appropriate culture and policies, to which we turn next.

According to one CKO, knowledge management is "20 percent technology and 80 percent cultural change" (Zack, 1999, p. 54). This statement reflects a widespread agreement among researchers and practitioners that similar to knowledge creation, knowledge dissemination (and management in general) requires an appropriate organizational *culture*. In the literature on knowledge management, there is little agreement on *what* culture specifically promotes dissemination. However, few researchers or practitioners would disagree with the proposition that the dissemination of knowledge requires a belief that "superior knowledge is a competitive advantage" (McDermott & O'Dell, 2001; O'Dell & Grayson, 1998) and a value that sanctions knowledge sharing and frowns on its private hoarding (Earl & Scott, 1999).

Both of these are consistent with the cultural facet of the multi-facet model. A basic assumption regarding the competitive advantage of knowledge is entirely consistent with the basic multi-facet model's assumption that learning is essential for improved performance. And a cultural norm of knowledge sharing can be produced by the joint operation of organizational commitment, which dictates that knowledge should be shared, and the values of inquiry, integrity, and transparency, which encourage seeking knowledge from others. Thus, we assume that knowledge creation and knowledge sharing are promoted by the same organizational culture.

In addition, we assume that knowledge creation and knowledge dissemination require the same psychological conditions. We have already seen that organizational commitment is required for knowledge sharing. Psychological safety is also required, albeit for a different reason. Learning requires safety to reduce the anxiety of the learner (recipient of knowledge) due to public exposure of error. Dissemination also requires that the knowledge source trusts that sharing knowledge will not prove harmful and preferably will be beneficial.

One of the lessons learned from the experience of CKOs is that *leadership behaviors and policies that promote dissemination* are one of the critical factors that determine their success. They require high-level sponsorship that extends beyond visible CEO support. The CKO must make the senior executive team and prominent line managers believe in knowledge management—a goal that is indivisible from winning and retaining personal trust. Such trust may initially derive from the CKO's track record, but before long it is sustained only by visible results (McDermott & O'Dell, 2001). Once convinced of the value of knowledge management, top and middle managers can help the success of dissemination efforts in a number of ways.

Under the guidance of their CKOs or consultants, they must select the appropriate knowledge strategy (see below), tying dissemination efforts directly to business goals and core tasks. Hansen and associates (1999) make a useful distinction between codification and personalization knowledge management strategies.

[In a *codification* strategy] knowledge is carefully codified and stored in data bases, where it can be accessed and used easily by anyone in the company. . . . [In a personalization strategy,] knowledge is closely tied to the person who developed it and shared mainly through direct person-to-person contacts. The chief purpose of computers at such companies is to help people to communicate knowledge, not to store it. The general rule, therefore, is that organizations that rely on explicit knowledge should adopt a codification strategy and those that rely on tacit knowledge should adopt a personalization strategy. (p. 107)

CKOs must model knowledge sharing themselves and encourage other managers to do the same, making subordinate managers responsible for the success of dissemination in their own units. They need to continually emphasize the importance of knowledge sharing and cooperation by incorporating these behaviors in member evaluations and rewarding accordingly. Finally, they need to institute proper measurements to facilitate the identification of best practices and the tracking of performance levels (O'Dell & Grayson, 1998).

❖ DEMYSTIFYING DISSEMINATION

Davenport and Prusak (1998) pointed to a central puzzle regarding the dissemination of knowledge:

How can an organization transfer knowledge effectively? The short answer, and the best one, is: hire smart people and let them talk to one another. Unfortunately, the second part of this advice is the more difficult to put into practice. (p. 88)

On one hand, there is nothing more simple and natural than creating and sharing knowledge; in the end, it is just a matter of people talking with each other. However, quite often the simplest, most obvious behaviors are the most difficult to produce in practice.

Ironically, the response to this puzzle is often mystification. Attempts to define and categorize knowledge have become increasingly complex and difficult to apply. Abstractions are thrown at problems or used as a kind of magic wand rather than as rigorous conceptual tools (Lane et al., 2002). Huge investments are made in sophisticated knowledge management systems and technologies that often fail to produce the desired results.

From the perspective of the multi-facet model, the way to cut through mystification is the understanding that systematic dissemination, like knowledge creation, begins with the establishment of OLMs. These OLMs must be tightly focused on the knowledge that organizational members feel they need and on the places in the organization where such knowledge exists or is being created. Indeed, the very first OLM in a knowledge management process may be the one that determines needs and maps existing knowledge resources (see Chapter 11 on knowledge management at Hewlett-Packard).

Bringing people together to talk is necessary but insufficient for producing dissemination. The transfer of knowledge, especially tacit knowledge, from one person or group to another is a very difficult process. Precisely because knowledge is complex and situated in context, there is a need for clearly structured models for representing and packaging knowledge. Theories of action, for example, can help individuals and groups make their knowledge explicit and more easily transferable.

There will always be gaps in understanding and differences in interpretation that need to be recognized and addressed. Furthermore, know-how that has been proved effective in one context cannot be automatically applied in different contexts. Rather, it needs to be tested against the new conditions and shaped accordingly. In this respect, knowledge dissemination cannot be held as distinct from experimentation and knowledge creation (see Chapter 12, on Chaparral Steel).

As illustrated in Chapter 3 ("The Cultural Facet"), the nature of the talk and the norms of behavior have a strong influence on knowledge creation. The cultural norms of inquiry, issue orientation, transparency, integrity, and accountability are equally important for dissemination. By the same token, these norms are likely to be enacted when there is a high degree of psychological safety and commitment to the organization. Managers cannot impose these norms and psychological conditions on members of an OLM, but they can foster them through mindfulness, modeling, and rewarding individuals and groups who experiment with them (see Chapter 6 on leadership and managerial channels of influence).

This chapter concludes our presentation of the multi-facet model of organizational learning. In the following chapters of the book, we apply the model to case studies of knowledge creation and dissemination in a variety of contexts. As will be seen, the multi-facet model offers an analytical framework, or template, for systematic comparison, and a guide for action.

PART III

Applying the Model

8

Inside an OLM

*Postflight Reviews in
the Israeli Air Force*

In this chapter, we present an in-depth analysis of after-action reviews, the most frequently discussed type of organzational learning mechanism (OLM) in the literature on organizational learning. The literature on this OLM describes after-action reviews in numerous settings, including high-hazard plants (Carrol, 1995, 1998), Microsoft (Cusumano & Selby, 1995), British Petroleum (Gulliver, 1987), and the U.S. Army (Baird et al., 1997). These descriptions focus on the procedural aspects of the after-action reviews and the stages that are followed. They also focus on how to conduct after-action reviews that produce lessons learned that are valid and have an impact. Our objective in this chapter is to further demystify organizational learning by examining the learning dynamics in after-action reviews: What goes on beneath the surface of the procedure- following activities? How do

AUTHORS' NOTE: This chapter is based on Ron, Lipshitz, and Popper (in press).

participants think and feel? How do they learn from the review process? How does the Israel Defense Force Air Force (IDFAF) actually learn?

We chose to study postflight reviews owing to their reputation as a "best practice" in the Israel Defense Force and in Israel in general. Air Force officers are in high demand in executive courses as lecturers on postflight reviews.

The importance of postflight reviews in the working life of the air-crews is evident from their integration into the working routine of the squadron. Training days begin with a 30-minute briefing for the aircrews that are scheduled to fly. Occasionally, the briefing includes a review of relevant lessons learned from past missions. Next, the aircrews who fly in the same formation (fighting units of two to eight planes) attend short formation briefings facilitated by the formation leaders ("number ones"). Assignments to the number one position are not based on seniority, a unique practice of the IDFAF that is designed to accelerate the development of junior officers. This means that rela-tively junior pilots may lead and later debrief pilots who are their senior in rank and experience, a practice that has direct implications for the postflight reviews culture.

A typical mission lasts between 30 and 60 minutes and is followed by a 45-minute formation postflight review, facilitated by the formation leader. Typical training days consist of the cycle of formation briefing–mission–formation postflight review, repeated two or three times, with occasionally an additional nighttime cycle. Each day concludes with a 60-minute squadron level postflight review attended by all formation aircrews and representatives of the relevant support units. This review session is facilitated by the squadron commander, one of the two deputies, or a veteran formation leader.

Formation postflight reviews are conducted in various designa-ted locations in the squadron. These are equipped with VCR and TV screens for reviewing flight films recorded by cockpit-mounted VCRs. Morning briefings and daily squadron postflight reviews are con-ducted in a central briefing room equipped with maps, VCRs, and overhanging TV screens. Postflight reviews account for 40% to 50% of training and operational time on flying days, a proportion that is reduced in wartime owing to heavier workload and the requirement for longer rest periods. Aircrews spend more time on reviewing their missions than in executing them. This time allocation explains one pilot's assertion that in regard to skill improvement, "flying without reviewing is equivalent to not flying."

Formation and daily squadron postflight reviews focus on different issues. Formation postflight reviews focus on what happened during the mission and how each pilot flew in combat exercise. The entire group reviews each pilot's video record meticulously. Particular attention is paid to errors, rule infractions, inappropriate actions that resulted in suboptimal outcomes, causes of error, potential remedies, and alternative actions that should have been taken. Daily squadron level postflight reviews deal more with output: mission accomplishment and the functioning of the formations as units. They focus on errors that are generally relevant due to their pervasiveness, excessive risk, or rule infractions that require disciplinary action. Based on these criteria, pilots select their own film segments for review in the daily postflight reviews. In practice, formation postflight reviews focus on learning, and daily postflight reviews focus on knowledge dissemination and social control functions, as will be elaborated later in this chapter.

The chapter is based on observations of debriefings and on in-depth interviews with 13 pilots and navigators, a representative sample of the aircrews of a squadron of F-16 two-seat combat airplane. All the interviews began with the open-ended question, "How would you describe the postflight reviews to a person who has not seen one?" The answers to this question provided a wealth of information on the nature of the postflight reviews and the functions that they fulfill. Ostensibly, the function of postflight reviews is to improve pilots' and navigators' performance by learning from their experience. To our surprise and the surprise of officers who read the final report, the reviews fulfill a variety of additional functions or purposes. These additional functions of the postflight review mean that learning went beyond the detection and correction of error by individual pilots. Table 8.1 presents verbatim quotes from the interview protocols that illustrate how the functions were expressed by the pilots and navigators.

❖ LEARNING FUNCTIONS

Postflight reviews fulfill three basic functions: learning functions, social control functions, and psychological functions. Altogether there are seven specific learning functions that we divided into three process and four output functions. The four output functions are improving individual performance, improving formation performance, improving training methods, and developing the doctrine and standard operating procedures of the squadron and of the IDFAF.

The three process functions are the construction of a valid mental model of the pilots' actions during the mission, learning from others, and learning from failure. We labeled them "process functions"

Table 8.1   Postflight Review Functions

Functions	Illustrative Quote
Learning	
Constructing valid mission representation	Quite often we simply do not remember what actually happened during the mission. Without the VCR, we'll miss about 40% of what happened.
	Before the postflight review, our picture of what happened in the sortie is subjective. In the formation postflight review, we try to construct a more objective picture by comparing what each of us saw from our perspective. By contributing our parts of the puzzle, we can construct a more complete and accurate picture.
Improving individual performance	If you don't debrief after flying, you may as well not fly at all [said with reference to improving performance].
	I can fly without debriefing for a while. In the long run, though, my performance will suffer.
	I personally believe that without postflight reviews, I would not care as much as I do about my performance, which will therefore regress. Postflight reviews keep you on your toes. I attribute the high performance of flight units to the fact that everybody knows that our actions will be scrutinized by others. Every pilot will tell you that as soon as we make a bad mistake, the humiliation of this being seen by everybody at the daily postflight review jumps right up in front of our eyes. So people learn to "fly the postflight review," that is, to act in a manner that will look good in the postflight review.
Improving formation performance	The postflight reviews deal with a variety of issues, including flying in formation and air combat tactics and doctrine.
Improving training effectiveness	Daily postflight reviews provide numerous points for improving the design of training.
Developing doctrine	I transfer relevant comments that I hear in daily postflight reviews directly to a squadron Standard Operating Procedures (SOP). It's really a copy, one level down, of how the Air Force works [comment made by the squadron's deputy commander].
Learning from others	Because we cannot observe all our errors, we sometimes find it difficult to admit that we made them. This is particularly true in the case of ambitious and competitive people, that is, most pilots. One of the things that we learn from experience is that errors are bound to occur so that making one is no big deal. Having others present in the postflight review,

therefore, helps to catch errors which we might otherwise either miss altogether, or notice but misinterpret. Furthermore, observing the errors of others helps us avoid them ourselves.

Learning from failure

When [a cadet in flight school] begins to "tell stories" during debriefing, the instructor cuts him short: "Stop the stories and come to the 'match-point'—why did you fail?"

Ultimately, good pilots are distinguished from bad ones by their ability to stand up and say, "That's my error"—and then avoid it the next time around.

Social control

Disciplining and fixing culpability

The business of the daily postflight review is holding people accountable for their errors.

The squadron is a small, closely knit social system. Exposing a severe error unbecoming your experience or status is not as bad in the formation postflight review, with few people around, as in the daily postflight review, with the commander saying in the presence of 50 people, "This is a very serious matter," pointing out some aspects that did not even occur to you.

Occasionally you make such a stupid mistake that you pray the VCR was not working or that the postflight review will be skipped that day.

Monitoring performance

During the flight, each pilot is locked inside the cockpit, and formation postflight reviews take place in small closed groups. The daily postflight review is when everybody can observe how everyone else performed. I learn who to assign to which mission, and we all learn with whom we would like to fly in formation [the squadron commander].

Communicating intent

The daily postflight review is a communication channel that can be used to influence the squadron [the squadron commander].

If postflight reviews focus only on results, they encourage competitiveness so people will do everything to succeed, regardless of procedures and doctrine. This is less likely if postflight reviews focus on process.

Socializing

I learned to surf as kid, and like everybody else I did not think twice when I fell, expecting to improve through mere experience. When I learned to ski, as an experienced pilot I debriefed myself each time I fell: Why I did I fall and how could I avoid it? Operating this way became second nature.

(Continued)

Table 8.1 (Continued)

Functions	Illustrative Quote
Psychological	
Social comparison	Proving the existence of a dark human need, some pilots are happy to observe others fail. I assume they feel that their own performance looks better this way.
Recognizing and rewarding	Every time pilots speak at the postflight review their status is enhanced—provided that the contribution makes sense.
	The daily postflight review is definitely an arena for rewarding whoever deserves reward and punishing whoever deserves to be punished.
	Every person is naturally happy to hear a good word, all the more so when it is broadcasted to the whole tribe in the daily postflight review.
Generating involvement	The postflight reviews are an open, democratic social system.
Bonding	Postflight reviews are the campfire around which the tribe sits to share the day's events, except that it's done in a structured fashion. It's a sort of a summary, an opportunity to show off successful experiences and learn from less successful experiences, a catalyst for sharing, publicly and candidly, positive and negative feelings and opinions.
Building resilience	Pilots and navigators are required to withstand stressful situations, be it the postflight review, air combat, or falling into enemy hands. Strengthening one's ability to withstand stresses is an ancillary outcome of participation in postflight reviews.

because they facilitate the accomplishment of the output functions. They form the core of the learning process in the postflight review, so understanding how they operate can shed considerable light on how this OLM works.

Several researchers (Kim, 1993; Senge, 1990; Wack, 1985) suggest that organizational learning is concerned with changing managers' shared mental models. Lessons learned based on distorted mental models are not likely to be valid. Owing to the speed with which events take place in air combat, aircrews sometimes form distorted mental models of what happened in the air. The postflight reviews help to improve mental models by three means: the removal of time and other distracting pressures, the VCR records, and the input from other participants, who help to correct misinterpretations of the meaning of the objective events.

Because postflight reviews are carried out in group settings, it is possible to benefit both from the input of informed colleagues, as was noted before, and from reviews of their performance. Some researchers have defined learning in general and organizational learning in particular as the detection and correction of error (Argyris & Schön, 1996). Other researchers dispute this definition as too narrow and suggest that learning from success is as important as learning from failure (Ellis et al., 1999). Echoing the facilitative effect of the costs of error on organizational learning (see Chapter 5), virtually every pilot described the essence of the postflight reviews by a triple mantra-like slogan: "What happened? What went wrong? How can we do better next time?" Thus, although postflight reviews are held after every mission irrespective of its success or failure, the attention of participants is still focused on failure.

❖ SOCIAL AND CONTROL FUNCTIONS

Like all OLMs, postflight reviews are social activities that take place within formal organizations. Therefore, they fulfill social and control functions that go beyond learning itself. These functions include disciplining and culpability fixing, socialization, monitoring performance, and communicating commander's intent. The daily postflight review offers the squadron's commanders an opportunity to monitor the performance of individual pilots and navigators—including their behavior in the postflight review itself. It enables commanders to note repeated performance problems, breaches of safety regulations, and other impediments to the squadron's functioning.

When pilots break a rule, particularly safety regulations, they are reprimanded, or worse, by the squadron commander in the daily postflight reviews. Errors of judgment are not punished, but public disclosure of error is difficult for two reasons. On the emotional level, there is loss of face. On the cognitive level, there is the requirement to supply a plausible explanation. Pilots are expected to identify their errors, try to explain them in a reasonable fashion, and suggest alternative courses of action. "Owning up to an error," said one pilot, "and coming up with a satisfactory explanation for 40 other people is a considerable intellectual effort."

Disciplining and culpability fixing involve the inherent conflict between punishing subpar performance and tolerating error for the purpose of learning. This function has to be fulfilled with tact: Overdoing the control function can cause irreparable damage to the psychological safety essential to learning. Strict monitoring and holding people accountable may entail a punitive stance that is inconsistent with a nonevaluative and safe atmosphere that promotes learning (Edmondson, 1999; Schein, 1993). The squadron's commander recognized this conflict:

> If I charge a fine for every error, people will stop disclosing their errors—it's as simple as that. And if I avoid disciplining altogether, they will get the message that "everything goes." That's why the postflight review is an intricate business that must be handled with judgment and care.

The commander's dilemma is partly mitigated by the fact that the pilots recognize the legitimacy of disciplinary action. As one pilot said, "Flying is hazardous, and without a disciplining framework, there are bound to be crashes."

An interesting by-product of the disciplining and culpability-fixing function is that pilots learn to "fly the postflight review." In other words, they learn to fly in a manner that will pass the scrutiny of others. Another interesting effect is that it raises the vigilance of participants in the formation postflight reviews. No one wants to gloss over bad performance in the supportive surrounding of the formation review, only to be caught in front of the entire squadron in the more formal daily review.

The postflight review is an arena for socializing pilots to the learning norms that contribute to its effectiveness. This process begins in flight school and continues throughout active service until it becomes second nature to the pilots. Interestingly, this intense socialization influences the pilots' behavior in all spheres of life. For example, one pilot noted that

> I, and in my opinion every pilot, learned to debrief everything that I do and goes wrong. If I put the baby to sleep and he keeps crying or if I fall from the surfboard, I automatically ask myself: What happened? What went wrong? How can I do better next time?

We believe that control, disciplining, and culpability fixing can be carried out simultaneously with learning only because the learning norms and the practice of debriefing are so deeply ingrained among the pilots and navigators. We return to this point when we discuss how psychological safety is achieved in the highly critical milieu of the postflight review.

Daily postflight reviews engage the squadron's command with groups of pilots and navigators, including those who are only part-time in the squadron. This provides the commanders with an opportunity to exercise leadership and to communicate their intents. The postflight reviews provide a forum in which they can explicitly make their agenda known by pronouncing their policies and objectives. It also offers opportunities for making this agenda known implicitly through their behavior and reactions to the information revealed by the VCRs and to the behavior of the other participants during the postflight reviews.

❖ PSYCHOLOGICAL FUNCTIONS

Psychological functions concern the effects on the participants of participating in postflight reviews. They include resilience building, bonding, involving, recognition and reward, and social comparison. Participation in postflight reviews helps build resilience by teaching participants to endure the intense stress experienced when their errors are exposed in public. Participation in the postflight review also strengthens the emotional ties of pilots and navigators to the squadron and to their colleagues. One interviewee referred to them as "the gathering of the tribe around the campfire." Because of their reputation as a best practice and their importance in the Air Force, postflight reviews have become a kind of bonding ritual. In addition to sharing their errors with each other, participants affirm their membership in an elite group, in an elite unit, and in a unique process at the vanguard of the defense of the State of Israel. The postflight reviews are also a conduit through which participants can be directly involved in changing routines and procedures of the squadron and the Air Force at large.

Postflight reviews involve the two most important activities of the flight squadrons: flying and debriefing. Behavior in the postflight review, not just performance in combat, is a source of social recognition and reward—or the opposite. Pilots and navigators are expected to behave nondefensively and to make apt comments and suggestions. These behaviors influence the position of participants in the formal and informal social order in the squadron. Similar to every group of people who engage in comparable tasks or occupy comparable roles in organizations, participants in postflight reviews compare their performance to those of other participants (Festinger, 1954).

The various functions of the postflight reviews reveal the dynamics of learning in them. Learning is principally driven by the high costs of error: injury, death, or capture. In general, postflight reviews are designed to produce improvements in four areas: personal performance, squadron performance, doctrine, and training methods. To achieve these improvements, participants are concerned with three issues: What happened (the construction of a valid mental model of the mission); what went wrong (the detection of error); and what should be done to prevent or correct the error in the future (drawing of lessons learned).

The VCRs provide objective input for answering the first two questions. Input of fellow navigators and pilots contributes to the validity and utility of the answers to the last two questions. Monitoring and disciplining provide additional motivation for learning. Communicating the commander's intent sets specific goals for learning. Socialization helps to internalize norms of behavior that facilitate learning (see below).

The psychological functions support learning in two ways. Resilience building, as well as recognition and reward, helps participants struggle with the threat and loss of face generated by the public exposure of failure, social comparison, and culpability fixing. Bonding supports socialization and generates organizational commitment and involvement, which motivate pilots to draw lessons regarding doctrine and training methods, and not just in regard to themselves.

❖ PSYCHOLOGICAL SAFETY AND LEARNING
    CULTURE IN A HIGH-THREAT ENVIRONMENT

Socialization and bonding point to the cultural aspects of the postflight reviews that, together with the psychological aspects of participation, are key for a full understanding of the dynamics of learning in the review process. In Chapter 4, we noted that psychological safety is essential for productive learning. The high degree of transparency produced by the VCR records, the rigorous search for errors, and the requirement for accounting for one's own errors in a plausible fashion seemingly create an environment that is highly threatening, particularly in the daily reviews. Indeed, interviewees referred to the difficulty of participating in the postflight review:

> Every pilot will tell you that as soon as we make a bad mistake, the humiliation of this being seen by everybody at the daily postflight review jumps right up in front of our eyes.
>
>   Occasionally the postflight review simply kills you: "Why did you make this error? Here you were shot down. Here you screwed

up the formation. Here you flew below some limit. There you broke some safety rule. Here I was shot down because of you."

Sometimes nothing goes your way, just as on other occasions everything does go your way. That is why postflight reviews often require you to be strong.

How do pilots and navigators learn productively in the postflight reviews in spite of this difficulty?

The answer lies in three factors: the postflight review culture, the psychological safety that it engenders, and the participants' long process of socialization into the postflight review culture. Pilots and navigators refer to a unique "debriefing culture" that is essential for rigorous inquiry. Analysis of the interview protocols and observation of formation and daily reviews showed that this culture consists of the five norms specified by the cultural facet of the multi-facet model: inquiry, integrity, issue orientation, transparency, and accountability (see Table 8.2).

Ed Schein, who studied organizational cultures (Schein, 1985), suggested that in addition to norms and values, organizational cultures consist of basic assumptions that are taken for granted by the organization members. The postflight reviews are based on a number of such deeply and commonly held assumptions:

- Personal experience, particularly if it is publicly reconstructed, provides an opportunity to learn and improve.
- Errors of judgment, but not rule infractions, are inevitable and represent opportunities for learning.
- Learning from experience is best accomplished by those who have participated in the experience.
- Learning is best done in group settings because individuals can benefit from sharing their knowledge with one another.
- Individual and group learning should be shared by other member units in the organization.

The cultural norm of issue orientation, coupled with a belief that errors are inevitable, reduces the loss of face generated by public exposure of error. All participants in the review make errors, and each one in turn is critiqued and has errors exposed. Furthermore, because the norms of inquiry, integrity, issue orientation, transparency, and accountability are so deeply ingrained, the loss of face generated by breaking them is greater than that which is generated by the public exposure of error. Finally, the VCRs ensure that criticism is based on hard evidence, thereby protecting participants from arbitrary criticism and enabling them to refute unjust criticisms.

Table 8.2   Postflight Review Values

Value	Behavioral Manifestations	Illustrative Text
Inquiry	Pilots point out their errors and say what they should have done. Other participants disagree and the argument continues until everybody is satisfied with the conclusions.	We always check what we have done and ask how we can improve. Always ask questions and never take anything for granted.
Integrity	Pilots point out their errors and try to explain what caused them and what they should have done instead. No defensive reactions to the comments of others.	The biggest benefit from the postflight review is that it forces you to recognize your errors for yourself in order to be able to account for them in public. I have yet to meet a pilot who lied in the postflight review.
Transparency	Transparency is achieved by the VCRs. Pilots, however, point out their errors and do not try to argue their way out of them.	Because of the VCR, the post-flight review is an act of mental striptease. People who admit that "That was an error. I need to improve here," are highly regarded.
Issue orientation	The discussion is totally focused on the VCR records and their implications. There are no attempts to apportion blame. Lower-rank participants take part in the discussion. Participants of higher rank talk more, but it can be attributed to their more extensive experience because there are no shows of deference to them.	I know that my opinion counts, and if I think that it's relevant, I will say it even to the commander of the Israel Defense Force Air Force or the world's number one ace. The opinions of someone with more flying hours under his belt count more though. Yesterday I flew as number one with a close friend who is 2 years my elder. In the postflight review, he expressed his anger at some things that I did [during the sortie] in no uncertain terms, and I responded in kind. To an outsider, it must have seemed that there was really bad blood between us. In fact, we agreed to disagree—and that was that. Having unloaded whatever

		bothered us, we went on to other issues without holding any grudge whatsoever.
Accountability	Participation in postflight reviews is taken for granted. Implementation of lessons learned depends on their acceptance by the individual pilot.	Because postflight reviews are essential, we show them respect: We arrive on time, ready to review the videos and make comments, and all data sheets are properly filled out beforehand.
		The most important thing that I do in self-debrief is prove to myself that I made the error and that it was my responsibility. If I succeed in that, I will improve. If, on the other hand, I come to the conclusion that it was someone else's responsibility, I may end up being correct—and foolish. Taking on responsibility is essential for doing better next time around.

Trust is an important component of psychological safety (Chapter 4). Two types of trust that contribute to psychological safety are present in the postflight reviews. The first is trust in other people. Owing to the norm of issue orientation, participants can trust that the criticism of their colleagues is not motivated by blame seeking or malice. The second is trust in the system. The postflight review process is trustworthy because it is fair (all participants are subjected to the same treatment), issue oriented, and evidence based.

The psychological safety present in the postflight reviews differs from the sense of security engendered by the ability to cover up one's errors and by the presence of colleagues who are willing to collude in this venture. The latter is dysfunctional for learning and likely to produce a lingering apprehension of having to pay for both the original error and the subsequent cover-up.

Pilots and navigators undergo a long process of socialization in which they internalize the assumptions and behavioral norms of the postflight review culture. This process begins right from flight school:

When a cadet begins to tell stories during debriefing, the instructor cuts him short: "Stop the stories and come to the 'match point.' Why did you fail?"

This long process of socialization selects out those individuals who cannot withstand the criticism. Those who survive acquire the resilience to withstand failure and to accept criticism in the service of learning.

❖ WHAT CAN MANAGERS LEARN FROM POSTFLIGHT REVIEWS?

According to conventional wisdom, it is impossible to draw general lessons from unique cases. The uniqueness of the postflight reviews is salient on many dimensions. Looking just at the most prominent ones, the fact that the squadron is an elite military unit sets it apart, not just from non-Israeli military and civilian organizations but from most units in the Israel Defense Force. Pilots and navigators are a highly selective professional population who undergo a long process of deliberate socialization to the postflight review learning culture. The task structure of the squadron is unusually conducive to learning, first because of the feasibility of VCRs to collect high-quality data and second because learning (training and, more generally, preparing for the next operation or war) is a major task of the military. Finally, both cost of error and proximity to the core task of the organization are high.

Nevertheless, the case of the postflight reviews offers some lessons for managers and consultants who wish to improve processes of learning in a certain organization:

1. Similar to all best practice examples, the case sets a standard for high-quality learning. Managers of any system can use these standards to evaluate the frankness of the interchanges among participants and the rigor in which the detection and correction of error is pursued in their own OLMs.

2. It pays to invest in collecting good data for learning through technical means and by instituting the proper culture and policies. The Israeli Air Force places enormous effort and resources in obtaining such data. Culture and psychological safety are all the more important for obtaining good data when technical means such as VCRs are not feasible, as is the case in most situations. Good data can also be collected by instituting policies that require careful documentation and retention of data throughout the duration of projects or in conjunction with task performance.

3. It is important to explicitly set precise performance objectives and clear standards for satisfactory performance. In the post-flight reviews, performance standards are set by the mission's objectives. Thus, pilots said that preflight briefings, in which objectives are stated, are actually part of the postflight debriefing.

4. Learning questions are important. Even with all of the technical tools for creating transparency, learning is stimulated by good thought-provoking questions. In the postflight reviews, there are always four questions. The first three are posed explicitly by participants: What happened? What went wrong? How can we do better next time? The first question leads to a better mental model of the reality. The second question frames the learning. The third question generates "actionable" knowledge to be put into practice. The fourth question is, why did the situation go wrong? This question leads to a satisfactory explanation, or theory, that constitutes new knowledge.

5. After-action reviews provide an opportunity to exercise leader-ship, announce objectives, and bolster policies that are designed to achieve them.

6. The psychological safety necessary for productive learning can be fostered, even in a highly exposed and threatening environ-ment. This kind of safety is not based on mutual protection from criticism but rather on fairness, trust in the system, and trust in others.

Finally, the most important lesson is that introducing or improving learning processes is challenging—but doable. On one hand, it requires much more than developing a vision or pronouncing a mission that includes organizational learning. On the other hand, it does not require the transformation of the organization to a "learning organization." The postflight reviews are cultural islands in which pilots and navi-gators work on improving the core task of their organization. The Air Force has tried but never succeeded in disseminating this process to support units and noncombat flight squadrons. However, the Air Force never puts resources into these dissemination efforts that are compara-ble to those invested in postflight reviews in the combat squadrons.

Everyone with whom we spoke—pilots, navigators, and high-ranking commanders—all agreed that the Air Force reaps great bene-fit from the postflight reviews. It continually generates and applies cutting-edge knowledge and skill that make the Israel Air Force a top performer in its field. It has done this by sharply focusing efforts on developing an appropriate OLM and a learning culture in the area that is most important to the organization's success. This is a lesson that is certainly applicable to any organization.

9

Is Training Organizational Learning?

I n the preceding chapter, we presented a case that illustrates how organizational learning looks according to the multi-facet model. In this chapter, we argue why one type of learning activity, training, which is often regarded as organizational learning, should not be regarded as such according to the model.

Training denotes a varied family of practices ranging from basic-skill training for workers to leadership development and executive education for potential COOs, CFOs, and CEOs. The ubiquity of these programs is such that "corporations, world-wide, spend annually billions of dollars" (Liedtke, Weber, & Weber, 1999, p. 404). There is also a growing tendency to bring training in-house, with more than 1,000 companies setting their own internal "universities" ("Extending the Learning Curve," 1997). Granted that the agents of learning in organizational learning are the organization's members, does any learning by individual members contribute to organizational learning? Alternatively, do extensive training programs constitute organizational learning?

Our answer to this question is that training per se, which aims at improving the performance of individuals or groups, should not be confused with organizational learning, which aims at improving the performance of organizations. There is an important distinction between *training*, which is learning *in* the organization, and *organizational learning*, which is learning *by* the organization. However, training programs can generate organizational learning when they move beyond the skill development and evolve into organizational learning mechanisms (OLMs).

In this chapter, we clarify this distinction by looking closely at the relationship between training and organizational learning in five organizations. We begin with a negative example by analyzing the case of Computer Chips International (a pseudonym), a company that unsuccessfully used training as the strategy for creating a "learning organization" (Ford et al., 2000). Then we will demonstrate how training evolved into organizational learning in three organizations frequently mentioned as learning organizations: Johnsonville Foods, Motorola, and Dell. Finally, we will look at Bell Laboratories, which offers an instructive example of training design using an organizational learning mind-set in order to capitalize on and add to knowledge available in the organization.

❖ COMPUTER CHIPS INTERNATIONAL

Ford and associates (2000) described and analyzed an organizational learning project carried out in the Data Shaping Division (DSD) of Computer Chips International (a pseudonym), a large manufacturer of computer chips. In the early 1990s, Computer Chips International (CCI) engaged the Organizational Learning Center at MIT to "transform the DSD into a learning organization by implementing organizational learning in a subunit of the DSD" (Ford et al., 2000, p. 74). This division had some 100 engineers working in four units of product development and one support unit. The strategy for accomplishing this transformation was to instill the "five disciplines" of the learning organization (Senge, 1990): personal mastery, shared vision, mental models, team learning, and systems thinking. The project was led by a 10-member, in-house "Implementation Team" within the Data Shaping Division as the site for the breakthrough (our term) project.

The rationale behind the intervention was that, if members of the Implementation Team learned and practiced the five disciplines, effective learning would gradually become an integral part of organizational life and spread throughout the organization. In order to make this happen, the members of the Implementation Team underwent systematic training in each of the five disciplines. In their account of this learning process, Ford and associates (2000) repeatedly described the change process in terms of the acquisition and application of *skills*:

> The Implementation Team held a meeting very early in the project at which they described their personal visions, and members subsequently reported informally on their private attempts to develop personal mastery skills. (p. 76)

> The Implementation Team considered developing their own mental model skills to be one of the most important parts of organizational learning. . . . The Implementation Team frequently and regularly used a variety of tools recommended in the literature to develop mental model skills. (pp. 76–77)

> Although espoused as a desired skill by the Implementation Team and . . . management, little of evidence of a strong awareness of a need or focus on team learning was found. (p. 77)

> Systems thinking activities included managing a relatively simple but dynamic system through simulation, . . . causal loop diagramming sessions, workshops with engineers to elicit and articulate important relationships that link product development processes. . . . Despite a significant amount of activity and practice for developing systems thinking skills, no infrastructures were put in place for this discipline. (p. 78)

> Although developing competence in some of the disciplines appears slow, the speed of skill development and dissemination is consistent with the experience of other organizations. (p. 80)

These quotations all reflect an attempt to move from learning *in* the organization to learning *by* the organization. The program's investment in training was fairly successful in improving the skills of members of the Implementation Team. However, attempts to transfer this knowledge beyond this team were largely unsuccessful. As a result, the expected transformation of the DSD to a learning organization never occurred, and the project was eventually abandoned in the wake of reorganization.

This failure was particularly puzzling because the organization provided all of the necessary preconditions for success: ample assistance, leadership, time, and upper management support (Ford et al., 2000). The researchers hypothesized that there was an inherent contradiction between organizational learning and CCI's organizational culture. They concluded that CCI was dominated by an "engineering culture" (Schein, 1996), which focuses on pragmatic problem solving, designing "humans out of systems rather than into them" (Ford et al., 2000, p. 74). In our opinion, however, this hypothesis is highly tenuous because the researchers never actually conducted a systematic study of the organizational culture. Rather they inferred the dominance of an engineering culture based on the fact that the organization's upper management consisted primarily of engineers (Ford et al., 2000).

The researchers also hypothesized that failure stemmed from the lack of formal structural mechanisms for integrating the newly acquired skills into the actual functioning of the organization:

> A common weakness across the disciplines was a lack of learning and information infrastructures that could have facilitated the dissemination and utilization of organizational lessons and skills. . . . Therefore, the Implementation Team was unable to share knowledge significantly beyond their own group. They also had little success in utilizing the knowledge they had acquired . . . to improve the DSD's operations. . . . If the DSD had been able to wait for and perceive the benefits of the Implementation Team's learning work, broader commitment might have developed. . . . Patience is needed before significant improvements due to organizational learning can be recognized. (p. 74)

This second hypothesis is more plausible because the lack of infrastructure was clearly documented in the case.

The case of CCI is particularly informative because training was aimed at imparting skills and ways of thinking considered to be essential for organizational learning. However, the progression from individual to organizational learning never occurred. This case reflects experience with many organizations that fail to make this transition from "learning *in*" to "learning *by*." The fundamental error, as we see it, stems from an assumption that there is a logical progression from individual to organizational learning. This assumption contributes to anthropomorphism, one of the sources of mystification, which sees organizational learning as individual learning writ large (see Chapter 1). It leads to the belief that if everyone in the organization is learning, then the organization is learning. However, this belief confuses two logically distinct types of learning (Bateson, 1979).

Skills and new ways of thinking are extremely important for improving the quality of organizational learning, but they are not the starting point. To the contrary, a large up-front investment in training may be counterproductive. After having put a great deal of valuable time and effort into developing these skills, organization members are often frustrated because they lack the means for using these skills in ways that can have an impact on learning at the organizational level. Although Ford and associates (2000) called for "patience," there is little evidence in the case to suggest that developing individual and group skills through training would have eventually generated organizational learning.

From the perspective of the multi-facet model, the project at Computer Chips International was fatally flawed because it lacked a well-developed structural facet, which makes learning *organizational*. The establishment of OLMs that focus on specific work-related problems or issues would have enabled individuals to learn on behalf of the organization and to disseminate this knowledge throughout the company. This case, however, does not mean that training never functions as a means for promoting organizational learning. To the contrary, the following three case examples illustrate how learning *in* the organization *can* become learning *by* the organization when training programs actually evolve into OLMs.

❖ JOHNSONVILLE FOODS

The evolution from learning *in* to learning *by* an organization can be observed in the case of Johnsonville Foods, a Wisconsin-based sausage manufacturer. Johnsonville was a financially sound but traditional organization that underwent a transformation into a learning organization (Honold, 1996). This process consisted of four phases: individual learning, group learning, intergroup learning, and ongoing learning (Honold, 1996).

Individual Learning

The goal of Johnsonville Foods CEO-owner Ralph Stayer was to develop "an organization where people took responsibility for their own work, for the product, for the company as a whole" (Stayer, 1990, p. 67). His method for achieving this goal was to "'get people into a learning mode' . . . [under the theory] that people who were learning would be more open to change" (Honold, 1996, p. 27). Johnsonville Foods began, accordingly, to offer employees three individually based learning programs. First, they could draw $100 from a Personal Development Fund, provided they spent it on learning any subject that they wanted. Gradually some two thirds of the workforce became involved in some type of formal, often job-related, education (Stayer, 1990). Second, they could learn about themselves in a Personal Development Workshop, for which they could also draw from their own Personal Development Plan. Finally, they could "spend a day with any other employee of the company [in order] to see beyond their own jobs and how their work impacted the product and the customer . . . and to explore options for personal development planning [and career opportunities]" (Honold, 1996, p. 27).

Group Learning

As people began to apply job-related learning in their work, teams began to form spontaneously to tackle a variety of problems. This led to the formation of cross-departmental "Quality of Working Life Teams" that dealt with companywide issues such as food choice for the vending machines and aligning the company's disciplinary procedures to fit its changing culture.

Intergroup Learning

As line workers began to take responsibility for their work and to organize themselves in work teams, they began to assume responsibilities normally performed by supervisory personnel or staff functions, such as budgeting, scheduling, quality control, and the hiring and training of new workers. To help them perform these tasks, workers were encouraged to take relevant training courses. In order to promote individual learning, the compensation system changed from one based on wage scales for positions and across-the-board pay raises to a "pay-for-performance" system. The system specified skill requirements for some 80 positions in the company, and pay was partly based on the number of requirements that line workers showed they had mastered by passing an evaluation.

The process by which the new system was developed illustrates the shift to the intergroup level phase in the evolution of learning at Johnsonville Foods:

> Tim Lenz, an employee in Johnsonville's manufacturing facility, was one of many who were frustrated with the company's hourly compensation strategy. . . . In 1990, he went to the vice president of manufacturing and proposed that a group of employees work together to rethink the hourly compensation system. The vice president not only approved Lenz's suggestion, he also agreed to work with the team as needed throughout the design process.

Lenz hung a note on the plant bulletin board, inviting other employees to help him try to improve the hourly compensation system. . . . Approximately 12 people signed up to help. After several introductory meetings, eight of these volunteers made the commitment to be members of the hourly compensation design team.

During one of the initial meetings, the team members decided that they needed some assistance from member services. "We invited a member of our company's [HR] department to join the team, because we knew that those skills would be necessary, and knowledge about compensation would help us determine the right system for our company," says Lenz. Because the team members had little or no expertise in the compensation area, this HR person was able to conduct initial research for the team and gather useful data to assist them in the compensation system's design.

As part of the research process, team members also conducted focus groups of employees at Johnsonville to determine their needs and expectations, benchmarked other companies to evaluate different types of compensation systems, and talked with consultants to generate ideas. . . . One particularly helpful research project was a site visit and one-day seminar on skill-based pay sponsored by Aid Association for Lutherans, a fraternal benefits society in Appleton, Wisconsin. This seminar helped the team determine what type of compensation structure would work within Johnsonville's culture. (Peters, 1994, p. 129)

The need for a compensation system that promoted learning triggered the transition from individual to organizational learning. In order to accomplish this transition, Lenz created an OLM to work on the issue of compensation. This OLM interfaced with other groups and individuals both inside and outside the company in the process of learning.

Ongoing Learning

The next step in the evolution of Johnsonville Foods seemed almost natural: Cross-functional teams began to form as "sales people started to meet with the accounts receivable department to ensure there was a common understanding on credit . . . and the information systems people began to include their internal customers on meetings to prioritize their work" (Honold, 1996, p. 31). Learning became a way of life in Johnsonville Foods, in line with Stayer's vision for the company.

The first stage in Johnsonville Food's process was not, strictly speaking, learning *in* the organization. Whereas most learning *in* the organization programs are work related, learning at this phase was neither necessarily work related nor did it necessarily take place in the organization. Beginning with its second phase, the process became a bona fide organizational learning program. The various departmental and interdepartmental teams that were formed dealt with organizational problems and produced changes in Johnsonville Food's work processes and behavioral norms. Although some learning in the organization was still carried on (training workers in new skills), these learning activities were subordinate to the goal of changing work processes.

Johnsonville Food's case demonstrates how learning *in* the organization and a skill-based reward system motivated organization members to begin and sustain a bottom-up process of OLMs development. Training in Johnsonville Foods was not initially focused on work-related subjects, but it led to the emergence of OLMs. This step set the stage for organizational learning. It also had more enduring effects on the organization than the skills-focused program at Computer Chips International because the latter never developed the essential structural component. It is not entirely clear why this transition took place naturally at Johnsonville but not at Computer Chips International. In this case, it seems likely that the leadership of Stayer played a crucial role. Perhaps the most important thing that Stayer did was to *not* stand in the way but to allow employees to set up OLMs to address real needs and problems (see Chapter 6).

Whereas Johnsonville Foods had a training *program* that evolved into a set of OLMs, Motorola institutionalized its program as an in-house *"university,"* which evolved into a single mega-OLM that centralizes this organization's work- and product-related research.

❖ MOTOROLA UNIVERSITY

"Operating on an annual basis of $200 million, . . . Motorola University is arguably . . . the most impressive of the . . . more than 1,000 corporate universities which have sprung up in the USA since General Motors pioneered the first institution of this kind in 1955" ("Extending the Learning Curve," 1997). Although *individual* development has been traditionally used in Motorola as a vehicle for *organizational* change, how it has been used changed dramatically from traditional training in the 1970s to an in-house university that is a mega-OLM for "exploring beyond the known boundaries of [the company's] business and its industry . . . [and generating] for itself new models or maps for making sense of the market" (Baldwin, Danielson, & Wiggenhorn, 1997, p. 52).

In 1979, Motorola's CEO Bob Galvin set up Motorola Training and Education Center (MTEC) with two missions: to upgrade the skills of all Motorola's employees and to expand participative management in support of Motorola's Six Sigma method for improving product quality (Baldwin et al., 1997; Wiggenhorn, 1990). MTEC was located outside the Human Resource Department to underscore that its charter was not so much to educate people as to be an agent of change, with an emphasis on retraining and redefining jobs. MTEC developed a 5-year training program that included statistical process control, basic industrial problem solving, effective presentation, effective meetings, and goal setting. An evaluation study conducted in the early 1980s showed that in spite of its apparent success (e.g., MTEC was using 50,000 hours of employee time in a typical plant of 2,500 workers), the program failed to deliver its hoped-for results. Although product-shipping goals were met, quality was not improving (Wiggenhoen, 1990).

Several causes were identified for the failure. Workers were complacent and lacked motivation to learn, complicated by the fact that a high proportion lacked basic reading and arithmetic skills required for the new quality-promoting work processes. Senior mangers did not emphasize quality and did not encourage workers to apply what they learned to their work. Part of the solution for the first problem was to upgrade the status, rewards, and recruiting of production workers. The solution for the second problem was to enlarge the scope of training to management levels. A 2-week program was designed "to send a message to the company about achieving quality through the integration of efforts across functions, a message not just about quality of product but about quality of people, quality of service, quality of the total organization" (Wiggenhorn, 1990, p. 76). To ensure participation, Galvin and 11 senior managers, who constituted MTEC's board, invited themselves and everyone else at the top to participate.

Around the same time, MTEC also started an annual event for senior management during which the CEO picked a topic of interest to be discussed by top executives with the help of experts. Between 1985 and 1987, 200 top executives spent 17 days each in the classroom learning about manufacturing, global competition, and cycle time management. People at lower level, right down to production workers, participated in portions of the same program (Wiggenhorn, 1990).

Concurrently with the changes in training of managers, MTEC changed its operation mode in the training of production workers. As the magnitude of the problem of inadequate reading and arithmetic skills of the (often immigrant) production workers became evident, the charter of the institute changed from providing continuous training to every employee to providing remedial math and language instruction to a large portion of the workforce as well. Realizing that this task was not within its area of expertise, MTEC turned to community colleges and similar institutions for help. This move eventually led to the formation of Motorola University, which replaced MTEC in 1989. The university is essentially a strategic alliance between Motorola and institutions of higher education that cooperate in the development of curriculum and training of instructors to meet the specific needs of Motorola employees and support the achievement of its strategic objectives.

The university's leadership development program, Vice President Institute (VPI), demonstrates how it applies action learning to promote participation, increase the relevance of learning, and fuse educational activities with the pursuit of strategic objectives (Eller, 1995). The 2-year program opens with a 5-day seminar in which VPs are presented with issues and problems that span the business units to which they are responsible. They then form teams that are responsible for developing and implementing solutions to these issues and problems (e.g., what will Motorola's structure look like in 2005?). Following the seminar, the VPs meet regularly to work on their programs, acquire additional knowledge and skills, and continue the process of networking begun in the seminar. The goals of the program are to (a) teach the VPs about Motorola's unique heritage so that they understand why the company has outstripped its competition and is uniquely positioned to grow, (b) help VPs explore ways to invent new technologies and businesses, (c) expand VPs' social networks in the organization, and (d) provide VPs with opportunities for personal growth.

More recently, Motorola has evolved from an institution resembling teaching-oriented colleges to full-blown research universities, underscoring its analogy to an OLM that produces knowledge that is directly relevant to its parent organization. For example, the university's College of Learning Technologies (CLT) is responsible for providing "learning solutions through the use of CD-ROMS, Web-based systems, instructor-led training, on-line communities of practice, video and satellite conferencing to Motorola world-wide" (Rucker, 1999, p. 3) so that "MU will continue to provide the 'right knowledge, right now' for Motorola and its customers" (Rucker, 1999, p. 6). E-learning is naturally particularly suitable for this mission. A specific example of this activity is the development, in cooperation with Carnegie Mellon University, of an architecture of "Just-in-Time Lectures" that enables users worldwide to access educational material of various types (text, video, virtual reality) as the need arises on the job.

Next we turn to Dell, the successful computer manufacturer that has learned to use e-learning to an even greater extent than Motorola, employing it as a vehicle for institutionalizing on-line learning.

❖ DELL LEARNING

Dell Computer Corporation is a producer of computer system products with offices in 37 countries and distribution in more than 170 (Coné, 2000). Until the crash of NASDAQ, the company enjoyed a phenomenal rate of growth that translated into 500% employee growth between 1996 and 2000. Such blessings, however, are not problem free:

Massive expansion means between 200–300 new employees a week. How do you keep new staff up to date with dozens of new products and dozen more skills? As important, how do you maintain a corporate culture when the majority of your workforce has been with the company for less than two years?" ("Dell Takes a Stroll in the Park," 2001, p. 23).

Like Motorola, Dell traditionally emphasized training. It too developed its own university with a mission to "ensure that people had the knowledge and skills to keep pace with the firm's hyper growth" (Coné, 2000, p. 59). However, in 1995, the company changed its emphasis on class learning to a delivery approach that relies on e-learning. The mission of the new entity, Dell Learning, was to (a) align learning with key business initiatives, (b) make learning directly available to everyone who needs it, (c) create clarity around competencies required for continued success, and (d) provide consistency, where needed, through global curricula (Coné, 2000, p. 59).

The basic idea was to provide Dell's employees, from line workers to top executives, with exactly the knowledge they needed just when they needed it on the job. Furthermore, it put the workers themselves in charge of accessing and utilizing this knowledge. Learning materials were accessible through Dell's internal Web site. They included materials that ranged from tools designed to support routine managerial tasks (e.g., hiring, assimilating new employees, and compensation planning) to background materials like case notes and key note transcripts. In Dell's terminology, the traditional paradigm of class learning was replaced by "stealth learning," in which the boundaries between working and learning are intentionally blurred. In our terms, Dell

University, as an in-house provider of training, was replaced by Dell Learning, an in-house institution that promotes and supports on-line/external OLMs. The reliance on e-learning "makes learning ubiquitous and a natural part of the job" (Coné, 2000, p. 60).

The e-learning format has some noteworthy advantages. It increases the control of learners, allowing them to tailor learning to their needs and schedules and to pace it according to their needs or abilities. It increases the scope of access compared with the time and space limitations of classroom learning. Evaluation modules that are attached to instructional units allow the organization to track and measure both the time spent and progress made in learning.

At the same time, e-learning is not free of limitations. It is expensive, requiring considerable investment in design expertise and IT infrastructure. It is limited to technology-based skills, which excludes, for example, interpersonal skills or team relationship building. It is interesting that even at a computer company like Dell, experience demonstrated that people were actually more comfortable with *classroom* learning, which explains the basic rationale underlying "stealth learning": Keep the act of learning out of learners' awareness. Consistent with this insight, "self-paced online courses [in Dell Learning] were supplemented by instructor-led workshops and seminars" (Murray, 2000, p. 17).

Studies evaluating Dell's return on its investment in Dell Learning show that Dell Learning paid off in some $75 million in reduced costs, increased sales, improved productivity, better customer service, faster new-hire orientation and training, and reduced turnover (Coné, 2000; "Dell Takes a Stroll in the Park," 2001).

Dell's experience is one of the clearest illustrations that we can cite of the importance of leadership support for the success of organizational learning. It is the belief of Dell's founder and CEO Michael Dell (who was involved in Dell Learning in a variety of roles) that "when learning is this important to the business, it's everybody's job—especially mine—to get behind it" (Coné, 2000, p. 65). As a *visionary*, he defined Dell Learning's unique character, which "makes every intermediary in the learning process (e.g., instructors) a target for elimination" (Coné, 2000, p. 63) and dedicated its missions and targets to those of the business. As a *sponsor*, he funded and commissioned new programs, which he then launched personally. As a *governor*, he chaired the Board of Regents of Dell Learning, "which sets policy, supports, directs, and reviews the operation of education within Dell" (Coné, 2000, p. 66). As a *subject matter expert*, he reviewed and wrote several sections of a training program on the Dell business model. As a *faculty member*, he taught in a program on strategic leadership at Dell (in which the faculty consists exclusively of Dell top executives). As a *learner,* he stressed his own learning—from employees, outsiders, and particularly customers—in his speeches and presentations. Finally, as a *marketing officer,* Michael Dell "sent personal e-mails to his team to let them know that he expected 100% participation" in a program on ethics, values, and the legal aspects of management, which the company mandated for all managers (Coné, 2000, p. 70).

Whereas Johnsonville Foods illustrates the emergence of OLMs as an outcome of training, and Motorola illustrates how centralized in-house training evolved into a mega off-line OLM, Dell illustrates how learning *in* the organization became an online/external agency OLM. The knowledge was provided by an external agent, a computerized knowledge dissemination system that functioned as a consultant or coach, which was immediately available to organization members whenever they needed it on the job.

❖ BELL LABS

We conclude our discussion of learning *in* organizations by examining training at Bell Labs' Switching Systems Business Unit (SSBU; Kelley, 1993). Two assumptions underlie Bell Lab's program for enhancing the productivity of the SSBU engineers: (1) The best way to improve performance is to change the ways professionals work rather than install new computers, and (2) in organizations that attract top people (like Bell Labs), the real difference between stars and medium-low performers lies in the strategies that their members use, not their innate abilities (Kelley, 1993). Consistent with these assumptions, the first step in developing the program was the identification of star performers. Members of this group were nominated by both their managers and their peers. Peer opinion was important because experience showed that managers tended to overlook behaviors like coming up with new ideas and helping others. According to colleagues, these were the behaviors that distinguished real stars.

Next, members of the star and middle performers groups were asked individually about their definitions of productivity, how they knew they were productive, and what exactly they did to be productive. Based on the answers to these questions, an "expert model" of engineers was constructed consisting of nine work strategies: taking initiative, networking, self-management, teamwork effectiveness, leadership, followership, perspective, show and tell, and organizational savvy (see Kelley, 1993, for exact descriptions of these strategies).

Although the two groups agreed on these broad strategies, they disagreed about their relative importance and on the detailed tactics of which they are comprised.

The next phase was the development and pilot testing of a curriculum by 16 engineers who were selected from the two original groups that participated in the previous phases of the program. The primary task of the program was "to make the critical work strategies concrete, accessible, and learnable" (Kelley, 1993, p. 135). The curriculum included nine modules for each of the work strategies that, in turn, included discussion groups, work-related exercises, rating scales for evaluating strategy performance, and homework practice exercises. The final version was a 6-week program administered by members of the development team and later on by engineers who participated in the program. The use of peer instructors was based on recognition of the fact that "knowledge professionals value the real experts on productivity in their laboratory or law firm, not trainers who breeze in, teach a day-long workshop, and then breeze out" (Kelley, 1993, p. 134).

Between 1989 and 1993, more than 600 of SSBU's engineers participated in the program. Self-evaluations of the program's effectiveness showed 10%, 20%, and 25% improvement immediately after the program, 6, and 12 months later. More impressively, a survey of graduates' superiors using behavioral rating scales showed that participants improved more in terms of skills relevant to the program than members of a control group.

The relationship between learning *in* and learning *by* was reversed at Bell Labs. It created an off-line/internal OLM for the purpose of improving the effectiveness of its training program. The output of an intensive and systematic process of organizational learning was a new training paradigm uniquely fitted to the organization's needs.

❖ DISCUSSION AND LESSONS LEARNED

What lessons can be drawn from the five case studies of learning *in* the organization discussed in this chapter?

1. *Training is not equivalent to organizational learning.* The goal of training is improving individual performance. The defining characteristic of organizational learning is organizational level changes in practices, procedures, norms, and routines. This is not a mere conceptual quibble. The case of Computer Chips International shows that training does not necessarily add up to organizational learning, either in theory or in practice.

2. *Properly managed, training (and learning in the organization in general) can and should lead to organizational learning.* We chose Johnsonville Foods, Motorola, and Dell for analysis, not because they illustrate this conclusion but based on the reputation of their programs for learning *in* the organization. The evolution of these programs into mega OLMs was a *finding* of our analysis.

3. *Make learning relevant to core tasks of the organization.* Consistent with the multi-facet model's proposition that organizational learning is more likely to succeed if it is related to the organization's vision, business strategy, or core activities, all four exemplars can be related to one of these entities. At Johnsonville Foods, learning was a central element of Stayer's vision of an organization in which managers and employees take full responsibility for their work. Engaging in learning was essential to support the constant need for new skills and to carry out independent initiatives. For Motorola, learning was essential for enabling workers to implement its Six Sigma program, which was the key to maintaining competitive advantage. At Dell, learning was indispensable for sustaining its phenomenal growth. Finally, for Bell Labs, an R & D institution, learning was essential for improving the productivity of the engineers whose performance was the absolute determinate of the organization's success.

4. *The process is the product.* This adage intends to capture the fact that once an organization begins to experiment with the institution of OLMs and compatible change in its culture and policies, it is already engaged, however modestly, in organizational learning. All four organizations learned that training alone failed to meet their requirements for know-how. Their learning *in* programs took shape through processes of trial and error that were deliberate to varying degrees. Motorola University emerged from a series of transformations that began with the failures of organizationwide training programs. The program at Bell Labs was based on a study comparing star and middle performers (the quintessential form of learning) and continued to evolve in response to the changing need of the institution. Based on his own experience, Stayer summed up this process of learning to learn as follows:

> First, just start. Don't wait until you have all the answers. When I set out to make these changes, I had no clear picture of how these new systems would interact with one another or with other company systems and procedures, but if I had waited until I had all the answers, I'd still be waiting. A grand plan was impossible; there were too many variables. I wasn't certain which systems to

change; I just knew I had to change something in order to alter expectations and begin moving toward my goal. (Stayer, 1990, pp. 74–75)

5. *The leader's commitment is crucial.* At Johnsonville Foods, Motorola, and most notably Dell, leaders played a critical role by instituting OLMs, placing learning high on the organization's agenda, devoting the necessary time and resources, and setting a personal example.

In conclusion, properly developed and supported, training can be used as a foundation or entry point for the introduction of organizational learning into organizations. At the same time, the four best practice cases analyzed in this chapter show that learning *in* the organization should not be confused with learning *by* organization.

10

High-Quality Organizational Learning

Why Do Some After-Action Reviews Work and Others Don't?

A brief report that appeared in the Israeli daily *Maariv* on 2 July, 1997, raises a question about the quality of learning from after-action reviews:

> On 31 June 1996, a foot soldier carrying a wireless set was electro-cuted when the set's antennae made contact with an overhead high tension electric cable. This was the sixth accident of this kind in the Israel Defense Forces. A committee appointed to investigate the acci-dent discovered that specific instructions issued based on lessons learned from the previous accidents had not been followed. (p. 4)

The report clearly documents a failure in organizational learning. Five accidents were followed by after-action reviews, yet the same acci-dent occurred again, and with a lethal outcome, on a sixth occasion. The Israel Defense Force is not the only organization that fails,

AUTHOR'S NOTE: This chapter was written in cooperation with Neta Horin-Naot and is based on Norin-Haot.

occasionally, to learn from its experience. Why or when do such failures occur, and what can be done to avoid them?

An obvious cause of failures of learning is a low-quality learning process. As we pointed out in Chapter 2, the mere existence of organizational learning mechanisms (OLMs) is insufficient to ensure productive learning. In Chapter 3, we presented five cultural norms that increase the likelihood of productive learning. In this chapter, we offer a more inclusive list of factors that influence the probability that lessons learned from after-action reviews will be remembered, thereby lowering the likelihood that past errors will be repeated.

The factors were identified in a study that compared two episodes of low-quality and two episodes of high-quality after-action reviews in an elite unit of the Israel Defense Forces. The unit operates a variety of OLMs, the most important of which are after-action reviews. Every combat or training mission is followed by an after-action review, and preparation for operational missions includes a review of relevant lessons learned from similar missions. After-action reviews in the unit vary in quality. Some are considered exemplary by the officers and soldiers who participated in them; others are regarded as a waste of time. The principal criterion on which these judgments are based is the effectiveness of assimilation, namely, the long-term implementation of lessons learned. The episode at the beginning of the chapter is an example of failure according to this criterion.

Using assimilation as a criterion for determining the success of after-action reviews makes sense because long-term implementation of lessons learned prevents repetition of accidents and errors. There are two qualifiers for this criterion. First, the lessons learned have to be valid, that is, effective solutions to the causes of the problem. In addition, they have to be reviewed periodically to test their continued relevance to the organization's mode of operation, as well as to changing environmental conditions.

A serious limitation of the assimilation criterion is that it requires the passage of time in order to know if a given learning process was successful. To correct this limitation, we decided to study the ways in which the *processes* that produced effective or ineffective assimilation differed systematically. This way we hoped to complement the *outcome* criterion of assimilation with criteria that pertain to the after-action review *process*.

Owing to its unorthodox and dangerous combat methods, the elite unit under study experiences training accidents. The study concerned four reviews of such accidents. The first step was to ask some 30 officers to identify after-action reviews that represented high- and low-quality reviews and, based on their evaluations, select two high- and two low-quality reviews on which there was consensus regarding their quality. The reviews spanned a period of several years and were sequenced as a low-quality review, two high-quality reviews, and a low-quality review. We interviewed every available officer who participated in each review and analyzed all the documentation that was available on them.

The accidents required more complex after-action reviews than the postflight reviews discussed in Chapter 8 because of the complexity of the exercises, the number of persons involved, the severity of the outcome, the uncertainties regarding their causes, and the number of required changes. To convey a sense of the two types of reviews, we present an outline of one example of each.

❖ LOW-QUALITY AFTER-ACTION REVIEW

The review concerned the death of a soldier during a dangerous combat exercise. The review proceeded in four phases: information gathering, drawing of lessons learned, implementation, and assimilation.

Information Gathering

As soon as he was informed that a soldier was missing, the exercise commander convened a debriefing on the ground to assess the situation and begin a search. The unit's commander conducted a more systematic review after the soldier was found dead. Although the information-gathering phase is intended only to ascertain the facts of the accident, the commander drew some key lessons learned during this phase. The corps to which the unit belonged appointed an external investigative committee that four hours later began interviewing officers and soldiers who participated in the exercise. Another external investigation was launched by the military police, as required by the Israel Defense Forces regulations. The phase of information gathering continued for 2 days.

Drawing of Lessons Learned

We could not obtain reliable details on this phase either from the interviewees or from the documents (which we take to indicate its shallowness). The usual format requires the commander of the exercise, the officers in charge, and other participants to provide information on the objectives, planning, and execution of the exercise from their different perspectives and answer the questions of the unit's commander and other officers who conduct the review. At the conclusion of this process, the unit's commander decides on lessons learned regarding training procedures, combat doctrine, and logistics.

Implementation

Three committees were appointed by the unit's commander to translate the lessons leaned into changes in training procedures, combat doctrine, and logistics. The changes were summarized in a document that was presented in a conference attended by the unit's high- and middle-rank officers. This phase continued for 2 months. The overall duration of the review was markedly short for an accident that involved the death of a soldier.

Assimilation

To ensure assimilation, the lessons learned were refreshed in several "safety symposia" in the period following the after-action review. The after-action review of a similar accident some 2 years later (the high-quality process below) revealed that some key relevant lessons learned were never implemented.

❖   HIGH-QUALITY AFTER-ACTION REVIEW

This episode occurred under the successor of the commander who succeeded the officer who commanded the unit during the low-quality review. The two accidents were similar—a soldier who disappeared during an exercise of the same combat technique was later found dead. The two reviews consisted of the same four phases.

Information Gathering

The deputy commander arrived on the scene as soon as the soldier was declared missing. He debriefed the officers and soldiers to assess the situation and direct the search. Several additional debriefings were held later, both on the grounds and in the commander's office. No conclusions were drawn at this stage. The external investigations by the Military Police and the committee appointed by the corps commander began their work shortly after the accident. This phase continued for 3 days.

Drawing of Lessons Learned

An initial after-action review was held in the unit 4 days after the accident. Its report did not identify the causes of the accident but proposed three hypotheses, one of which was considered the most plausible. In addition, it offered 22 recommendations. Two of these were the same recommendations of the external committee in Episode 1, which had not been assimilated. The commander accepted most of the recommendations (this phase continued for 5 days).

Implementation

Eight days after the accident, the commander appointed five committees to study in depth the conclusions and lessons learned of the initial review relating to different subjects (e.g., training and standard operating procedures). Each committee was headed by the most senior officer knowledgeable on its subject. The committees were instructed to conduct extensive investigations and not to limit themselves to narrow issues relevant to the accident. The five committees were coordinated by a steering committee headed by a senior officer. The committees prioritized their agendas and dealt with subjects relevant to routine operations of the unit first. Proposed lessons learned were tested by the training and operational subunits and the results were fed back to the committees, which changed them if necessary. Detailed instructions for implementation were issued to the relevant subunits and units of the corps. The set of final lessons learned and the review process were documented in detail. This process continued for 3 months.

Assimilation

During the next 2 years, the unit held several symposia to refresh the lessons learned, and their implementation was closely inspected. An investigation 3 years after the accident showed that all the lessons learned were operative.

Why did the two cases produce such different assimilations? An examination of their outlines (Table 10.1) reveals that although they followed the same four phases, the, low- and high-quality reviews differed in their breadth and duration. Finer grained analysis produced seven more specific attributes that could account for their different outcomes:

- The commander's leadership style
- The extent to which the review was systematic
- The review's (low vs. high) place in the unit's agenda
- The productiveness of the internal inquiry
- The effectiveness of the external committee
- The plausibility of the lessons learned
- The effectiveness of the implementation and assimilation processes

Table 10.1 After-Action Review Process in the High- and Low-Quality Cases

	High-Quality Process		Low-Quality Process	
Phase	Duration	Comments	Duration	Comments
Information gathering	3 days	Several debriefings held on the grounds and in the base. No conclusions are drawn.	2 days	Two debriefings held on the ground. The commander draws some key lessons learned during this phase.
Drawing of lessons learned	5 days	An initial after-action review headed by a senior officer proposes three hypotheses and 22 recommendations (including 2 by the external committee). The commander accepts most of the recommendations.	? (See next column)	? No documentation available on this phase (an indication of shallowness).
Implementation	3 months	The commander appoints five committees headed by a steering committee to study the conclusions and lessons learned of the initial review and related subjects in depth. Final lessons learned formulated and documented after testing by training and operational units. Detailed instructions issued to all relevant units.	2 months	The commander appoints three committees to translate the lessons leaned into changes in training procedures, combat doctrine, and logistics. Changes summarized in a document that is presented in a conference attended by the unit's high and middle rank officers.
Assimilation	3 years	Several symposia held to refresh the lessons learned. Close inspection of their implementation. An investigation shows that all the lessons learned are operative.		

These attributes can be used both to guide effective reviews and to evaluate their quality. We now discuss each of them in detail.

Leadership Style

Chapter 6 proposed that leadership is a key influence on the probability that organizational learning will take place and that it will be productive. The comparison between the low- and high-quality reviews showed that this factor is especially important when the conditions for learning are difficult. After-action reviews of fatal accidents take place under trying circumstances. The unit is pressured by higher echelons, the media, and the families of the dead and injured soldiers. There are strong feelings of sorrow, guilt, and fear among those who were directly involved and unit members whose friends have died or are likely to be punished. Everyone worries that results of the after-action review may affect him personally. Two behaviors distinguished between commanders of the high- and low-quality reviews. The first, *support*, was specific to their circumstances. The other, *receptiveness*, is relevant to any process of organizational learning.

Support. The commanders of the unit in the high-quality reviews supported their subordinates by being sensitive to their emotional needs and shouldering responsibility for the outcomes of the review. Both were explained by a commander:

> My principal concern was to preserve the unit. Fatal accidents can cause units to fall apart, and to preserve them you must take care of their people. The officer in charge of the exercise was a reservist who expected to return home after a short period in service. Instead he faced the prospect of going to jail, possibly for a long period. Such experiences destroy people. At the outset of the review, I told the participants that they should relax because I was responsible for whatever happened in the unit, for better or worse. I tried to impress on them that I trusted them and that they were not alone.

In contrast, the commander during a low-quality review was visibly stressed and left an impression that his only concern was to save his own skin:

> In four meetings, he and other officers screamed at four different junior officers. . . . What disturbed me most was that our commander was willing to take responsibility for success but not for failures. It

is impossible to draw [valid] lessons learned when you know that if, god forbid, something happens, you will be left on your own.

Receptivity. The purpose of after-action reviews is to introduce required changes in current practices and procedures. This purpose is not likely to be achieved if the commander is not receptive to the suggestions and opinions of others. The commander may reject or not implement them outright, or signal through his reluctance to listen that making suggestions, to begin with, is a waste of time. Overruling the objections of others, the commander of a low-quality review decided on lessons learned that were subsequently not followed in practice and rescinded by his successor. The same commander rejected suggestions involving new techniques or novel ideas because "We tried it before. It will not work." As a result, "Instead of going forward with new methods and technologies, the unit went backward. A week after he left, his successor began to adopt the suggestions that were rejected."

Systematic Design of the Review Process

Other researchers of after-action reviews offered the following guidelines for conducting after-action reviews:

- Invite the right people.
- Appoint a facilitator.
- Revisit the objectives.
- Go through the project (i.e., action) step by step.
- Ask what went well? Find out why these aspects went well and express the learning as advice for the future.
- Ask what could have gone better.
- Ensure that participants leave the meeting with their feelings acknowledged.
- Record the meeting.

These guidelines are appropriate for relatively simple, one-shot reviews, such as the postflight reviews described in Chapter 8.

The criterion of systematic design is intended for complex reviews such as those discussed in the present chapter. It specifies the assignment of committees to investigate a broad range of issues, manning them with persons that have relevant professional and organizational authority, providing them with sufficient resources, appointing a steering committee to coordinate their work, and monitoring their progress periodically through meetings that critique and integrate their work. High-quality reviews were designed according to this prescription:

Work was divided among several committees. One analyzed the training program. Other committees analyzed operational plans (to find if the training program was compatible with them), the unit's combat doctrine, and so on and so forth. The committees were headed by senior officers and composed of senior and middle-rank officers with the best expertise on their subject matter in the unit. Each committee had a detailed plan with specific goals, subgoals, and a timetable. All the committees met every 2 days to present their findings, discuss them, and decide on how to proceed.

Compare this with the testimony of a participant in a low-quality review who said that "I do not remember a real process. The most serious debriefing was conducted on the grounds about half an hour after the accident, and that was it."

This quote points to another important principle of systematic design: Separate information gathering from making conclusions and the drawing of lessons leaned. The separation is important for conducting a thorough information search, basing lessons learned on all potentially available information, and preventing commanders from committing themselves to premature conclusions that they will have difficulty reversing. The quote shows that the commander of the low-quality review violated this principle. Lessons leaned were drawn at an early stage of the after-action review, the stage which should have been devoted to gathering information. In contrast, the commander of the high-quality review took deliberate steps to separate the two phases. At the beginning of a preliminary debriefing, he instructed participants that the objective was to gather as much information as possible soon after the accident and that he would make no conclusions based on this debriefing. An added benefit of his clarification was that "it helped people to talk freely without worrying about the consequences of what they were saying."

The Place of the Review in the Unit's Agenda

In Chapter 5, we claimed that when the learning effort is closer or more relevant to the core mission, there is a higher likelihood that it will receive resources and attention, catch on, and succeed. Safeguarding soldiers' lives is high on any fighting unit's agenda. Nevertheless, the high- and low-quality reviews differed in the extent to which participants remembered them as central or marginal in the unit's ongoing operation. The difference can be attributed to the attention that the different commanders paid to the review process. One high-quality review was actually headed by the commander himself. He was deeply involved in all its activities and saw to it that the review and its outcomes were presented to the unit's senior officers, who were therefore familiar with its details. Another indication of a review's place in the unit's agenda was the time that was devoted to it relative to other tasks. A participant in a high-quality review remembered the following:

> We thought that the review was of high quality and so felt obliged, professionally and morally, to participate. All of us who participated in the review except for one officer were simultaneously engaged in other missions—the unit was particularly busy at the time with operational missions as well as maintaining its training operations. I was involved in the planning of an operation that took a long time. Although I did not downplay the importance of the review, I finally had to spend more time on that [other] operation.

The officer's efforts to participate in the review in spite of competing operational duties is a clear indication of its high place in the unit's agenda. Significantly, he and other officers felt morally obliged to participate because they perceived the review as a serious investigation into the death of a comrade.

Another indication of the review's place in the unit's agenda is participants' ability to remember its details. Participants in high-quality reviews remembered them in detail; those who participated in low-quality reviews had a hard time doing that:

> In my opinion, the process was a complete failure. I arrived to the unit 2 or 3 weeks after the accident, and they were already busy with the implementation of lessons learned. The accident could have happened a year rather than 2 months before I arrived. The review did not receive any special attention.

The place of the review in the unit's agenda sends a message about the importance of its lessons learned, which clearly affects the probability that these will be remembered and implemented.

The Productiveness of the Internal Inquiry

This criterion pertains to the learning process itself: To what extent do the processes of gathering and analyzing information by the unit's members enable them to draw valid conclusions and lessons learned? According to the multi-facet model, a positive answer to this question depends on two factors: (1) the extent to which the culture in the after-action reviews conforms to the learning norms and (2) the extent to which participants feel psychologically safe during the review process. We did not find evidence for accountability in either low-or high-quality reviews, and participants in both types of reviews exhibited integrity. The latter was most clearly observed in the reports of the external committees in both types of reviews, which included candid admissions of errors by officers who testified to the committees. For example, the officer who supervised one of the exercises admitted that he had not reviewed the safety regulations before the exercise (as required) because "We do this exercise routinely." Another supervising officer admitted that he neglected to check the area in which the soldier was found dead. Similar to the pilots and navigators in Chapter 8, members of this unit attributed the norm of integrity that was ingrained in it to the long process of socialization of its members:

> Right from basic training in the unit, we are told to report after any exercise on what we did [correctly] or failed to do with an emphasis on the latter. . . . Reporting truthfully is a norm that is part of the culture of the unit. Compared to other organizations with which I am familiar, people here are honest, and you can obtain from them something that approximates the [objective] truth.

Our analysis did show consistent differences between the high- and low-quality reviews in terms of inquiry, transparency, and psychological safety:

Inquiry. The following quote from a participant in a low-quality review demonstrates lacking inquiry:

> Although my roommate OKed the exercise, no one came to talk with him. . . . The debriefing on the ground did not find anything unusual. The commander decided on some minor changes and that was it. I do not remember any follow-up discussions. During the internal review, we were hardly asked two and a half questions on the accident, and most attention was paid to the injury of a soldier during the search.

Lacking inquiry is shown in the above quote through the narrow and unfocused information search, the fact that no attempt was made to go beyond the obvious ("anything unusual"), and the making of quick decisions without serious analysis. Not surprisingly, the status quo was left essentially unchanged, in spite of the fact that a soldier had been killed. Compare this with the manifestation of inquiry in a participant's description of how interim conclusions served to broaden and deepen the analysis in high-quality reviews:

> During an after-action review, you try to map all the factors that may have determined the outcome. You begin from the present and go backward looking at the training course, the operational process, beliefs, behaviors, and then—based on common sense, and debriefs, many debriefings—you focus and come to a conclusion. Now this is your understanding of the accident, but different people may come to different understandings from different perspectives. That is why it is important to take into account the information and conclusions of other committees and the external investigation. At the end, you come to a reasoned conclusion based on your analysis and that of others in relation to training, safety, combat doctrine, and so on.

Transparency. Manifestations of transparency were usually associated with those of integrity, inasmuch as both entailed disclosure of error. Here is how one participant in a high-quality review described how the two values were manifested in the learning process:

> The unit is generally characterized by openness [i.e., transparency] and truthfulness [i.e., integrity]. I do not think that anyone tried to hide something or to force something on others. Everyone said his mind. Other people could be angry or disagree with him, but he was heard. I attribute this to the spirit of the unit, which is influenced by the commander as well as the way we debrief right from basic training, particularly the way in which errors are dealt with in them.

The following quote underscores the subtle distinction between integrity and transparency. Integrity is admitting error to yourself or others when it is discovered (as opposed to becoming defensive), whereas transparency is allowing others to observe your actions so that they provide you with valid feedback on them:

> There was openness at least to hear what people had to say. There were different committees, and people came to say what they knew and thought. In the final analysis, the intention is not to cover up or falsify what has happened. People truly wish that accidents

will not be repeated. Listening to people with different perspectives allows you to come to different conclusions.

Psychological safety. Psychological safety is important for productive learning. In its absence, participants become occupied with defending themselves instead of trying to understand what went wrong and how to improve for the future. Commanders' sensitivity and support played a decisive role in the presence or absence of psychological safety in the reviews that we studied. One officer described how the commander's leadership style and lack of sensitivity lowered his psychological safety this way:

> The atmosphere during the review was uncomfortable. It had an effect on me and must have affected the others. An officer was late, and the commander let him know that in his customary threatening style. A soldier was seriously injured when he fired a flare during the search. As the subject came up in the review, I remember saying that I did not order to fire the flare. I must have been anxious because I would not have mentioned it otherwise. One officer ran to call a medic instead of helping the injured soldier. My impression during the incident was that he was shocked, but in the review he said that he was acting deliberately. In my opinion, he was trying to make his actions look better.

The Effectiveness of the External Committee

The rationale for appointing external committees is clear: Enlist relevant expertise from outside the unit and correct potential biases in the work of internal reviews with a review by persons who can study it objectively. To be effective, external committees should possess expertise and objectivity *and be perceived to posses them.* The credibility of the external committee in a low-quality review was damaged irreparably because it included an officer who was on leave from the unit but scheduled to return as its commander. The credibility of another was destroyed because the accepted opinion in the unit was that its members lacked the required expertise to understand the exercise. Neither committee managed to affect the lessons learned that were decided on by the respective commanders. In contrast, participants in one high-quality review were impressed, not just with the objectivity and expertise of the external committee but by the time and effort that they put into their work. Ninety percent of the recommendations of this committee were accepted by the unit's commander.

The Plausibility of Lessons Learned

There are two methods to ensure that lessons learned will be implemented: Apply external force and generate internal commitment. Applying external force relies on monitoring the implementation processes and punishing those who are caught disobeying them. Generating internal commitment depends on convincing the unit's members that the review has unearthed the causes of the accident and that the lessons learned are plausible, that they provide effective and applicable remedies to these causes. The plausibility of lessons learned was often judged by *how* they were drawn. Thus, a participant in a low-quality review reported that its lessons learned were perceived as "panicky" because the commander decided on them at an early stage without waiting for the conclusion of the full review. In contrast, a participant in a high-quality review thought that "the review produced the correct lessons learned because it considered all the aspects of the accident and elicited a wide range of opinions from different persons."

Judgments of plausibility were sometimes determined by the compatibility of the lesson learned with the unit's culture. A key lesson learned in the low-quality accident was hotly contested as impractical. The underlying issue was a tension between safety and risk taking that was ignored in the review. The informal norm in the unit was that model fighters take risks to accomplish their missions. Ignoring this norm, the change in procedure decided on in the review limited soldiers' freedom of movement to increase their safety. The change was contested as "impractical" and was never implemented in spite of the risks involved. A high-quality review recognized the conflict between formal procedures that stress safety and the unit's culture and introduced new safety regulations in conjunction with a campaign that educated soldiers on the risks involved and that promoted the idea that model fighters avoid unnecessary risks.

The Effectiveness of the Implementation and Assimilation Processes

Implementation is often mentioned as the bottom-line criterion for high-quality organizational learning. Because of our interest in the prevention of repeated errors in the long term, we extend this criterion to include assimilation. The effectiveness of implementation and assimilation is partly dependent, of course, on satisfying the previous six criteria of the review process. As we'll show, these form a causal chain that extends from the commander's leadership style to successful assimilation. In addition, the low- and high-quality reviews differed in terms of specific actions that were taken in the latter and neglected in the former to ensure that lessons learned were implemented and assimilated. These included (a) detailed documentation of the lessons learned; (b) dissemination of the lessons learned to all relevant units with explanations of their underlying rationale, changes in mode of operation that they entailed, and risks that were involved in disobeying them; (c) close supervision and monitoring of implementation of the lessons learned; and (d) regular "refresher" conferences, in which the above are repeatedly illustrated with "war stories" on the accidents (such as the story of the original accident) that the lessons learned were intended to prevent.

As we have just mentioned, these six criteria form a causal chain with the commander's leadership style to determine the review's success or failure. The commander affected all the factors that differentiated between the low- and high-quality reviews, except for the external committee. He determined the design of the review process, and his leadership style influenced the productiveness of the learning process. Proper design had two outcomes: First, systematic data collection and analysis increased the probability that the causes of the accident would be identified correctly and that the correct lessons learned would be drawn. Second, involving as many unit members in the review as possible by assigning them to various subcommittees and testing the plausibility of preliminary lessons learned improved understanding of the rationale of new procedures and regulations and commitment to their implementation. The commander also determined the place of the review in the unit's agenda, which, in turn, determined the amount of time that they could devote to the process and sent a message to the unit at large regarding the importance of the review and the implementation of its lessons learned.

The receptivity of the commander and the latitude that he left to the committees to pursue their investigations were key factors in promoting the value of inquiry. The commander's support shielded members from fear and promoted integrity, transparency, and issue orientation.

The seven factors identified in this chapter are not limited to determining the quality of after-action reviews in military units. The extent to which the review is designed and carried out systematically, the leadership style, receptiveness and support of higher echelons, the productiveness of the learning process, the expertise and objectivity of external resources, the plausibility of the lessons learned, and the effectiveness of implementation will affect the success of assimilating lessons learned in every type of organization. For mangers who wish to maximize assimilation, the chapter has a general lesson beyond ensuring that the seven criteria are achieved: To succeed, they must see that the lessons learned win both the hearts *and* minds of the organization members. It is not sufficient that lessons learned be valid in some objective sense or in the opinions of experts. Unless the organization members judge them to be valid *and* important, they will not make the necessary effort to change their current patterns of behavior. That is why it is important to involve as many members as possible in the process, to let those who are directly involved participate in a meaningful way, and to persuade the remaining members of the organization of the importance of lessons learned through extensive communication and the symbolic value of serious support and resources.

11

Demystifying the Learning Organization I

The Case of Hewlett-Packard

When Peter Senge (1990) reframed the issue of organizational learning as the "art and practice of the *learning organization*," he transformed an esoteric academic concept into a popular vision of a brave new world of organization. This framing of the issue, however, created an implicit distinction between companies that learn and those that do not. Quite naturally, forward-looking, self-respecting CEOs wanted their companies to be identified as the former (Gerhardi, 1999). This distinction also implied that *becoming* a "learning organization" requires a deep and far-reaching transformation. Thus, before anyone could clearly define this distinction in operational terms, many managers aspired to fundamentally change their organizations either through an application of Senge's five disciplines or some other method. As we pointed out in the introductory chapter, this gap between the vision and practice persists and contributes to mystification.

Demystifying the learning organization means stepping back from "either-or" or transformational thinking. As we have pointed out in earlier chapters, organizational learning can be understood by observing the structural mechanisms (OLMs) that make individual learning *organizational* and at the contextual, policy, psychological, and cultural factors that influence the effectiveness of the learning processes that take place within these structures. Structural organizational learning mechanisms exist in some form in most, if not all, organizations. If they did not, organizations could not survive for long in a changing world. In this respect, talking about "the" learning organization creates a false dichotomy and distracts attention from the everyday managerial actions that promote learning, although not necessarily transforming the organization as a whole.

The claim that all organizations learn does not mean that all organizational learning is equal. The literature that has emerged over the past decade clearly indicates that some organizations, or organizational units, excel at knowledge creation and management. The question, then, is what actions managers can take to enable their organizations to learn more, faster, and better. In the next two chapters, we will take close look at exemplary organizations, Hewlett-Packard Consulting (this chapter) and Chaparral Steel (Chapter 12), in order to illustrate that they invest heavily in both OLMs and in policies that promote learning under a given set of strategic and task conditions. These observations suggest an observable, operative definition of the learning organization that can guide management action.

If any organization deserves to be an exemplar of organizational learning and knowledge management, it is Hewlett-Packard (Davenport & Prusak, 1998; Parskey & Martiny, 2000). Founded in Dave Packard's Palo Alto garage in 1939, HP was ranked 11th in the Fortune 500 in 2005 with $73.061 billion in revenues, more than 140,000 employees in 178 countries, and thousands of products in IT infrastructure, global services, business and home computing, imaging, printing, and Web-related applications. In an industry known for its turbulence and the meteoric rise and fall of companies, HP has maintained consistent growth and leadership. HP is also well known for an organizational culture that promotes technological and managerial innovation, employee commitment, and social responsibility.

This chapter examines two case studies of organizational learning at Hewlett-Packard. Although both cases illustrate productive learning, one of these initiatives was discontinued whereas the other spread and became institutionalized. By comparing the two cases, we will attempt to understand both the design of the learning organization and the factors that lead to more sustainable learning processes. The example of the successful program will show that organizational learning can be promoted in a gradual, but deliberate, process that does necessarily involve transformation or heroic measures.

❖ HP'S WORK INNOVATION NETWORK (WIN)

Zell (1997, 2001) tells the story of HP's "Work Innovation Network" (WIN). In 1990, a group of internal consultants from HP's Strategic Change Group began to teach HP managers how to improve the productivity of their units by organizing them as self-managing teams. The initial change strategy was to illustrate the benefits of self-managing teams to the wider organization by conducting intensive pilot projects with a small number of sites throughout the organization. These initial efforts led to reports of substantial improvements in quality, productivity, and responsiveness, which spread quickly throughout the company and generated great interest in work redesign. Within a short time, this group found itself unable to keep up with the demand for consulting services (Zell, 2001). In response, the consultants created WIN, through which participating managers met once each quarter for 2 to 3 days in order to learn about work redesign and autonomous teams.

WIN was based on a set of explicit principles for countering common barriers to the diffusion of innovation in organizations. The first principle was avoiding forced, top-down change by enabling managers to "pull" information and innovations that they needed on a just-in-time basis. Thus, participation in WIN was strictly voluntary and restricted to managers who expressed a willingness to actually experiment with self-managing teams. WIN itself was self-managed—the content and format of each meeting was planned by consultants and a rotating group of participating managers who continuously sensed the needs of the network.

WIN meetings were a forum in which managers could discuss their own redesign efforts among themselves as well as with the consultants. Networking was facilitated through seating arrangements and informal meetings in which participants could choose both their partners and the topics of discussion. Once participants began to implement redesign, they presented detailed cases at forum meetings. Peer consulting was used as a method for reflecting on experience and for developing skill in giving and receiving feedback. "Networking" allowed managers to maximize face-to-face communication among units, to facilitate the dissemination of information and knowledge, and to form alliances to push through changes that did not receive initial top-down support.

Creating a "safe environment" (that is, psychological safety) was considered extremely important for encouraging open and honest dialogue in which members felt comfortable sharing both their successes and failures. As WIN grew, some members began to feel that presentations became less personal and truthful:

A WIN member circulated an e-mail urging a return to presenting the whole picture of redesign efforts. "We're veering away from honesty," the memo said. "We need to return to personal disclosure about presenters' sources of pride and disappointment, because that's what the audience learns from most" (Zell, 2001, p. 81).

Maintaining a safe environment was also the reasoning behind the rejection of a suggestion to videotape the peer-consulting sessions.

Finally, WIN consultants introduced "action research" as a method for ensuring high-quality and relevant solutions, as well as systematic evaluation of both processes and outcomes. Participating managers were required to document their learning in "white papers" that described their objectives, methodologies, impact on organizational performance, and lessons learned. These papers were then distributed and discussed by the participants at each WIN meeting so that the learning could be disseminated, helping others deal with similar obstacles (Zell, 2001, p. 81).

According to participants' feedback, WIN was a very successful project. Eighty percent said they had received full return on their investment; more than two thirds said it gave them moral support and good ideas on how to implement self-managing teams. The WIN network was considered a more valuable source of information than HP's internal consultants and other sources of information. Anecdotal evidence provided some support for the effectiveness of the transition of self-managing teams, which was adopted in one or more units of a third of HP's twenty divisions.

In 1995, WIN's existence was threatened by a companywide effort to cut costs that banned all nonessential travel and meetings of over 20 people. WIN's leaders argued for treating WIN as a special case so as "not to send the wrong message" to the company. However, these efforts failed to persuade management, and the program was discontinued.

❖ THE HPC KNOWLEDGE MANAGEMENT INITIATIVE

HP Consulting (HPC) is the 4,000-employee-strong service wing of Hewlett-Packard. Its mission is to "ensure that customers get the greatest return from the products and services they buy from HP" (Parskey &

Martiny, 2000, p. 27). The HPC "Knowledge Initiative" was started to help HPC consultants to "tap into the knowledge of the broader HP organization to solve [clients'] business issues" (Parskey & Martiny, 2000, p. 28). Our analysis of the initiative is based on two insider accounts written by the managers of HPC's Global Knowledge Management Marketing and Global Knowledge Services (Martiny, 1998; Parskey & Martiny, 2000).

In 1995, a team of consultants interviewed HPC's clients on the effectiveness of the organization in using HPC knowledge in their work. The survey results, as reported to HPC management, revealed that clients believed that the value and depth of HPC knowledge is highly dependent on the consultants assigned to their project. These results were disturbing because HPC felt that it had to deliver ever increasing new and innovative services in a consistent, high-quality manner, regardless of the consultants assigned to the engagement. In order to meet this challenge, the survey concluded, HPC "must rapidly leverage our experience from one project to the next and from one part of the world to another" (Parskey & Martiny, 2000, p. 28).

The results of the survey overcame doubts among HPC consultants about the need for increased knowledge sharing and reuse in meeting customer demand. More important, HPC's new vice president and general manager realized that organizational learning and knowledge management were critical to the success of the business. In order to respond to this need, the general manager launched the "Knowledge Management Initiative" and remained actively involved in it throughout its operation.

HPC's senior management team set forth a vision in which HPC consultants "feel and act as if they have the knowledge of the entire organization at their fingertips when they consult with customers." (Parskey & Martiny, 2000, p. 30) Achieving this state required making this knowledge explicit and available. It also meant that consultants would have to know how to locate the specific information and knowledge they needed. Most important, it required willingness on their part to share their knowledge and to learn from one another's experience. The vision also linked these behaviors to an organizational reward system recognizing "those consultants that share and those that leverage others' knowledge and experience as the most valuable members of the HP team" (Parskey & Martiny, 2000, p. 30).

The project began with the establishment of the Organizational Learning/Knowledge Management (OL/KM) Team to lead the initiative. This team specified three measurable definitions of success for the initiative: learning from the success and failure of different projects, sharing knowledge among projects, and minimizing redundant "innovation" (reinventing the wheel). In addition, three mechanisms were established for achieving these objectives. The first mechanism was a "postproject review" process to facilitate learning from successes and failures of completed projects. The guidelines for running the reviews promoted openness and trust by setting a number of ground rules: All members of the project team would participate; lessons learned would be based on consensus; and the emphasis would be on learning rather than blaming or finding fault.

A second OLM, periodic "project snapshots," were instituted for ongoing efforts. This mechanism consisted of team meetings devoted entirely to identifying and documenting knowledge that had been generated in the course of the project so far and that could be used by other teams. The third mechanism, "learning communities," was defined as "informal groups of people that cross organizational boundaries and meet . . . face to face or through conference calls . . . to discuss best practices, issues, or skills that the group wants to learn about" (Parskey & Martiny, 2000, p. 39). The third objective, minimization of reinventing the wheel, was facilitated by developing generic versions ("genericizing") of tools that were developed by consultants to assess clients' requirements in connection with particular HP products.

Specific criteria were set for selecting the specific business issues for the pilot studies that would launch the initiative (Martiny, 1998). These criteria included high visibility and strategic importance for the success of HP, high readiness based on a business need for knowledge sharing, and a strongly committed leader. HP's SAP (a comprehensive organizational resource management package) practice in North America met these criteria and was of special interest because a previous knowledge management effort, based on the use of Lotus Notes database of lessons learned, had failed due to low consultant participation. Thus, the pilot project, which was dubbed "OWL–Orchestrating Wisdom and Learning," was expressly *not* technology driven. Rather it was designed to "develop a committed core consultant group that would identify, share, and leverage knowledge for the benefit of others in the organization . . . and then become advocates for the value of knowledge management" (Parskey & Martiny, 2000, p. 35).

The OL/KM Team that was assigned to lead the initiative began by knowledge mapping. A group of experienced consultants was asked to break down into key components or steps the consultant's core activity of selling or delivering a solution. On the basis of an analysis of specific examples for each component, they identified what the consultant needs to know, where this knowledge comes from, who "owns" it, what skills are required, what tools or templates exist or should be created, and what barriers exist to effective execution. Based on this information, the team developed a new solution delivery approach. It also developed a 5-day workshop to acquaint consultants with this approach, as well as the benefits of organizational learning/knowledge management.

The workshop was designed not simply to train the consultants but to involve them in the expansion of the KM initiative as well. Consultants were required to develop OL/KM implementation plans tailored to their business units' specific needs for creating, sharing, and leveraging knowledge. Learning communities formed and project teams shared their experiences in delivering new solutions to clients. New solutions were documented and made available to other consultants. Through these OLMs, the new delivery approach was spread throughout the entire North American SAP consulting business. It was credited with the decrease in clients' implementation cycles from 18 to 6 months (Parskey & Martiny, 2000, pp. 37–39).

At the same time that the Knowledge Management (KM) Initiative was started, HPC was deploying a project management methodology worldwide. The OL/KM Team made a strategic decision to use this program as a vehicle for integrating its tools into the core project management practices of HPC. Owing to its phased nature, project work was an ideal ground for project snapshots and postproject reviews. For example, the transition from the selling phase to the delivery of the solution represented a natural point for conducting project snapshots. To smooth the integration of project snapshots with project management, the OL/KM Team developed a project snapshot training module that was included in HPC consultants' training in project management.

Learning communities also became widespread in HPC. Martiny (1998) provides a detailed description of what went on when learning communities met:

During a learning community session, a consultant spoke up about a technical assessment he would be conducting the following day at a client site, and asked other participants for any experience or assessment tools they had used in similar situations. A participant piped in that he had recently completed the development of an assessment tool and reviewed how he delivered it successfully in a client engagement. He then sent the assessment tool electronically to the consultant in need. The second consultant evolved the assessment tool for his application, leveraging both the first consultant's experience and the tool to deliver the assessment to his client. At the next Learning Community session, the second consultant shared his newly gained experience including what worked well, what he had learned, and what he would do differently next time. He made the enhanced assessment tool available to the Learning Community and both he and the first consultant offered to be contacts for additional information or mentoring. (pp. 75–76)

According to Martiny (1998), learning communities were credited with reducing delivery time while improving quality through the sharing of best practices. They also increased productivity by facilitating the sharing of tacit knowledge and by helping to standardize proposal and presentation materials.

The solution development groups, which developed new products ("solutions" in HP jargon), found that knowledge mapping was useful for identifying what knowledge was needed—and sometimes already available—for developing or delivering new solutions. They held 2-day knowledge mapping workshops involving a wide range of consultants from around the world. These workshops also served as a catalyst for creating new relationships and forming "learning communities" among participating consultants (Parskey & Martiny, 2000, p. 41).

As project reviews and snapshots and learning communities took hold throughout HPC, the organization added new knowledge management roles and developed an electronic infrastructure and an incentive system to support them. "Knowledge service managers" were assigned responsibility for identifying local knowledge needs and priorities, as well as for providing and implementing appropriate solutions in the highly decentralized HPC organization. "Knowledge architect managers" and "solution development knowledge managers" developed tools and methodologies to enhance OL/KM in HPC. "Learning community lead people" were responsible for the conduct and smooth functioning of learning communities within their subject domains.

The role of "knowledge consultant" was created to overcome the difficulty of promoting and coordinating organizational learning in an organization that practices and is ideologically committed to decentralization. Knowledge consultants facilitated knowledge flow around HPC and linked the central OL/KM Team with the different field units. They reported directly to the OL/KM Team and maintained extensive personal networks and good understanding of local cultures. For example, knowledge consultants recommended that the focus on learning communities and project snapshots is less necessary for Japanese than for Western consultants, because the Japanese tend to be naturally adept at sharing tacit knowledge, which is difficult to verbalize or communicate directly. The outcome was that in Japan the focus shifted from learning communities to supporting the management of "explicit knowledge" by building a repository for sharing documents (Parskey & Martiny, 2000, pp. 46–47).

In order to support OL/KM, HPC developed a Web portal that allowed consultants worldwide access to a database of documents stored electronically. This portal was supervised by the "HPC Standards Board," which set guidelines for standardizing the elements accessible through the portal, knowledge structures, service portfolio development, and collateral creation. HPC management also instituted "Knowledge Master Awards," which recognized and rewarded individuals who exemplified the highest standards of knowledge mastery. These individuals received an all-expense-paid vacation or cash award, but the main idea was to make them role models for the rest of the organization. They received HPC-wide recognition, and their stories were widely publicized. These stories emphasized improved business results through leveraging and reusing of knowledge, as well as through fundamental values such as expertise, teamwork, and willingness to contribute to the overall good of the organization (Parskey & Martiny, 2000, p. 461).

As of the year 2000, HPC's OL/KM initiative was regarded as a success story. To sustain its success, the OL/KM Team intended to concentrate on three areas that, based on its experience, it identified as key success factors: cultivating leadership involvement and support, reinforcing OL/KM performance by developing OL/KM evaluation metrics, and developing a method for gauging the progress of entire units in terms of OL/KM. The common theme underlying all efforts was the integration of the OL/KM projects with HPC's core activities. Cultivating leadership involved the identification of OL/KM sponsors who would participate in prioritizing knowledge initiatives, setting clear expectations, and serving as role models. In addition, it meant incorporating knowledge-based measures into senior managers' roles and adding training in OL/KM to management development programs. Another important part of cultivating leadership was keeping sponsors involved and informed of progress, successes, and challenges in the wider HPC OL/KM initiative (Parskey & Martiny, 2000, p. 48).

The second area for reinforcing OL/KM performance was evaluation. Commitment to sharing knowledge was now considered to be an important behavior for HPC consultants. In order to promote this behavior and to use it as criteria for reward and promotion, HPC had to develop ways of measuring commitment to sharing knowledge for every role in HPC. There was also a need to educate senior management on the existence of these measures and to encourage their use in communicating expectations and monitoring progress.

HPC used a "maturity" of knowledge model as a method for gauging the progress of entire units in terms of OL/KM. Maturity models provided managers with "concrete tangible ways of . . . comparing explicit competencies at the program and project level relative to a standard" (Kam & Thomas, 2002, p. 4). HPC's knowledge maturity model divided the knowledge management capacities into five levels: ad hoc, repeatable, defined, managed, and optimized. The characteristics of each level were clearly defined so that they could be used as criteria for assessing the state of knowledge management in a particular unit.

❖ WHY DID WIN DIE AND THE KM INITIATIVE LIVE?

The case of both WIN and the KM Initiative illustrate how the creation of OLMs and the appropriate cultural norms can produce productive organizational learning. However, there is a critical difference between the outcomes of the two cases: WIN was allowed to simply die, whereas the KM Initiative was systematically expanded and institutionalized throughout the organization. The immediate explanation for this difference is that the latter received top management support, whereas the former did not. However, this explanation only points to deeper questions: What led management to support one initiative rather than the other? How did management support manifest itself?

In this chapter, we will use the multi-facet model as an analytical tool to help us answer these questions. We will systematically apply the model to these two cases in order to understand what may have led one project to become institutionalized whereas the other was only a fleeting, temporary OLM (see Table 11.1). Furthermore, the analysis will help us see more clearly what it means for learning to be *organizational*. In order to get there, the analysis will address the following questions: What was learned? Who learned and to what extent was the learning organizational? How did organizational learning actually take place? How did each of the structural, cultural, psychological, policy, and contextual facets influence learning?

What Was Learned?

Strictly speaking, this first question is not derived from the multi-facet model. However, before analyzing organizational learning, it is important to clarify whether some significant change took place that could be classified as learning. In the case of WIN, the learning involved the introduction of new methods for organizing (self-managing teams) and for overcoming barriers to innovation in change. These methods were based on a well-defined set of concepts and values. The methods were not aimed at any specific set of issues but could be applied generically throughout the organization. The learning in the KM Initiative focused on adding value to the customer by building capacity to systematically create new knowledge from existing, but scattered, knowledge.

Table 11.1   Comparing WIN and the KM Initiative at Hewlett-Packard

Categories	KM Initiative	WIN
What kinds of structural mechanisms (OLMs) evolved or were created for the purpose of learning?	Postproject reviews Project snapshots Learning communities Knowledge-Mapping Team Workshops Knowledge service managers Knowledge architect managers Solution development managers Knowledge consultants	Workshops Peer consultation
What other "tools" or technologies evolved or were created to support learning?	"Genericizing" tools Knowledge mapping Web portal Knowledge Master Awards Evaluation metrics for learning at both individual and unit level	Action research
What was learned? (not a facet)	How to maximize use of existing, but scattered, knowledge so that it adds value to customer	How to organize as self-managing teams to improve productivity, quality, and responsiveness: a clear methodology of five principles
Who learned? Did the organization learn?	The HP consultants and the organization, in the sense that it developed and institutionalized a new set of OLMs for improving performance	Managers and groups in different parts of the organization. The organization learned in the sense that the innovations advocated by the WIN initiators were disseminated and implemented widely in the organization. But *organizational learning* was limited because neither these innovations nor the OLMs were institutionalized.

(Continued)

Table 11.1 (Continued)

Categories	KM Initiative	WIN
How did the cultural values influence learning? **How did the psychological climate influence learning?**	There is insufficient data to analyze the learning culture and the psychological climate of the organization. However, both initiatives took place within the same organization, which is known for its unique, strong, and unified culture. There is no indication that the values governing learning in the KM Initiative were significantly difference from those in the WIN case. Indeed, a high level of learning was reported in both cases.	
How did policies or management practices influence learning?	• Management set clear learning goals for the project. • Training was linked to specific learning goals and action planning. • Management linked organizational learning into a broader change effort by integrating OLM components into changes in project management methodology. • Rewards and promotion linked to learning.	Management did nothing to support the learning or the OLM. In fact, management policy (restrictions on travel) unintentionally led to the demise of the OLM.
How did contextual factors influence learning?	• The learning was focused on improving the core mission (consulting, delivering knowledge to customer). • The structure of the consulting task and project management easily lent itself to OL/KM because both were based on knowledge. There was an easy integration. • Leadership was highly committed. The leadership of top management played a central role in initiating, supporting, and institutionalizing the learning. Top management also looked for leadership at lower levels.	• A generic kind of knowledge (self-managing team) was offered to managers and units with no particular focus on the specific task. • Formal leadership was not involved directly. The process was only semiformal, kind of a "guerilla movement."

Who Learned?

This question is important for distinguishing individual and organizational learning. Through WIN, managers in different HP units developed new skills and capabilities that they then applied, changing the way work was designed. These changes in work design were credited with improving performance on achieving business objectives. The organization learned in the sense that the innovations advocated by the WIN initiators was disseminated and implemented widely in the organization. But *organizational learning* was limited because few, if any, mechanisms were developed for systematically disseminating this knowledge or storing this knowledge in organizational memory. For the most part, dissemination and storage took place informally rather than through formal policies and operating procedures.

In the KM Initiative, on the other hand, both the HPC consultants and the organization learned extensively. The consultants developed a new appreciation for the importance of OL/KM, as well as a complex set of skills and methods for producing it. The organization learned in the sense that these values and methods were institutionalized through an extensive and relatively permanent set of organizational learning mechanisms and policies intentionally designed to reinforce them.

How Did Organizational Learning Actually Take Place?

From the perspective of the multi-facet model, the answer to this question can be found by looking at the organizational learning mechanisms (OLMs) employed by each project. Through OLMs, organizational members identified problems or opportunities, collected relevant information, processed this information, generated new knowledge, and disseminated that knowledge to where it was needed. There is a very clear contrast between the two cases in terms of the OLMs involved.

WIN functioned as a single, though complex, off-line OLM. It was a bit of a hybrid in terms of agency. The introductory workshops were off-line/external agent OLMs in which consultants passed their knowledge on to managers who felt that it would meet their needs. However, in more advanced stages of the WIN process, it became more of an internal agency OLM as managers presented their own cases, provided feedback, and consulted with each other on practice issues. To the extent that networking led to ongoing, informal information sharing and peer consultation among participants, then WIN also constituted an online/internal OLM.

The KM Initiative, on the other hand, involved a wide variety of OLMs. Postproject reviews were off-line/internal OLMs. Project snapshots also involved internal agents but occurred in much closer proximity to task performance. The learning communities, in which consultants shared information informally or through conference calls, were online/internal agent OLMs. Another OLM, the knowledge-mapping team, was set up in order to develop a method for service delivery using organizational learning and knowledge management.

The KM Initiative was particularly noteworthy, however, for the way in which one "generation" of OLMs spawned a whole new set of OLMs to meet various learning and information needs that arose as the project developed. The initial OLM, which could be called the knowledge-mapping team, was basically an off-line, external agent OLM. It developed both a new service delivery method to be used by the entire organization and a workshop for dissemination. The knowledge-mapping team was a temporary OLM and ceased to exist once the new knowledge was created.

The dissemination workshops were themselves off-line OLMs involving both external and internal agents (trainers and participants, respectively). The notable thing about these workshops was that this second-generation OLM functioned as a mechanism for disseminating a third generation of OLM for knowledge production and sharing. Participants in the workshops not only learned a new method for service delivery but also developed plans for tailoring postproject reviews, project snapshots, and learning communities to the specific needs and features of their units. Thus, one generation of OLM gave birth to another. In addition, linking new methods with the design of tailor-made OLMs constituted a combination of top-down and bottom-up learning strategies.

The existence of a wide variety of OLMs does not necessarily ensure that they will function efficiently or maximize the potential learning. A tremendous waste of energy could easily have resulted from multiple OLMs working on the same issues in parallel, by the "not invented here" syndrome, and by the tendency to "reinvent the wheel." This challenge was met by the creation of the roles of knowledge service manager, knowledge architect manager, solution development knowledge manager, and knowledge consultant. Each of these roles functioned as an off-line/external OLM for linking local OLMs, facilitating information sharing and coordination, and ensuring that local learning was disseminated throughout the organization.

In addition to creating a wide, diverse, and tightly linked network of OLMs, the KM Initiative also created a number of technologies, or tools, for supporting the organizational learning process. These technologies included knowledge mapping, the Web portal, genericizing tools, the Knowledge Master Award, and methods for measuring learning at both individual and unit level. In the WIN case, the only reported technology for supporting learning was action research.

Comparing WIN with the KM Initiative reveals a major difference in the OLMs created for the purpose of learning. WIN was based on one large and complex OLM. It clearly aimed at stimulating learning, and the networking among participants was intended to spawn new initiatives, but WIN did not invest directly in the development of new OLMs. The KM Initiative, on the other hand, made extensive use of a wide variety of OLMs and support technologies.

How Did Cultural Norms and the Psychological Climate Influence the Learning?

As pointed out in Chapter 3, OLMs are a necessary, but insufficient, condition for productive organizational learning. Productive learning requires behaviors driven by cultural norms of inquiry, issue orientation, transparency, integrity, and accountability (see Chapter 3). The enactment of these norms depends largely on a psychological climate of safety and commitment to the organization (see Chapter 4).

The available materials on the two cases provide very little descriptive material that would enable us to infer or compare the specific values and the psychological climate that characterized these two projects. Hewlett-Packard is widely recognized for a strong and unique culture. One of the explicit principles of WIN, for example, was creating a "safe environment" (psychological safety) that would encourage the participants to expose their errors as well as their successes ("transparency" and "integrity"). These norms were strongly enough felt for at least one participant in WIN to publicly object when he perceived that presentations were becoming less truthful and personal. There is no concrete evidence about the participants' commitment to the organization. Commitment could be inferred from the fact that they voluntarily participated in a program with no material reward, but there could be other equally plausible explanations.

Similarly, in the KM Initiative, the importance of creating a climate of psychological safety was espoused in the guidelines for the postproject reviews, which called for an emphasis on learning as opposed to blaming or fault finding. However, these guidelines rightfully belong to the leadership and policy facet (see Chapter 6) and do not say anything about the organizational members themselves. There is little evidence as to whether the HPC consultants experienced psychological safety, how deeply committed they felt to the organization, and whether their behavior in the various OLMs was guided by learning values or not.

How Did Organizational Policy Influence Learning?

The policy facet focuses on the formal and informal steps taken by management to promote organizational learning. The multi-facet model points to three policies that are particularly important for learning: commitment to learning, commitment to the workforce, and tolerance for error.

A look at the policy facet reveals a major difference between the KM Initiative and WIN. The KM Initiative was shaped and supported by a wide range of policies aimed at giving concrete expression to the organization's commitment to learning. For example, management set clear learning goals for the project. Thus, training was linked to specific learning goals and action planning to achieve those goals. Management linked the KM Initiative into a broader change effort by integrating OLM components into changes in project management methodology.

Most important, perhaps, learning was integrated into the organization's performance management system. Indeed, the organization invested effort in developing a new and sophisticated set of criteria and measurement tools for evaluating learning and learning-oriented behaviors at both the individual and unit level. A conscious effort was made to make managers aware of the existence, and the importance, of this new set of performance measurement tools. Finally, rewards and promotion linked directly to the learning exhibited through these tools.

In the case of WIN, on the other hand, no specific policies were developed or implemented to support learning or to disseminate beyond the program itself. To a certain extent, the lack of policy supports was an implicit, if not fully intentional, part of WIN's learning strategy. From the beginning, it defined itself as an alternative to change imposed from above. WIN adhered to such a radically bottom-up approach that it was described as "a bit of a guerilla movement" (Zell, 2001, p. 84). In retrospect, its advocates lamented not trying to cultivate top-level sponsors, which they saw as the root cause of WIN's demise when HP encountered financial difficulties.

Although we can say very little about the psychological climate and the cultural norms actually enacted by participants in both cases, we can identify aspects of HP policy that support learning. "Commitment to the work force" comes through most explicitly in official HP policy. For example, "employee commitment" is one of the explicit corporate objectives (*HP history and facts*, n.d.):

> To help HP employees share in the company's success that they make possible; to provide people with employment opportunities based on performance; to create with them a safe, exciting and

inclusive work environment that values their diversity and recognizes individual contributions; and to help them gain a sense of satisfaction and accomplishment from their work.

This objective reflects Hewlett-Packard's strong and unique culture, known as "the HP way." This culture, which influences both formal policy and informal management behavior, was originally instilled by its two inspirational founders, Bill Hewlett and Dave Packard and assiduously maintained by succeeding corporate leadership (*HP history and facts*, n.d.; Rogers, 1995a).

The "HP way," as it was understood at the time that these two cases took place, has been described as follows:

> When former employees reminisce about the HP Way, they toss around words like "integrity," "trust," and "team." They tell stories about how Hewlett and Packard regularly roamed the halls, talking with employees about their projects; how employees put on annual skits where they ribbed their bosses, including Bill and Dave; how co-workers were reassigned to new jobs rather than fired; how the company for a time implemented a shortened work week for all employees so certain individuals would not lose their jobs. "Everybody respected everybody else. Management was part of the team," Cottrell (former head of HP's European division) said. "Something you'll notice is that even retirees talk in terms of 'we.'" Following the founders' lead, managers were expected to know their employees and share with them what was going on in the company. (Dong, 2002)

The HP way clearly reflected a commitment to learning in both formal policy and informal management behavior. It mainly emphasized "learning-in" the organization; that is, providing individuals with opportunities for developing their task-related knowledge and skills. However, it also placed importance on information sharing (Dong, 2002; Kotter & Heskett, 1992, pp. 60–61).

It is more difficult to find direct evidence about policies that support a "tolerance for error" in the service of learning. As mentioned earlier, the KM Initiative emphasizing the importance of creating a climate of psychological safety was espoused in the guidelines for the postproject reviews, which called for an emphasis on learning as opposed to blaming or fault finding. *HP History and Facts* (n.d.) stresses "the importance of developing leaders who coach, relay good news and bad, and give feedback that works" and who "demonstrate self-awareness and a willingness to accept feedback and continuously develop." These espoused values are intended to encourage managers to be open about their own errors as well of the errors of others and, in doing so, to be a role model for their subordinates.

The evidence clearly indicates that overall HP culture is oriented toward fostering the psychological climate and values conducive to learning. The very emergence of both WIN and the KM Initiative programs, aimed at organizational learning and knowledge management, are reflections of this culture. However, this corporate culture was translated into concrete management policies mainly in the case of the KM Initiative. The contextual facet may help us understand the reasons why one initiative received more management attention than the other.

How Did the Context Influence the Learning?

The contextual facet focuses on factors that are not within management's direct control. These factors include error criticality, environmental uncertainty, task structure, proximity to core mission, and committed leadership. These factors create pressures to engage in learning but also posit conditions that shape and/or constrain learning. Although management may have no control, or no direct control over these factors, it must take them into account and adopt strategies for dealing with them.

Perhaps the biggest difference between WIN and the KM Initiative involved their proximity to the core mission of the organization. The learning in WIN was aimed at transmitting a generic kind of knowledge involving the use of self-managing teams and assimilation of innovation. As important as these tasks were, they were not directly related to the delivery of products or services. WIN was offered to managers and units throughout the organization with no particular focus on a specific task or problem. Essentially, the participants in WIN could apply this method to any issue, regardless of its strategic importance or proximity to the core mission of the organization.

The KM Initiative, on the other hand, was tightly focused on improving HPC's core mission. Indeed, delivering knowledge to customer *was* the core mission. The ability of the consultants to learn and improve their knowledge was critical for effective performance prior to the KM Initiative. The KM Initiative added an *organizational* component to this ongoing individual learning process.

A combination of environmental uncertainty and error criticality also created conditions that made the KM Initiative a strategic necessity. The learning was actually stimulated by environmental pressures—that is, customer perceptions that the quality of HPC services depended more on the individual consultant than on the organization as a whole. Management realized that if this perception was not addressed, it could lead to difficulty satisfying customers in the long term. Furthermore, because organizational effectiveness was closely associated with the individual performance of HPC consultants, any failures or errors on their part could be very costly. The success or failure of the entire business rested on continually building this knowledge base and making sure that it was as fully and equally distributed as possible.

There is no evidence to indicate that WIN, on the other hand, was a response to environmental uncertainty or error criticality. Rather, it was driven by the belief of a group of organizational members that they possessed knowledge that could be useful to others. And, as the case demonstrates, they were right. There were no apparent environmental or strategic pressures driving WIN. Given this context, the program succeeded admirably in meeting the needs of internal customers but was treated as expendable by management.

The structure of the HPC consultants' primary task, delivering knowledge to customers, also easily lent itself to organizational learning and knowledge management. It was relatively easy to bring together the relevant information for knowledge mapping and sharing because this information was held by the consultants themselves. The key was creating OLMs that bring together the right people at the right time. HPC's project structure lent itself to convening both interim and postproject reviews. Another challenge for the KM Initiative was making the tacit knowledge explicit and making sure that there were sufficient means and incentives for widely sharing explicit knowledge. The web of OLMs and technologies that HPC developed for accomplishing fit easily into the structure of the consulting task. In fact, the organizational learning and knowledge management became an integral part of HPC's project management methodology.

The issue of task structure was not really salient in the WIN case because the program focused on transmitting a generic set of management techniques rather than generating learning around a specific task or problem. It was implemented as an independent series of workshops without integration into a particular task arena. Participants were able to choose the specific issues or task areas they wanted to engage through WIN, but they had to design their learning according to the structure and timing offered by WIN. The learning that took place through WIN appeared to integrate well into the participants' work—at least for those who stayed with it. However, the WIN workshops were distanced from the places of actual task performance and involved significant travel, a factor that led to the program's eventual demise.

How Did Leadership Influence Organizational Learning?

In one sense, WIN was an example of grassroots, informal leadership. In fact, the WIN advocates, based on their ethic of self-management and bottom-up change, did not seek sponsorship or support from upper management. As a result, management did not identify with the program and could not be convinced that its contribution was important enough to override cost-cutting policies.

In the KM Initiative, on the other hand, the general manager of HPC recognized the strategic importance of organizational learning and knowledge management of the program from the very beginning. He made his commitment to learning clear and played a central role in starting, supporting, and institutionalizing the KM Initiative. Furthermore, top management emphasized the importance of fostering leadership at lower levels. Leadership in learning and knowledge management became an important criterion for promotion and the evaluation of manager performance.

❖ DEMYSTIFYING THE LEARNING ORGANIZATION

The Work Innovation Network and the Knowledge Management Initiative are both impressive examples of organizational learning in Hewlett-Packard. The very existence of these efforts would seem to justify calling HP a "learning organization" in which "people continually expand their capacity to create the results that they truly desire, where new and expansive patterns of thinking are nurtured, where collective aspiration is set free, and where people are continually learning how to learn together" (Senge, 1990, p. 3). However, looking at the learning organization in this way actually obscures the important differences between these two cases.

The difference between WIN and the KM Initiative was not that one represented better or more extensive learning. The difference was that the learning in the KM Initiative was simply more *organizational*. It was more organizational in the sense that it involved a more extensive system of tightly linked organizational learning mechanisms. Both WIN and the KM Initiative emerged from same organizational cultural context, but the latter was more organizational in the sense that it was grounded in a set of formal organizational policies. Finally, the KM Initiative was more organizational in the sense that it was initiated and supported by the formal leadership of the organization. As a result of these factors, the KM Initiative became institutionalized, increasing the likelihood that learning would be sustained and integrated into the everyday functioning of the organization.

By showing how learning can be made more organizational, the multi-facet model provides a framework for demystifying the learning organization. This framework can guide managers who aspire to building a learning organization by specifying the key factors that they must attend to. It suggests the potential effect of each factor and the steps that can be taken with it.

OLMs represent the basic tools that managers have at their disposal for making learning organizational and structuring it to address specific demands for knowledge. The policy facet points to additional tools that are largely within management's direct control. If designed and deployed appropriately, policies foster the psychological climate and cultural norms conducive to learning. The contextual facet, on the other hand, highlights the demands and constraints that impinge on any organizational learning effort. As illustrated in the analysis of these two cases, the degree to which a manager attends to these contextual factors may have a critical influence on the long-term viability of an organizational learning effort.

One advantage of the multi-facet model is that it provides an alternative to the either-or framing suggested by the learning organization concept. Managers may be inspired by visions of major transformation, but very few of them sit at the level where they can effect such systemwide changes. However, managers *can* use the multi-facet model to understand what *they* can do to be agents of organizational learning (Friedman, 2002).

The multi-facet model provides managers with a guide for taking realistic and practical steps toward fostering learning from any position in the organization. It suggests concrete actions that can be taken to clarify the demands for learning, identifying and adapting to the constraints, and marshalling the resources within their control. Our experience is that serious inquiry into these questions almost always leads to the discovery of some space for enhancing organizational learning.

The multi-facet model also implies that, given its particular contextual conditions, organizations develop their own unique configurations of learning mechanisms and policies in order to create the structures, psychological climate, and cultural conditions conducive to learning. From a managerial perspective, promoting organizational learning is a process of design: that is, consciously shaping learning-oriented mechanisms, policies, and practices in light of the demands, materials, constraints, and resources at hand (Shani & Docherty, 2003).

This design approach is based on the assumption is that there is no single method or formula for enhancing organizational learning. Because of the wide variety and complexity of organizations, learning has to be adapted to an organization's specific needs, characteristics, and circumstances.

12

Demystifying the Learning Organization II

The Case of Chaparral Steel

In the mid-1990s, Chaparral Steel, a "minimill" in Midlothian, Texas, received a great deal of attention for its success in competing with low-cost non-U.S. producers. In its first 8 years in operation, it grew from 250,000 tons of produced steel at start-up time to the 10th largest steel producer in the United States in 1998. Breaking all previous efficiency records in the process, Chaparral received the following laudatory analysis in *Fortune* magazine:

> Chaparral is remarkable because, like a sculling crew that pulls in flawless synchronism, it has all the basic elements of good management—customer service, empowerment, quality, training, and more—working in concert. As a result, it produces *steel* with a record low 1.6 hours of labor per ton, vs. 2.4 hours for other minimills and 4.9 hours for integrated producers. (Dumaine, 1992, p. 88)

According to *Fortune,* Chaparral Steel owed its success to observing general "principles of good management."

Dorothy Leonard-Barton (1992, 1995), who studied Chaparral Steel extensively, attributed its success to organizational learning. The former CEO of Chaparral Steel Gordon Forward himself stated that "we are a learning organization" whose core competence is the "rapid realization of new technology into products" (Leonard-Barton, 1992, p. 23). Here are some examples of organizational learning at Chaparral:

> Managers assume that the performance of any purchased equipment can be improved. . . . Some improvements are novel enough to be patented. The rolling mill equipment its vendor believed limited to 8-inch slabs is now turning out 14-inch slabs, and the vendor has tried to buy back the design. (Leonard-Barton, 1995, p. 11)

> When cooling hoses burst during the first few weeks of starting up the new . . . project, a group of operators, a welder, a foreman, and a buyer spontaneously gathered to discuss the problem, then scattered to seek solutions. . . . In this case (quoting a senior operator) . . . "Everyone telephoned some person they thought might know how to fix the problem—vendors, experts—and within three to four hours, we were getting calls back . . . and we worked the problem out." (Leonard-Barton, 1995, p. 10)

These examples reflect the dual mission that CEO Gordon Forward set for all employees: fulfilling their individual functions and continually improving production. In doing so, they were expected to solve production problems, improve production processes and equipment, import new knowledge into the organization, and share their knowledge with others (Leonard-Barton, 1992).

Exemplars of organizational learning like Chaparral are a double-edged sword. On the one hand, they inspire and invite learning through imitation. "By benchmarking against such companies," wrote Leonard-Barton (1992), "managers can derive principles to incorporate into their own particular visions" (p. 36). These exemplars may even tempt managers to take bold steps to transform their own companies into learning organizations. On the other hand, these exemplars may actually contribute to the mystification of organizational learning by feeding the gap between visionaries and skeptics (see Chapter 1). No matter how inspiring the ultimate vision, studies of these organizations rarely offer a well-marked path for getting there. Furthermore, the reality of promoting organizational learning is demanding, fraught with setbacks, and simply much more mundane than the heroic exemplars.

This reality may increase cynicism and the belief that organizational learning is nothing more than another fad or gimmick.

In this chapter, we shall argue that managers *can* learn from Chaparral Steel's example. In order to do so, however, they need a framework for systematic comparison that enables them to identify both the similarities *and* the key differences between their organizations and Chaparral. The multi-facet model presented in this book offers such a framework. Our reanalysis will build on descriptions of Chaparral Steel from previous studies and interviews with Gordon Forward rather than on original research (Kantrow, 1986; Leonard-Barton, 1992, 1995; Luthans, 1991; Preuss, 1998). It will show how Chaparral implemented a unique configuration of OLMs, especially the online/internal organizational learning mechanisms (OLMs). It will also identify features of Chaparral's learning culture, managerial policies, and leadership that make these OLMs effective. Finally, it will show how the particular design of learning at Chaparral was shaped, at least in part, by a specific set of contextual conditions. Such an analysis provides a more finely grained basis for comparison with other organizations and for understanding what principles can be adopted and what cannot.

❖ ORGANIZATIONAL LEARNING MECHANISMS AT CHAPARRAL

The scope and intensity of organizational learning at Chaparral can be attributed to the extensive use of OLMs, especially what we referred to in Chapter 2 as "online/internal agent OLMs." These mechanisms fuse work and learning together: The same people who do the work do the learning, and they do both at the same time and place.

> [After the introduction of a new product and production process,] the pulpit controls operator is carefully checking the timing on the line with a stopwatch. . . . He wants to achieve split-second timing. Asked who suggested he perform this function (which is often given to a process engineer elsewhere), he is surprised at the question: "No one." He considers it obvious that improvement is always part of his job. (Leonard-Barton, 1992, pp. 26–27)

Online/internal agent OLMs enable employees to produce changes in organizational routines, standard operating procedures, or norms of behavior while carrying out their specific functions.

The heart of online/internal agent learning mechanisms at Chaparral was constant experimentation carried out by everyone from management to the operators. There was no research and development department separate from production because it was considered to be a part of everyone's job (Leonard-Barton, 1992, p. 29). Employees at every level were expected to come up with ideas for improvements and, if possible, try out their own ideas on the spot.

Even operators were given opportunities to acquire and use the most advanced scientific knowledge, even if it meant travel (Kantrow, 1986). There were, of course, engineers and technicians working at Chaparral, but even they had line functions and worked closely with supervisors and operators so that experimentation was a joint project. Forward believed that putting operators, engineers, and maintenance workers in constant contact was the best and quickest means of testing out new ideas (Kantrow, 1986).

These experiments took place at the same time and at the same place as the production process. Innovation and experimentation were simply a part of everyday work routines. In the words of Gordon Forward:

> The lab is the plant. . . . Of course, we don't give the whole plant over to laboratory work, but the whole plant really is a laboratory— even though it's one of the most productive steel mills in the world. We don't stop operations to try crazy things, but we do try to do our research and development right on the factory floor. (Kantrow, 1986, p. 99)

The fact that experimentation and process improvements took place online meant that management had to tolerate disruptions to production. The great benefit was that the results could be implemented immediately without further engineering or testing because the experimental environment and final production environment were the same (Leonard-Barton, 1992).

Chaparral provided a rare and extremely valuable opportunity to observe internal/online mechanisms. Off-line OLMs are relatively easy to comprehend, identify, and institutionalize because they are based on a clear distinction between working and learning. Online/internal agent OLMs, on the other hand, are difficult to observe because they are tightly integrated into the flow of work itself. In many organizations, they are not fixed or formal entities but rather temporary structures that take shape as needed through informal interactions and interpersonal networks. Their informality makes them difficult to create and manage.

At Chaparral, online/internal agent OLMs did not evolve in some naturalistic way but rather from conscious management choice and design. The impetus for these design features was CEO Forward's own learning from experience in a large, bureaucratic organization (Luthans, 1991, p. 67). Forward jokingly compared big, separate research facilities to cemeteries because "good ideas are dying there all the time" (Kantrow, 1986, p. 2). He believed that no matter how much money was invested in R & D (an off-line/external agent OLM), this knowledge did not flow to the people who were supposed to use it. On the other hand, line workers and managers who came up with good ideas for change were unable to get this knowledge adopted and implemented by the organization (Luthans, 1991).

Because Chaparral Steel was created as a completely new, self-contained plant, it offered an opportunity to design an alternative from the bottom up. The idea of making R & D a line function was a strategic choice based on the belief that the key to maintaining competitive advantage as a low-cost steel supplier was combining manufacturing with technology. Thus, the physical and organizational structures of Chaparral were all carefully aimed at integrating work and experimentation through what we call online/internal mechanisms.

One of the key decisions in the design of online/internal mechanisms was keeping the number of employees at Chaparral Steel to less than 1,000. Small size facilitated both knowledge production and dissemination. It enabled employees to know each other personally, influencing the desire and willingness to share information. Even more important, it made it easier for employees to develop "transactive knowledge" (see Chapter 7 on dissemination). In other words, it was possible for every Chaparral employee to know whose expertise they needed in order to solve a problem or create an innovation. It also enabled them to know who might need or make good use of their own knowledge. Forward considered small size (in terms of number of employees) so important that he stated flatly that he "simply wouldn't consider" getting much bigger in the present location (Kantrow, 1986, p. 97). Rather than increase its scale of operations to stay competitive, Chaparral sought strategic opportunities that enabled it to maintain its small size.

The physical design of Chaparral Steel, which was related to size, provided an infrastructure conducive to the development of online/internal agent OLMs. First, all of Chaparral's operations were located in one plant, enabling employees to exchange information face to face without travel or sophisticated knowledge management technologies. Other features of the plant's physical design facilitated accidental meetings among all levels. The plant headquarters were situated in close proximity to the furnaces and mills as well as the employees' locker room (Leonard-Barton, 1992). Workers and line managers with ideas or problems did not have to go far to meet with higher levels of management. Indeed, they were likely to run into each other at least once or twice a day so that no one would have to wait very long to move information up or down. In fact, there was nothing really "accidental" about these meetings at all because they were facilitated by conscious design.

The organizational design of Chaparral complemented the physical design in enabling online/internal agent OLMs to take shape just about anywhere or anytime. The one-story headquarters building was symbolic of the flat organization that kept hierarchical distance and formality to a minimum. From the standpoint of management, informal on-the-spots meetings were neither interruptions nor distractions but rather integral parts their work. In addition, there was an intentional absence of the normal bureaucratic barriers to innovation. Chaparral employees were not required to follow bureaucratic procedures or receive management approval before trying out improvements. Decision making was delegated down the hierarchy so that even line supervisors could authorize tens of thousands of dollars for experiments without receiving permission from above (Leonard-Barton, 1992).

Rather than emphasize clear roles and a strict division of labor, management assigned both units and individuals to numerous tasks. Everyone had line responsibilities and operators performed 40% of the maintenance work. The company had a marketing department, but every employee was considered to be in sales (Leonard-Barton, 1992). Another unusual strategy for blurring boundaries was requiring all employees to work night shifts regardless of seniority. This strategy meant that organizational knowledge was not concentrated during particular hours but well dispersed across the entire 24-hour day (Leonard-Barton, 1992).

Requiring employees to fulfill multiple functions and develop multiple skills enlarged the scope of their interests, understanding, and involvement in Chaparral's operations and activities. It also increased the likelihood that employees would encounter and learn from people outside their functional specialty. This design feature made the organization more flexible, counteracted competition over turf, and encouraged knowledge sharing.

Not all organizational learning at Chaparral took place through online OLMs. There were also regularly scheduled, off-line meetings for discussing problems and ideas for improvement. However, a foreman estimated that "90 percent of the problems never make it to the morning meetings" because they are solved online (Leonard-Barton, 1995, p. 8). In other words, most problems were dealt with through the online mechanisms. This quote attests to the power and efficiency of these mechanisms.

Another common off-line OLM at Chaparral was travel. As mentioned, the company encouraged all employees to travel for the purpose of acquiring new knowledge. Teams of managers, foremen, and workers visited suppliers and competitors in the United States, Japan, and Europe. Gordon Forward observed that many important breakthroughs occurred during travel because the time together led to openness (Luthans, 1991). In addition, research projects were cosponsored with U.S. academic institutions to import cutting-edge knowledge into Chaparral Steel.

Whether or not new knowledge was acquired internally or from without, the efficient dissemination of knowledge was generated by the same features of the organization that promoted online/internal OLMs for experimentation. The intentional blurring of horizontal and vertical boundaries facilitated intensive networking and knowledge sharing among employees. The lack of bureaucratic barriers meant that results of experimentation and knowledge imported from outside could be quickly implemented and disseminated. Organizational members had no trouble imitating others and adopting their performance improvements as standard practice (Leonard-Barton, 1995).

OLMs for dissemination, however, were not left to chance. Chaparral used some well-planned strategies for making sure that knowledge was shared:

> For instance, in "commissioning" (ramping-up to problem-free production) of [a new mill] only two teams of operators are being trained. Each team works a twelve hour shift (with paid overtime). After the initial eight weeks of grueling schedule, these operators will be dispersed among the rest of the crews, to diffuse the knowledge they have created and assimilate about the idiosyncrasies of the [production] process. (Leonard-Barton, 1995, p. 13)

This method of disseminating knowledge by dispersing a highly skilled group of workers is common practice at Chaparral.

As this example illustrates, knowledge at Chaparral was transmitted primarily through people and interpersonal interactions. Face-to-face knowledge transmission was quicker and more efficient than engaging in a process of making knowledge explicit, generating written reports, translating it into formal procedures, and then transmitting it through training and support. It was also self-reinforcing and a bit risky. Because so much knowledge was transmitted informally and could not be accessed through written documents, people needed to interact and communicate directly with others if they wanted to stay on top of things.

❖ PRODUCTIVE LEARNING AT CHAPARRAL STEEL

Viewed through the multi-facet model, the existence of online/internal agent OLMs provided a necessary but insufficient condition for productive learning. Understanding productive organizational learning requires a systematic analysis of the culture, the psychological climate, specific management policies, and the context in which learning occurs. In this section, we look at each of these facets as they apply to Chaparral Steel.

The Cultural Facet

As described in Chapter 3, the cultural facet refers to the behavioral norms and the underlying values that regulate behavior in OLMs. The various accounts of Chaparral Steel provide ample evidence of the existence of the five norms that we consider essential for productive learning: inquiry, issue orientation, transparency, integrity, and accountability.

Norms of inquiry were clearly evident in Gordon Forward's description of the influence of his educational background on his role as the CEO:

> I feel my research background [showed me] how to deal with the mystery and intrigue of solving the puzzle. To me, the inquiry, the breaking through to new vistas, the finding of solutions, is what it's all about. (Luthans, 1991, p. 64)

This same norm of inquiry was reflected in numerous comments from workers to the effect that they were always asking questions and constantly trying to learn more about what they were doing (Leonard-Barton, 1992). It was also evident in the example given earlier of employees who doggedly pursued information and knowledge from a variety of sources in order to fully understand a problem and arrive at a solution.

Issue orientation was manifested by egalitarianism and respect for the individual, which were shared values in Chaparral Steel (Leonard-Barton, 1992). The strength of issue orientation at Chaparral was summed up nicely by this statement: "Knowledge is valued not so much for the pedigree of its source but for its usefulness" (Leonard-Barton, 1992, p. 36). Everyone's ideas were taken into consideration, regardless of function or level in the hierarchy. Indeed, the ideas and opinions of operators were especially valued because they were the closest to the work itself. Another element of issue orientation is the fact that innovations were usually seen as team efforts involving multiple inputs rather than individual accomplishments (Leonard-Barton, 1992).

Transparency was closely coupled with inquiry and issue orientation at Chaparral. Employees at all levels were encouraged to say what they think—even to the CEO. Gordon Forward put it this way:

> I actually like to deal in incomplete thoughts—in other words, a thought that you haven't really fleshed out yet, but one that you want to bounce off of someone. It's kind of like brainstorming. I've seen . . . more stilted structures stifle this kind of interaction. The approach was, "Don't talk to me until you've come to a conclusion." (Luthans, 1991, p. 70)

Chaparral employees repeatedly stressed that they freely shared their ideas even if they were unsure about their quality (Leonard-Barton, 1992).

Forward also gave expression to the norms of integrity (and inquiry), which we have defined as a willingness to admit ignorance or error:

> When you're operating in a technical field . . . trying to go one step beyond research, one of the things you learn fast is that you can't fool yourself. . . . You've got to be open in your questioning. . . . And you can't succeed by pretending to know things that you really don't. You have to go find them out. You have to try an experiment here, and experiment there, make your mistakes, ask your questions, and learn from it all. (Kantrow, 1986, p. 101)

The norm of integrity was also manifested in a millwright's report that he was actually pleased when someone less knowledgeable than he caught him in an oversight because it saved him from making a costly error (Leonard-Barton, 1992).

Finally, in Chaparral Steel's culture, accountability was expressed in a number of ways. The proper response to making mistakes was to admit them and then take action to fix them (Leonard-Barton, 1992). Because of blurred functional distinctions and the general ownership of problems, everyone was responsible for ensuring results, and no one could hide behind the claim that "it's not my job" (Leonard-Barton, 1992, p. 27). Accountability was also reflected in the wide latitude for experimentation but also in the demand to apply successful results. As illustrated in the description of the online/internal agent OLM, all employees were expected to act on and disseminate new knowledge.

The Psychological Facet

The published accounts of Chaparral Steel did not delve deeply into the psychological climate of the organization. Nevertheless, there was enough evidence to make inferences about both psychological safety and commitment to the organization. The clearly evident norms of transparency and integrity implied that employees experience a high degree psychological safety. In one telling quote, Forward provided an interesting perspective on this facet:

> In a research laboratory, risk is accepted as the norm, since the cutting edge is fraught with uncertainty. In contrast, risk is usually anathema in a production environment. . . . Chaparral managers avoid riskless projects because a "sure thing" holds no promise of competitive advantage. . . . This positive attitude toward risk permeates the company. . . . If everyone experiments, learns, and innovates, then neither success nor failure can be heavily personalized. (Leonard-Barton, 1992, p. 32)

To the extent that this statement reflected the thinking of organizational members in general, it contains two critical assumptions that apply to psychological safety. First, mistakes were considered not only normal but actually necessary occurrences, so there was no shame in making and admitting them. Second, everyone made mistakes, and most innovations were collective efforts. There was little fear of being blamed personally for errors.

The multi-facet model also maintains that people will expend the extra effort and take the risks involved in learning to the extent that they feel committed to the organization. Leonard-Barton (1992) described the workforce at Chaparral as "highly dedicated" (p. 33). The organization was deliberately understaffed and demanded much more of employees than most organizations, but employee motivation appeared to be very high and absenteeism very low (Leonard-Barton, 1992), providing some indication of high commitment.

The psychological climate and the cultural norms at Chaparral reinforced each other. Their positive strength accounted for the effective functioning of the online/internal agent OLMs. In this respect, Chaparral differs from organizations in which effective OLMs constitute cultural islands where learning norms may be more operative in OLMs than in the organization as a whole. Just as the online/internal agent OLMs were tightly integrated into the flow of work, the learning norms appeared to dominate the organizational culture as a whole.

Leadership

By this point, it should be obvious that the leadership of Gordon Forward, who was with the organization from its founding in 1973 until his retirement, played a key role in shaping Chaparral Steel as a learning organization. This is evident from the impact on the organization of his training as a researcher and his personal experience. It is interesting that the descriptions of Forward and interviews with him say little about his personality or leadership style. Instead these sources indicate two channels of influence (see Chapter 6) through which Forward and his top management team promoted the strategy of online/internal agency learning in Chaparral Steel. The first channel was Chaparral's overall mission. As we have already noted, workers in Chaparral Steel were assigned the dual task of performing their work and improving their production processes. The second channel was a set of policies that either promote organizational learning directly or supported it through human resource practices.

The Policy Facet

The multi-facet model points to three issues that need to be addressed by organizational policy in order to promote learning: tolerance for error, commitment to learning, and commitment to the workforce. In his interview with Fred Luthans, Forward said, "We don't have policies" but rather "basic ideas." This was, of course, stretching a point. However, Forward was expressing his disdain for bureaucratic rules and procedures that are "designed to catch the 3 percent who [are] trying to cheat in one way or another" (Luthans, 1991, p. 69). By minimizing the number of formal rules and procedures, Chaparral Steel manifests trust in its workforce, trust that they will rise to and meet the challenge of beating the competition through continuous innovativeness and superior efficiency.

From the founding of Chaparral Steel, management instituted policies to support the organization's multiple missions of production, problem solving, improvement of production and products, importing new knowledge into the organization, and sharing knowledge with others. These policies facilitated the development of online/internal agent OLMs and cultivated the cultural norms and psychological climate conducive to effectiveness.

Developing policies that promote a tolerance for error is one of the most difficult areas for management because it is not always possible to clearly distinguish between errors that stem from legitimate risk taking and those that stem from negligence or incompetence. Nevertheless, Chaparral had a policy that provided employees with the freedom to take risks. Gordon Forward explained this policy as follows:

> People say [risk taking] isn't very smart. But I respond that I think what they are doing is really risky. They ask, "What do you mean?" I say, "To me, the biggest risk, particularly in the business world of today, is to do nothing." Plenty of firms are afraid to take risks and I see this reluctance as a major risk itself. . . . The other thing is that people need the freedom to [achieve their goals]. We all figure we'll make some mistakes along the way, but that freedom is important. (Luthans, 1991, p. 69)

Tolerance for error is manifested in Chaparral Steel by the preference for new recruits who are risk takers and for deliberately taking conscious risks.

This policy was also evident in the story of one of the company vice presidents who, as a supervisor, purchased new equipment that totally failed and cost the company $1.5 million. He himself was not punished for his error. Furthermore, he explained that employees were rewarded for having new ideas by being given the freedom to test them out, even despite the obvious risks. The policy of tolerance for error clearly trickled down to managers who, as mentioned before, avoided projects that entailed little risk but also gained little. By the same token, mistakes were admitted and corrected rather than covered up (Leonard-Barton, 1992).

Chaparral's belief in people and commitment to the workforce was clearly articulated by Forward and expressed through its employment policies from the beginning of the company. Forward recognized that organizational commitment was governed by a norm of reciprocity. If Chaparral were to gain its employees' commitment, it had to show commitment to its employees. They had to feel that Chaparral had their interests in mind and that they belonged (Luthans, 1991).

Chaparral implemented this principle in treating all employees equally, investing in their personal development, and letting them share in the company's profits and wealth. For example, every employee was placed on salary rather than hourly wages, a manifestation and symbol of egalitarianism and respect for workers that contributed to organizational commitment. Bonuses for everyone were linked to company profits. There was also a profit-sharing scheme and a program through which most employees were stockholders (Leonard-Barton, 1995).

Not surprisingly, given the organization's multiple mission, many policies that expressed commitment to the workforce also expressed a commitment to learning. When Chaparral was first set up, management decided not to look for workers with industry experience. Rather, they sought employees who enjoyed hard work and had a high potential for learning so that they could be socialized into the unique learning culture of Chaparral (Leonard-Barton, 1992). Job applicants underwent a highly selective and rigorous screening process that included extensive interviews with Chaparral employees at different levels. Pay was structured in a way that rewarded learning and skill development as well as performance (Leonard-Barton, 1992).

Chaparral invested heavily in employee development and training that focused both on helping employees self-actualize and improve performance. Eighty-five percent of Chaparral's employees were enrolled in courses with direct or fairly direct relevance to their jobs. The company had an extensive apprenticeship program for every employee, which included courses on generic skills and company-specific knowledge as well as on-the-job training for workers. In order to keep supervisors excited about their work, they were encouraged to take time off from their jobs for paid "sabbaticals" involving work-related projects. Chaparral used these absences to give senior operators opportunities to fill in for their supervisors. As a result, they gained valuable supervisory training and experience (Leonard-Barton, 1992).

❖ THE CONTEXTUAL FACET

The final stage in our analysis of Chaparral Steel looks at the context in which organizational learning emerged. The contextual facet is different from all of the other facets because it focuses on factors over which management has limited or no control. Managers can set up OLMs as well as set policies and exercise leadership that influence the psychological climate and shape cultural norms. However, the contextual facets—error criticality, environmental uncertainty, task structure, and proximity to the core mission—are relative givens. They represent both opportunities and constraints to which managers must respond and adapt in promoting organizational learning. Thus, identifying and understanding the contextual facet is particularly important for managers wishing to apply the principles of organizational learning from Chaparral Steel, or any organization, to their own.

The most obvious contextual factor in understanding Chaparral's success was the fact that it was a greenfield site. Although Forward and his associates did not think in terms of the learning organization, they carefully designed and built the organization from the bottom up with the intention of integrating production and learning. They did not have to contend with and change the existing physical plant, organizational structure, and culture to promote learning. Managers attempting to apply the lessons of Chaparral in an existing organization would need to consider a very different strategy for getting there.

The case of Chaparral Steel is consistent with the contention that a relatively high degree of environmental uncertainty creates a demand for organizational learning. For Chaparral, the major source of uncertainty was defining and achieving competitive advantage in a changing industry:

> We realized that this business has traditionally been labor-intensive, capital-intensive, and energy-intensive, and from the beginning, we knew that we had to design all of those things out of it. That was the only way we could be competitive with Third World countries. (Luthans, 1991, p. 65)

Chaparral Steel was designed from inception to be an international low-cost supplier of steel products, but that meant competing with Third World companies with access to a much lower-wage labor force. From the beginning, Chaparral had to invent a new strategy for succeeding in an environment where most American producers had failed.

Essentially learning became a strategic imperative and part of Chaparral Steel's core mission:

> We are always trying to push back the technological frontier. . . . Maybe our largest challenge is to cut the time it takes to get technology out of the lab and into operations. The kind of lags that many industries experience would simply kill us. (Kantrow, 1986, p. 99)

To be competitive, Chaparral aimed at attaining 1.5 to 3 worker hours per ton by enlisting accessibility to the most advanced technology and to a highly committed innovative workforce (Luthans, 1991). To engage workers' commitment and encourage their innovativeness, Forward formulated a dual-purpose mission that called for the simultaneous manufacturing of cutting-edge products that require the invention of "test-the-limit" designs and the continuous improvement of production processes (to maintain cost advantage). Because both objectives require learning and experimentation, learning fused with task performance and wove itself into the organization's mission.

The question for other organizations that wish to learn from Chaparral's experience is whether the nature and degree of environmental uncertainty demands the same learning imperative. Learning is only one strategy for achieving competitive advantage. The fact that all organizations face increasingly intense competition in the age of globalization does not necessarily mean that learning needs to be defined as part of the organization's core mission. Conversely, managers who wish to promote learning need to take into account the proximity of their areas of responsibility to the core mission of the organization. The multifacet model suggests that units or processes that are ancillary to the core mission may not be able to attract the resources and commitment to learning evident in Chaparral and necessary for online/internal OLMs.

Superficially at least, error criticality does not seem to be a major driving force for learning in a steel manufacturing organization. Mistakes in steel manufacturing are costly but usually not fatal. Nevertheless, Forward did express the belief that, given the intense competition, any false move could prove fatal to the organization:

> We have to go like hell all of the time. If the price of what we sell goes up too high . . . all of sudden lots of folks will be jumping in. . . . We constantly chip away the ground we stand on. (Leonard-Barton, 1992, p. 24)

As evident from Forward's attitude toward risk, he believed that the greatest danger in the current situation is not taking risks, not pushing into the unknown for the purposes of learning.

The task structure is an important but often overlooked factor in shaping the potential for organizational learning. Chaparral was a minimill, which meant that it focused entirely on the production and sales of steel. In this respect, it was different from traditional U.S. steel producers that brought together mining, transport, and manufacturing of a wide variety of products, all under one organizational roof. Being a minimill made it possible for Chaparral to maintain its small size and to quite literally bring all its operation under one physical and organizational roof. As the case illustrates, these factors were extremely important in creating conditions for developing successful online/ internal agent OLMs and for minimizing bureaucratic constraints.

The fact that Chaparral manufactured a small number of very specialized steel products also facilitated organizational learning. It made it relatively easy for the company to sharply focus the relevant knowledge it needed, to match people with this knowledge, and to bring them together. Creating the necessary configurations of knowledge through online/internal OLMs would have been much more difficult if Chaparral were producing a wide range of products requiring different kinds of knowledge. Another factor that facilitated learning was the fact that Chaparral was producing a commodity and not a finished product made up of many different components with their own specialized technologies. It would have been much harder, though not impossible, to use online/internal OLMs for producing innovations in automobiles or even automobile manufacturing methods because automobiles involve so many different parts, materials, systems, and technologies.

Production technologies and work processes themselves also influence the ways in which learning can occur. Organizational learning structures are shaped and constrained by the structure of work, its pacing, its distribution across time and space, the numbers and types of people involved, the kinds of information involved in the work, and a variety of other factors. Leonard-Barton hinted at these differences in her description of learning at Chaparral:

> Just as continuous processing has great advantages for manufacturing over most batch processing, so the unimpeded flow of information aids learning more than fragmented, batch-processed information. (Leonard-Barton, 1992, p. 29)

The analogy between production processes and information processing can be turned around to suggest that information flow will be different in continuous processing environments than in large batch-processing environments. Woodward's (1965) classic study showed that relative to mass production, effective continuous process environments have shorter spans of control, more managers per worker, more skilled workers, lower formalized procedures, less centralization, higher verbal communication, less written communication, and a more organic structure. These features highlight the fact that, by nature, continuous process organizations emphasize problem solving, quick reaction times, and flexibility. The only major exception is that, according to Woodward's model, continuous process organizations require more levels of hierarchy, whereas Chaparral's productive learning flattened the organization.

It can be clearly seen that there is a kind of fit between these characteristics and Chaparral's extensive use of online/internal agent OLMs, as well as its learning policies and culture. Forward suggested that Chaparral itself is actually not so unique in this regard:

> We're not the only ones—there are others like us. Nucor does many of the same things, but it has a slightly different personality. . . . There are a number of quality minimills. We are all a bit different, but we all have to run like hell. (Kantrow, 1986, p. 97)

The point is not that continuous process manufacturing organizations are more likely to be learning organizations but that successful organizations adapt configurations to their particular tasks. Given similar strategic situations and similar technologies, organizations may develop very similar ways of learning.

❖ CONCLUSION

There is no doubt that Chaparral was a very effective and highly impressive learning organization. However, the multi-facet analysis shows that managers ought to be wary of blind imitation. Organizational learning can take many different forms, as reflected in the variety of OLMs. The effectiveness and intensity of learning at Chaparral was achieved through carefully crafted online/internal OLMs designed to fit the strategic situation, the task structure, and other factors. The idea of fit does not suggest a simple contingency model because there are simply too many factors involved to make such a model credible or useful in practice.

Perhaps the most important lesson from Chaparral itself was actually that managers need to take an experimental approach to organizational learning. On one hand, they need to systematically think through the kinds of OLMs and policies that are necessary, feasible, and appropriate, given the existing strategy, task, and culture. On the other hand, they need to take each step in implementing these OLMs and policies as an opportunity to see what works, what can be reinforced, and what needs to be done differently. Although it makes eminently good sense to see the learning organization as a holistic system, the way to get there, at least for most managers, is one step at a time.

13

Putting the Multi-Facet Model Into Practice

The preceding chapters of this book have presented a multi-facet model and case examples that enable us to see how organizational learning takes place and understand the factors that make it productive or unproductive. This chapter takes a final step toward demystification by illustrating how the multi-facet model can guide interventions aimed at generating organizational learning and knowledge management. We do so through an in-depth case study of a 1-year organizational learning project carried out with the staff of the New Education Environment (NEE), a program aimed at helping secondary schools in Israel work more effectively with students "at risk."

This goal of this chapter is not to provide a general model or recipe for fostering organizational learning. Given the wide variety and complexity of organizations, learning processes clearly need to be adapted to an organization's specific needs, characteristics, and circumstances (see Chapter 5 on the contextual facet). Accordingly, the need for

AUTHORS' NOTE: The chapter was written in cooperation with Dr. Michael Razer.

custom designing interventions to foster organizational learning is apparent from the case studies presented in this book. The postflight reviews in the fighter squadrons of the Israel Defense Forces Air Force (Chapter 8) developed incrementally over a long period of time. Chaparral Steel (Chapter 12), on the other hand, intentionally built learning mechanisms into the entire organization from the very beginning. Hewlett-Packard (Chapter 11) also took an incremental approach to instituting organizational learning and knowledge management.

The multi-facet model, however, does provide a useful framework for guiding this process of custom design interventions. Organizations learning mechanisms (OLMs), or the structural facet, are basic tools for making learning *organizational* and structuring it to address specific demands for knowledge. The leadership and policy facet points to tools that are largely within management's direct control. If designed and deployed appropriately, policies foster the psychological climate and cultural norms conducive to learning. The contextual facet, on the other hand, highlights the demands and constraints that impinge on any organizational learning effort. As will be seen in the following case study, the multi-facet model can help managers and consultants design and carry out a focused, systematic, and productive process of knowledge creation and dissemination.

❖ BACKGROUND

The New Education Environment (NEE) emerged in the early 1990s from a series of experiments sponsored by the Joint Distribution Committee-Israel (JDC-Israel)—a nongovernmental social service organization—in cooperation with local schools and the Ministry of Labor and Welfare. The goals of these experiments were to prevent dropping out and improve attendance, academic skills, achievement, student self-image, and social behavior. In 1996, the NEE program was formally adopted by the Israel Ministry of Education, leading to implementation in close to 100 schools nationwide.

The NEE goals were to be achieved by helping the staff of each school design and implement an educational environment that would meet the needs of its specific student population. The education environment was guided by five principles: (1) teamwork; (2) knowing each student from multiple dimensions (cognitive, behavioral, emotional, etc.); (3) personal learning plans based on differential instruction (instruction according to needs); (4) the use of information technologies in the teaching-learning process; and (5) an attractive, flexible, and technologically enriched physical space for learning (Cohen, Friedman,

& Eran, 1996). A series of evaluation studies attested to the program's overall effectiveness (Cohen-Navot, 2000, 2003; Cohen-Navot & Lavenda, 2003; Sulimani, 2002).

The NEE program was delivered in each school by a team of professional facilitators in team or organization development, psychology, pedagogy, and information technologies. NEE facilitators worked with teachers, administrators, and other school staff for a 4-year period but never directly with students or parents. Until the NEE program was adopted by the Ministry of Education, it worked in relatively few schools with a small number of facilitators. Many of these facilitators had been with the program from the beginning. Although they varied considerably in style and approach, they shared a common ethos. They also enjoyed considerable autonomy and freedom to experiment for the purpose of ongoing development.

In the 3 years after going nationwide, the program expanded rapidly, taking on approximately 30 new facilitators, who were organized into four regional teams. New facilitators had little time for formal training and even less for gradual socialization into the program's principles and ways of working. As a result, it was difficult to determine whether new facilitators really understood and agreed with the program's principles or practiced them in the field. In addition, the program was constantly evolving, and no one could really say exactly what it had become or where it was going. This lack of clarity made it even more difficult to explain the program to new client schools and to train new staff, who felt they were not receiving proper support from management. Finally, there was no system or process for harvesting the knowledge gained from experience by program staff in a wide variety of new settings.

The regional directors believed that the lack of clarity and coordination among regions was exacerbated by conflicting approaches. Each region considered its own approach somewhat unique and guarded its autonomy. There was little cross-fertilization or knowledge sharing among teams, especially from one region to the next. However, because they were working with the Ministry of Education and with school networks that cut across regional boundaries, there were increasing demands for consistency and joint accountability among the regions.

❖ DESIGNING THE ORGANIZATIONAL LEARNING
   PROCESS: AN ACTION SCIENCE APPROACH

In order to deal with these challenges, the national director of the NEE invited us to propose a process for achieving greater clarity and coordination in the face of rapid expansion. In our proposal, we framed the intervention goals as (a) developing an explicit, unified, and agreed on perception of the NEE intervention strategy and (b) improving the ability of the program staff to systematically draw and apply knowledge from their experience. The product of the first goal would be the formulation of an explicit NEE program theory based on best practices (Argyris & Schön, 1996; Chen, 1990; Friedman, 2001a; Rogers, Petrosino, Huebner, & Hacsi, 2000). Making the program theory explicit was intended to reduce ambiguity and uncertainty among the program staff. The product of the second goal would be the development of organizational learning mechanisms suited to the task of systematic and ongoing knowledge creation and management.

The intervention process itself was composed of six stages to be implemented over a 1-year period: (1) mapping the current state of program knowledge and organizational learning as perceived by program leadership, (2) building program theory and fostering a learning culture, (3) mapping the learning mechanisms in the organization in general, (4) extending the theory-building process to the entire staff, (5) final processing and formulation of program theory, and (6) implementation of ongoing learning mechanisms. Each stage involved the creation of an organizational learning mechanism assigned to address a particular set of questions and to produce a tangible output. These stages were designed in a modular fashion so that at the end of each one, a decision could be made to continue or terminate the learning process. The entire intervention—design, implementation, data collection, analysis, testing, writing, and dissemination—was carried out in close collaboration between the consultant and the NEE management group. One of the regional directors was assigned to coordinate this process, and she took a leading role in the knowledge creation and dissemination.

Whereas the multi-facet model provided a guide to diagnosing the learning context and the development of learning mechanisms, action science (Argyris, Putnam, & Smith, 1985; Friedman, 2001a) provided an intervention strategy as well as a set of conceptual and analytical tools for capturing, making explicit, and displaying the knowledge implicit in NEE practice. The idea of an action science was introduced by Torbert (1976) and later picked up by Argyris (1980) and Schön (1983) in an attempt to overcome inner contradictions in normative social science research and its application to professional practice. In their seminal book *Action Science*, Argyris, Putnam, and Smith (1985) attempted to "articulate the features of a science that can generate knowledge that is useful, valid, descriptive of the world, and informative of how we might change it" (p. x).

From the perspective of organizational learning, the central objective of action science is to increase the conscious choices organizational members have, both individually and collectively, over their mental models, their goals, and the strategies they use to achieve these goals. Action science is concerned with producing "actionable knowledge" that can enable people to produce desired outcomes in specific practice settings (Argyris, 1993, pp. 2–3; see Chapter 7 for a more in-depth discussion of this approach to knowledge). The main analytical tool for making knowledge explicit and crafting new actionable knowledge is the concept of mental "theories of action" implicit in behavior at both the individual and aggregate (group, organizational) level (Argyris & Schön, 1974, 1978; Friedman, 2001a). A theory of action includes a description of the situation, an implicit goal, and an action strategy for achieving that goal under the given conditions. Theories of action explain and predict behavior (if one acts in such and such a way, the following will likely occur) and guide action (in order to achieve this goal, under these conditions, do the following).

The goal of this chapter is not to advocate the use of an action science approach for every situation of organizational learning. It is most appropriate in practice situations, like the one described here, that are characterized by uniqueness, instability, uncertainty, and conflict. These situations involve mostly nontechnical "wicked" problems, described in Chapter 4. Action science is useful for engaging these problems because it combines a method for making knowledge explicit with a theory of how people reason-in-action (Argyris & Schön, 1974). This theory claims that under conditions of psychological threat, people employ Model I theories of action aimed at maximizing unilateral control, protecting oneself and others, and maintaining rationality. Model I inhibits productive inquiry and limits individual and organizational learning. In order to overcome these barriers, action science advocates learning to produce a Model II theory of action driven by the values of generating valid information, free and informed choice, and internal commitment. From an action science perspective, the effectiveness of both researchers and practitioners requires an ability to produce Model II or its equivalent.

Stage 1: Mapping the Situation

This first stage was guided by two basic questions: What are the main gaps in the organization's knowledge of its practice? What are the existing organizational learning mechanisms, and how well do they operate? The first question aimed at distinguishing those features of the NEE intervention strategy that could be clearly articulated and agreed on by the program directors and those features that were either unclear or contested. The second question aimed at understanding how the organization had attempted to deal with these issues so far and why these attempts had not been sufficient.

In order to address these questions, the national director set up a learning team composed of the four regional directors, two veteran facilitators, and her. The two veteran facilitators, who were not members of the management group, represented the program's main areas of expertise: team building–organizational consulting and psycho-pedagogy. This learning team was a temporary off-line/internal learning mechanism that was established only for the purpose of learning. Although a consultant (Victor Friedman) did much of the actual data collection and analysis, all findings were discussed and authorized by the learning team.

The data for mapping was collected through semistructured, tape-recorded interviews with all of the members of the learning team. These interviews aimed at identifying the points of high uncertainty, ambiguity, or conflict in light of changes in the program's task environment. The interview data were analyzed and integrated into two diagnostic "maps" (see Figure 13.1 and Figure 13.2), one addressing the state of program knowledge and the other describing the organization's learning system. The multi-facet model served as a general framework for analyzing, interpreting, and mapping the interview data, though the actual content of the maps stayed close to the language and meanings expressed by the interviews.

These maps were a means of collecting information from scattered sources and integrating it into a relatively coherent picture of the situation. They were intended to be comprehensive enough to capture the essential features of the problem but simple enough to enable organizational members to "see" what they "knew" but could not clearly express. The maps also provided a baseline for evaluating progress and change as a result of the intervention process.

Both maps placed the current situation into a historical context that traced program develop over three generations: the founders, the second generation of gradual development, and the current third generation of rapid expansion. The first map focused on the contextual facet. It showed how changes in the task environment had increased uncertainty as well as error criticality. It then showed how these changes affected the core mission ("program theory") from the time of the founders until the current state. It attempted to distinguish between three kinds of "knowledge": explicit and consensual knowledge (specific principles and practices on which they agreed), implicit and consensual (very general and ill-defined principles and practices on which they agreed), and areas of uncertainty and ambiguity (features of their practice that they either questioned or about which they felt there was significant disagreement).

Figure 13.1 Mapping the Development of NEE Program Theory

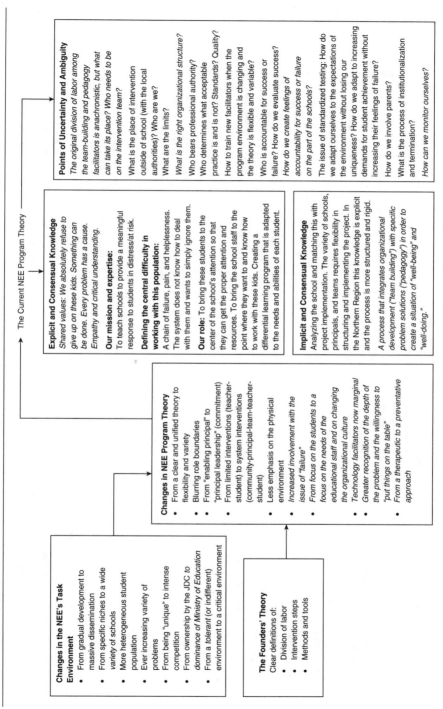

The Current NEE Program Theory

Changes in the NEE's Task Environment

- From gradual development to massive dissemination
- From specific niches to a wide variety of schools
- More heterogeneous student population
- Ever increasing variety of problems
- From being "unique" to intense competition
- From ownership by the JDC to dominance of Ministry of Education
- From a tolerant (or indifferent) environment to a critical environment

The Founders' Theory

Clear definitions of:
- Division of labor
- Intervention steps
- Methods and tools

Changes in NEE Program Theory

- From a clear and unified theory to flexibility and variety
- Blurring role boundaries
- From "enabling principal" to "principal leadership" (commitment)
- From limited interventions (teacher-student) to system interventions (community-principal-team-teacher-student)
- Less emphasis on the physical environment
- Increased involvement with the issue of "failure"
- From focus on the students to a focus on the needs of the educational staff and on changing the organizational culture
- Technology facilitators now marginal
- Greater recognition of the depth of the problem and the willingness to "put things on the table"
- From a therapeutic to a preventative approach

Explicit and Consensual Knowledge

Shared values: We absolutely refuse to give up on these kids. Something can be done. Every problem has a cause. Empathy and critical understanding.

Our mission and expertise:
To teach schools to provide a meaningful response to students in distress/at risk.

Defining the central difficulty in working with this population:

A chain of failure, pain, and helplessness. The system does not know how to deal with them and wants to simply ignore them.

Our role: To bring these students to the center of the school's attention so that they can get the proper attention and resources. To bring the school staff to the point where they want to and know how to work with these kids. Creating a differential learning program that is adapted to the needs and abilities of each student.

Implicit and Consensual Knowledge

Analyzing the school and matching this with project implementation. The variety of schools, principals, and teams requires flexibility in structuring and implementing the project. In the Northern Region this knowledge is explicit and the process is more structured and rigid.

A process that integrates organizational development ("team building") with specific problem solutions ("pedagogy") in order to create a situation of "well-being" and "well-doing."

Points of Uncertainty and Ambiguity

The original division of labor among the team-building and pedagogy facilitators is anachronistic, but what can take its place? Who needs to be on the intervention team?

What is the place of intervention outside of school (with the local authorities)? Who are we? What are the limits?

What is the right organizational structure?

Who bears professional authority? Who determines what acceptable practice is and is not? Standards? Quality?

How to train new facilitators when the program environment is changing and the theory is flexible and variable?

Who is accountable for success or failure? How do we evaluate success? *How do we create feelings of accountability for success or failure on the part of the schools?*

The issue of standardized testing: How do we adapt ourselves to the expectations of the environment without losing our uniqueness? How do we adapt to increasing demands for student achievement without increasing their feelings of failure?

How do we involve parents? What is the process of institutionalization and termination?

How can we monitor ourselves?

NOTE: Italics indicate a correction, addition, or change made in the original based on the feedback session.

227

Figure 13.2 Mapping the Learning System of the NEE Program

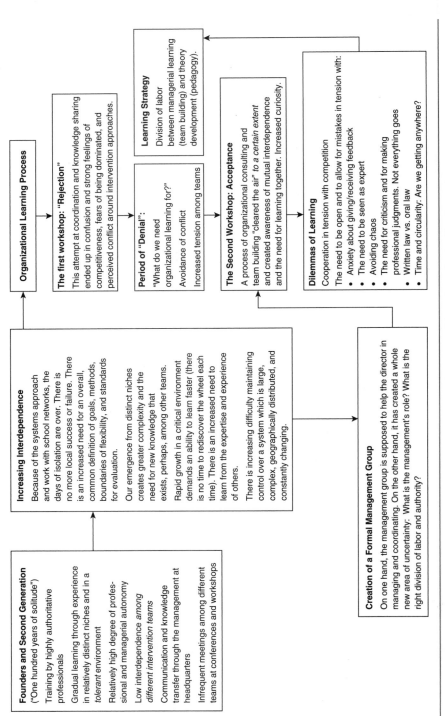

Founders and Second Generation

("One hundred years of solitude")

Training by highly authoritative professionals

Gradual learning through experience in relatively distinct niches and in a *tolerant* environment

Relatively high degree of professional and managerial autonomy

Low interdependence *among different intervention teams*

Communication and knowledge transfer through the management at headquarters

Infrequent meetings among different teams at conferences and workshops

Increasing Interdependence

Because of the systems approach and work with school networks, the days of isolation are over. There is no more local success or failure. There is an increased need for an overall, common definition of goals, methods, boundaries of flexibility, and standards for evaluation.

Our emergence from distinct niches creates greater complexity and the need for new knowledge that exists, perhaps, among other teams. Rapid growth in a critical environment demands an ability to learn faster (there is no time to rediscover the wheel each time). There is an increased need to learn from the expertise and experience of others.

There is increasing difficulty maintaining control over a system which is large, complex, geographically distributed, and constantly changing.

Organizational Learning Process

The first workshop: "Rejection"

This attempt at coordination and knowledge sharing ended up in confusion and strong feelings of competitiveness, fears of being dominated, and perceived conflict around intervention approaches.

Period of "Denial":

"What do we need organizational learning for?"

Avoidance of conflict

Increased tension among teams

The Second Workshop: Acceptance

A process of organizational consulting and team building "cleared the air" *to a certain extent* and created awareness of mutual interdependence and the need for learning together. Increased curiosity.

Learning Strategy

Division of labor between managerial learning (team building) and theory development (pedagogy).

Dilemmas of Learning

Cooperation in tension with competition

The need to be open and to allow for mistakes in tension with:

- Anxiety about giving/receiving feedback
- The need to be seen as expert
- Avoiding chaos
- The need for criticism and for making professional judgments. Not everything goes
- Written law vs. oral law
- Time and circularity: Are we getting anywhere?

Creation of a Formal Management Group

On one hand, the management group is supposed to help the director in managing and coordinating. On the other hand, it has created a whole new area of uncertainty: What is the management's role? What is the right division of labor and authority?

NOTE: Italics indicate a correction, addition, or change made in the original based on the feedback session.

The second map focused on changes in the learning mechanisms, the policy facet, the psychological climate, and the cultural facet. It showed that learning in the "first" two generations took place through an on-line/internal agency mechanism. This kind of OLM was appropriate for the early, experimental stage of the program in which *the work itself was learning* and the organization was relatively small (see Chapter 12 for an analysis of on-line/internal OLMs at Chaparral Steel). Once the program became more established and expanded, the "summer workshop," an off-line/internal OLM, was set up to facilitate knowledge sharing.

As the map illustrates, the first summer workshop did not generate productive learning because of low degree of psychological safety. A climate of competitiveness, fears of domination, and perceived conflict prevented the program staff from enacting the cultural norms conducive to learning. Part of the problem was that the regional directors, who were all new in their function, felt uncertain about their roles, authority, the division of labor, and ways of working together. On the other hand, the map reflects the organization's commitment to learning. Despite the initial failures, it continued to invest in learning and set up two parallel OLMs, one in which the program directors worked on managerial issues and one in which the learning team worked on program theory.

The thing that the map did *not* show was a *substantive* conflict among the regional program directors. In fact, not one of the interviewees was able to specify a single substantive issue on which there was clear and fundamental disagreement. All of the interviewees *believed* that there were serious conflicts, and they could point to experiences in which attempts at learning had ended in explosions. However, no one was able to say exactly what aspects of the program theory were being contended.

Both maps were presented and tested with the learning team in a 3-hour session in January 2001. Testing meant that the participants were asked the following questions: Did the maps capture the reality of the situation as they experienced it? Did they see their own perceptions of the situation in the map? Did they see errors, misinterpretations, or gaps in the map that needed to be corrected or filled in? The italicized portions of the map represent aspects that were either revised or added on the basis of this process of feedback and testing.

After suggesting a number of changes and additions to the first map (the program theory), the learning team was easily able to reach consensus about the key areas of uncertainty. The learning team members also confirmed most of the second map (the NEE learning system), but there was heated discussion about the perceived conflict among the regional directors. This discussion provided an opportunity, unavailable in the interviews, to directly observe and openly discuss the cultural norms being enacted in the learning team. For example, at certain points in the group discussion, someone would say something and someone would disagree. Then, almost instantly, everyone would start talking at once so that no one could hear anyone else and the discussion essentially dissolved. At that point, the consultant would usually have to shout over the commotion in order to bring the group back to order. This pattern repeated itself a number of times.

The members of the learning team espoused the cultural norms conducive to learning (transparency, inquiry, integrity, issue orientation, and accountability). They also considered these values to be a central feature of their work with the schools. However, they also admitted having trouble enacting these same values among themselves:

> You know, it's really strange. All day long we sit and listen to people. But we don't do among ourselves what we do in our work in the field. . . . Each of us does some kind of self-critical process, but we don't do it here. In other words, what we do on the outside, we don't do here. That strategy of intervention you just described (based on the cultural norms), are we familiar with it? And how!!!! We do it every single day, but we don't do it amongst ourselves— not at all. I act completely differently here. I shout in order that people will hear me. What we do as facilitators, we don't do [here].

Thus, a key part of the intervention strategy was to help the learning team clearly see the gaps between their espoused theory and the "theory-in-use" they were enacting in their actual behavior.

During this session, as in the interviews, the learning team members talked a great deal *about* history and conflict but always at an abstract level. Despite the consultant's probing, they were unable to clarify what had actually *happened* and what the conflicts were about. When this pattern became clear, we made the following intervention:

Consultant: You are arguing about history, about reality 5 years ago. The question is, how would you know that you are mistaken? You can each express your opinion as many times as you want, but there is a real question as to how you are going to actually determine what happened. On what basis can you decide? Everyone has a strong opinion, but how might you discover that the position you have taken is wrong?

The intervention strategy here was to shift their focus from the history to the effectiveness of the way in which they dealt with history. This particular comment was aimed at raising the need for both inquiry ("how you are going to actually determine what happened?") and integrity ("how might you discover that the position you have taken is wrong?").

Later in the discussion, the consultant explicitly stated that our intention was to help them increase their ability to learn by putting the values into practice:

Regional Director:	I think that there were things that were very painful, and by the way, they are repeating themselves today. There are things in the culture of the larger organization (of which the program is a part) that hurt me in a very personal way. These things repeat themselves, and it's impossible to discuss them.
Consultant:	Impossible?
Regional Director:	Impossible! For example, it is impossible to make an orderly criticism of the organization. You always come up against a lot of anger. And these things keep repeating themselves.
Consultant:	If I understand you correctly, you are saying that the culture of this organization, of which you are all a part . . . by the way, I heard a lot of discussion of history. If you are saying that it is impossible to discuss history, that statement is not exactly correct. Today you have spoken a great deal about the history, but if you listened carefully to the way in which you talk about the history, it would be clear why you keep repeating the same history.
Regional Director:	How do we talk?
Consultant:	I would bet you a $100 that in all of the talk about what happened in the past, no one asked each other a real question.
(Long Silence)	
Consultant:	Any discussion like the one you've been having would never bring you to either understanding or change.
Veteran Facilitator:	There is no listening.
Consultant:	I did not say that there was no listening. Perhaps there was no listening. I don't know. I don't know what was happening

in people's heads, but I do know what you said and did. As I see it, it's not just you, and it is not by chance. I am now revealing my own theory. I work with a theory that says that it is possible to predict this approach, which is rooted in your reasoning and behavior and which can be changed. And there is a puzzle here: What prevents you from asking questions so that you might truly understand each other? Part of what I want to do together with you in the theory-building process is to learn how to deal with these kinds of situations in a way that will enable you to test . . . because, in effect, when you say "that's the way it was" or "that's what I do," you are stating a "theory" or a "hypothesis."

National Director: You mean it's an interpretation.

Consultant: Yes. So the question is how to act in a way that enables me to test this perception or interpretation. It's easy for me to negate someone else's interpretation, but how can I discover if I am mistaken? I attribute to you that it is important not to be mistaken, but when you are facing an opposing interpretation, there is a dynamic that prevents you from testing your own interpretation or hypotheses. Thus, one of the things that I wish to do with you—in addition to collecting data and theory building—is to help you learn how to help you relate to what you know—in your everyday practice—as an hypothesis or an interpretation, and learn how to test it, to test and even disconfirm it. Does that make sense?

Veteran Facilitator: That would certainly make the process of working easier.

This intervention was actually a reframing of the problem facing the learning team. Rather than accept the regional director's claims that it was impossible to discuss history in this group because of the organization's culture, we suggested that it was *their own behavior* that made it impossible.

The evidence of this reframing was easily observable (e.g., no one asked each other a nonrhetorical question), and it was not difficult for the learning team members to recognize the absence of this very simple behavior. Because the reframing attributed the problem to some very simple behaviors (not asking questions), it also suggested that the solution would be much easier than changing the organization's culture. The consultant then suggested that it *was* possible to act in ways conducive to learning and that doing so was a matter of *personal choice*, which could be exercised with a little help. By the end of this session, the learning team had confirmed the validity of the two maps, identified the values that needed to be fostered in their learning culture, and stated their commitment to moving to the next stage.

Stage 2: Building Program Theory and Fostering a Learning Culture

The goal of the second stage was to build an initial version of the program theory that would address the specific areas of uncertainty and ambiguity specified in the map. Here the team continued its function as an off-line/internal agency learning mechanism—collecting information, analyzing it, and drawing conclusions. The data for this theory-building process was drawn from "personal case studies" written by the learning team members. The team members were given freedom to choose their cases as long as the case illustrated at least one of the areas of uncertainty or ambiguity identified in the map and described a situation in which the case writer was personally involved and took action toward the resolution. The consultant recommended a standard format for writing the case, based on the double-column format used in action science (e.g., Argyris & Schön, 1974, pp. 48–52; Senge et al., 1994, pp. 246–252). Team members were asked to write their cases using two parallel columns. In one column, they were asked to write what they, and others, said or did. In the other column, they were asked to write their unspoken thoughts and feelings. However, team members were allowed to write it in any way they wished.

The learning team met for a half-day session once a month from February through June in order to analyze and discuss these cases. Members of the team inquired into the case writer's reasoning and shared their own experience of dealing with similar problems. They also tried to distinguish those aspects of their practice on which there was clarity and consensus and those that required further clarification or decision making. After each session, tape-recorded transcripts were analyzed, and key elements in the program theory of action were identified. These analyses were documented and disseminated to the members of the learning team. They were then read out loud at the beginning of the next session, discussed and tested for validity. Thus, from session to session, the contours of NEE program theory became clearer and subject to critical inquiry.

During each session, the consultant presented one concept or tool, mostly drawn from action science, that the team members could use to put the learning values into practice. For example, the double-column case mentioned earlier provided a means of fostering *transparency*. The concept of espoused theories versus theories-in-use (see Chapter 7) was a particularly useful tool for guiding *inquiry* into the gaps between the kinds of behavior they intended to produce and what was reflected in their actual behavior. This conceptual tool also fostered *integrity* because it helped them see and accept their errors. The "ladder of inference" was used as a tool for fostering *inquiry* and testing (see Argyris, 1982, pp. 470–471; Senge et al., 1994, pp. 242–252). It helped the participants more closely connect their claims and interpretations with concrete data and information they had collected. It also oriented them toward trying to understand the reasoning behind the positions of others rather than simply rejecting or stating counterclaims.

It is far beyond the scope of this chapter to describe all of the features of the NEE program theory that were made explicit through this process. One example should suffice to illustrate the learning process. The case discussions revealed that the definition of the target population was a major source of ambiguity in the program. First, there was no single agreed-on definition of the target population, which was variably defined as "at risk" (Hixson & Tinzmann, 1990), "disadvantaged" (Kashti, Arieli, & Shlasky, 1997), or "underachievers" (Sulimani, 2002). Second, the NEE intervention, although ultimately intended to benefit students, was aimed entirely at helping school staff. Nevertheless, it was unclear in what sense the teachers could be considered the "target population" of the program.

Between the third and fourth case analysis sessions, the consultant asked the learning team members to read a study that described a process of producing actionable knowledge (Sykes & Goldman, 2000). The participants, however, were more intrigued by the substantive content of the study, which focused on the issue of social exclusion (Golding, 1995; Klasen, 1999; Rosenfeld & Tardieu, 2000). This concept struck them as remarkably descriptive of the problem facing the schools with which they were working.

The students in these schools generally came from lower socioeconomic levels; new immigrant groups; ethnic minorities; and/or family situations characterized by breakdown, violence, and neglect. Although they had the potential to succeed, they became caught up in a cycle of chronic failure and disruptive behavior. These students were generally unwanted in normative classrooms and were placed in a variety of special schools or classrooms that were typically characterized by disorder, severe behavioral problems, little academic achievement, violence, and alienation. Thus, rather than offer opportunities for social mobility, the school system functioned largely as a mechanism of social exclusion.

The really novel insight among the learning team, however, was that many of the teachers and administrators working with these students underwent a process of exclusion as well. Few of them received the special training and support required to succeed in this extremely difficult task. Many teachers regarded these assignments as a form of punishment. With a few rare exceptions, these teachers experienced chronic failure, constant fear of violence, and feelings of helplessness and despair (see the vignettes in Chapter 3). They displayed high levels of absenteeism; low motivation; and verbal aggressiveness toward students, peers, and parents. Teachers typically reacted to problems by blaming and punishing students, creating a vicious cycle of mutual recrimination, rejection, and alienation.

Principals who managed these frameworks faced a perpetual crisis situation characterized by inappropriate teaching methods; extreme and disruptive behavior; violence; and feelings of failure, exhaustion, and burnout. They felt abandoned and excluded by the social and institutional environment that held them accountable for the school's poor performance but failed to provide meaningful help and support for solving these extremely difficult problems. Many principals reacted by blaming the teachers, who then felt increasingly unsupported, abandoned, marginalized, and alienated from the system. The result was the creation of set of interlocking cycles of exclusion.

Thus, the learning team came to frame the problem as one of exclusion and to see the schools themselves as being the target population. This framing shifted the focus from individual deficits to a systemic view of the problem. It also accounted for the strikingly similar atmosphere and behavioral dynamics that the facilitators encountered in almost every school the NEE worked with, although there were great superficial differences among them. This way of viewing the problem represented a new way of thinking about the program's practice. It also enabled the regional directors see that despite superficial differences in their approaches to intervention, they shared a deep common understanding of the problems they were facing.

Stage 3: Extending the
Theory-Building Process to the Entire Staff

According to the original proposal for this project, the next stage should have been mapping the existing organizational learning mechanisms in the NEE program. However, this stage was passed over for budgetary reasons and because it was not considered critical. Instead, the management group decided to move to what was originally the fourth stage: extending the theory-building process throughout the organization.

The mechanism chosen for this next stage was a 3-day seminar for all 35 NEE facilitators and directors from all over the country. This seminar, which was held in July 2001, was an off-line/internal agency OLM that served both dissemination of knowledge that had been generated in the process so far and the production of new knowledge. It was designed and implemented jointly by the management group and three outside consultants. The management group now understood the principles of the learning process, so they were eager to play an active role in the design of this organizational learning mechanism. In addition, there were still concerns about the destructive potential of bringing the entire staff together, so they wanted to be sure that the design of the seminar would take the risks into account.

The goals of this seminar were to draw on the tacit knowledge of the entire staff in developing the NEE program theory, promote a programwide learning culture, and institute mechanisms for ongoing learning. This seminar was carried out in accordance with the same intervention strategies used in the previous stage but now adapted to an intensive 3-day format involving a larger number of people. Prior to the seminar, each facilitator prepared two personal cases—one describing a particular success in facilitating the program and one describing a situation characterized by difficulty or failure. During the seminar, these cases were analyzed and discussed in a variety of small- and large-group formats that brought together facilitators from different regions.

The case discussions focused on the process of entering the schools, developing productive relationships with the principal and the teachers, dealing with resistance, the limits to the intervention, and teamwork among the facilitators themselves. The outcomes of the analyses were then shared and discussed in plenary sessions. These cases provided a very rich database for identifying key elements of program theory as well as key dilemmas and challenges. They also enabled facilitators to see and openly compare their intervention approaches. These focused case discussions were balanced by dialogue sessions (Isaacs, 1999) held at the beginning and end of each day for the entire staff. The purpose of these sessions was to allow for more open, creative thinking as well as to create space for inquiring more into issues and concerns that came up in the separate case discussions.

This seminar built on and added to the theory-building process of the previous two stages. For example, the cases illustrating facilitators' intervention strategies began to be interpreted in terms of reversing social exclusion. The discussions around these cases raised the intense emotional and practical difficulties of getting a firm foothold in these systems. At one point in the seminar, the feeling of going into these schools was compared to the feeling of venturing into a "putrid swamp." The swamp image had a galvanizing effect because it perfectly captured the feelings of desolation, despair, danger, and hopelessness that characterized these schools. Anyone who ventured into them—including facilitators—risked being sucked down into the cycle of exclusion and despair.

Defining this feeling, however, immediately raised the question, what enabled the NEE facilitators to survive and in many cases help these schools turn around? This question constituted a central puzzle addressed by the inquiry process toward the end of the seminar. The facilitators pointed out that the key was establishing interpersonal relationships of a very special kind. They called this feature of their practice "forming a different connection"—"different" in the sense of being very different from the existing relationships among the students, teachers, administrators, and parents.

They also pointed out that this "different connection" began with relationships among the members of the team who intervened in each school. In fact, it was the relationship between the facilitators that seemed to account for successful interventions. This kind of relationship was not only a means for survival in these difficult environments but also a means for reversing the cycles of blame and rejection among teachers and students, administrators and teachers, teachers and teachers, and even between teachers and parents. This different connection was not the whole program theory. However, it was the foundation on which the intervention was built.

The seminar achieved the goals of drawing on the full staff's tacit knowledge and of fostering a learning culture. In addition, it had a very positive effect on the psychological climate among NEE staff. The seminar was the first time in the program's history that the NEE staff had an affirmative experience learning together. The participants came away with a much clearer sense that despite variations in approach and style, their practice was based on a common core set of values and practices. The competitive and defensive atmosphere that had characterized past meetings had been replaced by collaboration, mutual appreciation, and joint inquiry into a common set of problems.

Stage 4: Final Processing and Formulation of Program Theory

The seminar and the previous stages had generated a large body of data that still needed to be processed in order to make key aspects the program theory explicit. The seminar data was analyzed, and insights about NEE practice were then compiled into a document and distributed to all of the seminar participants, who were asked to provide feedback on their accuracy and comprehensiveness (testing). After these comments and corrections were incorporated into the analysis, an interim document was then presented to the NEE management group.

Although the management group confirmed that this document reflected the major themes that were raised in the process so far, they felt that it did not yet provide the specific explicit knowledge that they needed to make their practice more easily understood and transferable. At this stage, the initial learning team was disbanded, and an in-depth analysis of the data was carried out by the consultant and one of the regional directors. Because they were generating knowledge for others based on their data, the pair constituted an off-line/external agent OLM.

The work at this stage involved selecting key themes that had emerged in the earlier stages and analyzing existing data to tease out the specific intervention strategies involved. In order to deepen our analysis, the consultant sought out new cases that more clearly illustrated how facilitators dealt with particular issues or practice problems. The goal at this stage was to identify best practices and make them explicit. The results of these analyses were categorized, conceptualized, and organized into coherent set of intervention strategies that were then documented and tested with the management group and a few veteran facilitators. This analysis helped identify key gaps that still remained in our understanding of the program theory. In order to address these gaps, we held a 1-day seminar for the entire NEE staff in January 2002 that was similar to the one held during the summer.

One example of this in-depth analysis and conceptualization was the development of the idea of forming different connections that had emerged during the summer seminar. Although this idea resonated strongly with the entire NEE staff, it was still too vague and ill defined to be communicated or made "actionable" by others. In order to explicate this strategy, we reviewed the existing data and asked facilitators for additional cases that illustrated the nature of this relationship and the ways in which it was formed. Eventually the consultant came up with a very specific theory of action for forming a different connection (see Figure 13.3).

This theory consisted of four main components. The box to the left of the figure (Problem Framing) described the key features of the problem situation as perceived by the program facilitators. The box to the far right (Outcomes) described the specific characteristics of the different connection that the facilitators wanted to create; these were the goals. The boxes in the middle represented the four action strategies that we identified as critical for achieving these goals. These strategies

Figure 13.3 A "Theory" of "Forming a Different Connection"

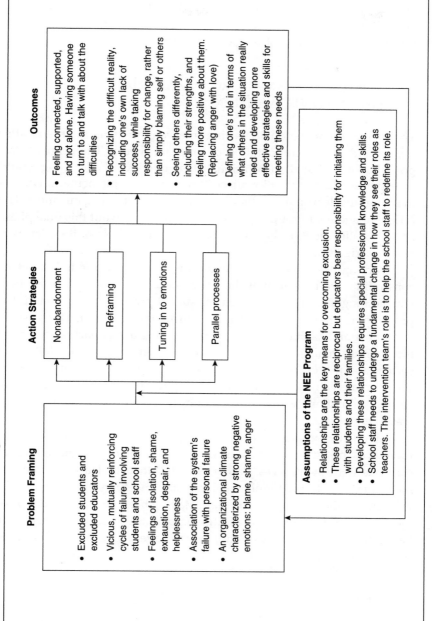

Problem Framing

- Excluded students and excluded educators
- Vicious, mutually reinforcing cycles of failure involving students and school staff
- Feelings of isolation, shame, exhaustion, despair, and helplessness
- Association of the system's failure with personal failure
- An organizational climate characterized by strong negative emotions: blame, shame, anger

Action Strategies

- Nonabandonment
- Reframing
- Tuning in to emotions
- Parallel processes

Outcomes

- Feeling connected, supported, and not alone. Having someone to turn to and talk with about the difficulties
- Recognizing the difficult reality, including one's own lack of success, while taking responsibility for change, rather than simply blaming self or others
- Seeing others differently, including their strengths, and feeling more positive about them. (Replacing anger with love)
- Defining one's role in terms of what others in the situation really need and developing more effective strategies and skills for meeting these needs

Assumptions of the NEE Program

- Relationships are the key means for overcoming exclusion.
- These relationships are reciprocal but educators bear responsibility for initiating them with students and their families.
- Developing these relationships requires special professional knowledge and skills.
- School staff needs to undergo a fundamental change in how they see their roles as teachers. The intervention team's role is to help the school staff to redefine its role.

were nonabandonment, reframing, "tuning in" to emotions, and parallel processes. The specific actions taken to carry out each of these strategies were also described and illustrated in detail (see Razer, Friedman, Sulimani, & Sykes, 2003; Friedman et al., 2004). Finally, the box at the bottom represented the fundamental assumptions in which the program's intervention strategies were grounded.

❖ ENDING THE FORMAL ORGANIZATIONAL LEARNING INTERVENTION

The formal organizational learning intervention came to an end after 1 year with the documentation of program theory. The original proposal had envisioned an additional stage in which the learning would be expanded and institutionalized through the implementation of formal ongoing learning mechanisms throughout the organization. The NEE management group expressed a desire to carry out this final phase and a specific action plan was prepared. Nevertheless, the plan was never carried out.

Although the lack of continuation was partially due to budgetary constraints, we believe that the main obstacle was simply that there was no longer a strong felt need for such a process. On one hand, the program had matured considerably during the past year. The tensions and uncertainties that had been so threatening a year earlier were now much more manageable. The regional program directors felt more certain about their roles and confident in their ability to manage the program as well as to coordinate among themselves. Communication among the regions was now much improved and knowledge sharing was a matter of routine.

Given the pressures faced in simply carrying out the program, there was no felt need to create a special set of off-line OLMs to continue with the process. Rather, they felt that the learning could be incorporated into the regular regional staff meetings and the periodic meetings of the entire program staff. Having been given an initial push by the formal learning process, the regional teams saw themselves as being able to function as online/internal agent OLMs—that is, carry out learning as an integral part of their everyday practice.

❖ EPILOGUE

Although the formal intervention ended in January 2002, the learning process continued. During the course of the year, the regional director assigned to coordinate the organizational learning process became deeply involved in developing the program theory itself. When the formal process ended, she took on a semiformal role as the "knowledge manager" for the program. She continued to develop and refine the program theory through an ongoing process of analysis, conceptualization, testing, and refinement. This knowledge was formalized and eventually published in a report titled *The New Education Environment: Action Strategies for Intervention* (Razer & Friedman, 2003). This report was not intended to be a complete description of program theory nor a systematic manual of operating procedures. Rather, it was intended to explicate and disseminate actionable knowledge about key aspects of program theory at a specific point in time.

The knowledge that was created in the process continues to develop and be disseminated through new mechanisms. Reframing the issue of at risk students as a problem of "social exclusion" had an impact on the thinking and discourse of the wider institutional environment. An Israeli college of education is using this knowledge to develop a set of programs aimed at making "inclusion" a form of professional educational practice.

❖ DEMYSTIFYING THE ORGANIZATIONAL LEARNING PROCESS

The objective in presenting this case study has been to illustrate how putting the multi-facet model into practice can help demystify the process of fostering organizational learning. The key to demystification was using the multi-facet model to structure and focus the learning around specific learning questions. The intervention was framed as an attempt to help the organization generate knowledge that was critical to its performance. Tools and changes in culture norms were introduced simultaneously with the introduction of OLMs and in a piecemeal fashion, one norm at a time as required by the inquiry process.

This case study provides a contrast to the image of learning organizations that undergo major cultural transformations as a prerequisite to learning. Organizational learning in the New Education Environment took place prior to this intervention and continued after the intervention officially ended. However, as the case illustrates, changes in the organizational context—such increased environmental demands, task uncertainty, and the high cost of error—created strong pressures to upgrade the NEE's learning capacities. Special OLMs were set up for generating and disseminating knowledge about the organization's core practice. However, once a sufficient portion of the organization's tacit knowledge was made explicit, these special OLMs were no longer necessary.

This learning strategy also modeled and fostered issue orientation by keeping the focus on generating knowledge about specific problems in task performance. The starting point for learning was always identifying the *task-related* uncertainties rather than the interpersonal conflicts and group dynamics that often grew out of these uncertainties. The reasoning behind this strategy was that interpersonal relations and group dynamics, for all their importance, were generally not the crux of the problem. Furthermore, because interpersonal issues are usually the most threatening, it may be counterproductive to make them the focus at the beginning of the process when the participants are still unsure about the learning culture and their own skills of inquiry.

At first, it took some effort to maintain an issue orientation in an organization so highly oriented toward interpersonal relationships. As illustrated in the feedback session on the map, it was quite natural for the regional directors to focus on interpersonal conflicts. This focus, however, led quickly to high levels of abstraction when little was learned and frustration mounted. Focusing the inquiry and gradually fostering the cultural values through the use of conceptual tools led to a significant change in the psychological climate in the learning team. As the team members became better at inquiry, they were able to be more open about perceived conflicts (transparency) and to test their perceptions openly. As a result, they discovered that most of the differences among them were not as significant as they had feared. To the contrary, they increasingly discovered common ground. As their skills improved, they became better at engaging the threatening, interpersonal issues in ways that led to learning rather than frustration and anxiety.

This case also illustrates the role of leadership in organizational learning. The decision of the national director to invest time, attention, and financial resources placed organizational learning at the center of the organization's agenda for an entire year. In addition, the organization leadership set a personal example by initiating the learning process among them before extending it to the entire organization. The program management also played a leading role in designing and monitoring the summer seminar, which clearly expressed the organization's commitment to learning. Finally, the regional manager, who stepped into the role of leading the knowledge creation process, ensured ongoing learning and dissemination after the formal intervention ended.

All of this was possible without heroic or charismatic leadership because the organization already had a tradition of learning. The norms of a learning culture were already a part of the NEE's espoused theory, and they were operative in certain parts of the organization. The intervention simply strengthened them and removed obstacles to their realization. The temporary OLMs under the consultant's guidance provided a psychologically safe environment that neutralized the existing dysfunctional relationships, and the consultant modeled all the values, which may have helped participants to acquire them by imitation.

At the early stages of the process, the consultant's role was to carry out the data collection and analysis and to facilitate the learning process. Although the intervention was heavily influenced by action science (Argyris et al., 1985; Argyris & Schön, 1974, 1996), systems thinking (Senge, 1990), and the concept of dialogue (Isaacs, 1999), it was not necessary to train the organizational members in these skills in order to generate productive learning (see Ford et al., 2000, for the opposite approach). Rather, the intervention strategy was based on the assumption that team members would gradually adopt and internalize the tools they found useful for learning. The consultant's job was to demonstrate how these tools could be employed, point out instances when they could be useful, and help participants craft their attempts to use them. As the intervention developed, organizational members themselves were increasingly able to employ these tools effectively and enact the cultural values. By the end of the planned intervention, they were able to carry this process on their own.

14

Before We Go . . .

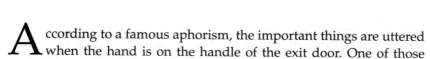

A ccording to a famous aphorism, the important things are uttered
when the hand is on the handle of the exit door. One of those
important things is reflected in a story told by one of the authors of this
book:

> When I was a graduate student working as teaching assistant for
> Argyris, one of the students in my section claimed to have mas-
> tered by the middle of the semester the fine arts of double-loop
> learning and Model II. His statement struck me as totally pre-
> sumptuous. After all, it had taken me 2 years of very hard work to
> even scratch the service. I was more than skeptical—even a bit
> scornful—and I shared my scorn with a more experienced TA. Her
> response surprised me. "You know," she said, "if I could teach
> someone to do this stuff in five minutes, I would do it!"

Of course, we are not arguing that organizational learning can be
brought into the 5-minute range. The moral of this story, however, is
that there is a real virtue in trying to demystify something as important
as organizational learning.

The multi-facet model presented in this book is our contribution
to this process of demystification that should serve researchers and

managers alike. In this final chapter, we will highlight some of the main ideas intended to guide you—whether you are a manager, consultant, or a researcher—in using the model. The model is not intended to be a "cookbook" because such an approach would oversimplify the real complexities and difficulties of the field. Rather we have provided a set of diagnostic concepts and thinking tools for understanding and fostering organizational learning.

In developing our model, we have taken a multidisciplinary approach, integrated existing conceptualizations and research findings, and used concepts with clear and direct relationship to organizational reality. Although we believe that the multi-facet model is widely applicable, its concrete manifestations will vary considerably from organization to organization. We have attempted to illustrate the power of this model for understanding organizational learning by applying it in a wide variety of contexts such as the military (postflight reviews in the Israel Defense Force Air Force; postaccident reviews in the Israel Defense Force), schools (the New Education Environment), heavy industry (Chaparral Steel, Globe Metallurgical), high-tech (Hewlett-Packard, Dell, Motorola, Microsoft, IBM), the food industry (Johnsonville Foods), R & D (Bell Labs), and the oil industry (BP, Shell). We have also used the model to analyze organizational learning as both a routine part of task performance (postflight reviews) and as a response to accidents. Finally, the model has been developed and applied in a number of different national cultures (Australia, Israel, the United States).

By now, you should be familiar, perhaps overly so, with the idea of organizational learning mechanism (OLMs). We have pointed out that these structural mechanisms are the organizational equivalent of the central nervous system for processing information. Carrying this analogy one step further, we can say that specific OLMs are like the brain cells of the organization. The importance of this concept is that it takes a rather amorphous, disembodied process and makes it observable and tangible. It provides a means through which you can literally *see* organizational learning in action—and get your hands on it.

The concept of OLMs offers managers a tool for identifying and mapping the organizational learning that is already taking place, the logical starting point for any effort at improvement. The five types of OLMs can help in the analysis and design of organizational learning, guiding systematic thinking about how learning best fits into specific work processes. The OLM concept should help managers focus on who needs to be learning, when it should take place, and how to get the people together for this to happen. OLMs provide managers with choices; they do not always have to be as intensive as the on-line/internal approach employed at Chaparral, for instance.

From a theoretical perspective, the OLM concept distinguishes between individual and organizational levels of learning, showing how individual learning becomes organizational. Making organizational learning more easily observable offers researchers a tool for studying the phenomenon. In this book, we have refrained from trying to develop a formal contingency model that links OLMs with specific types of work or other features of the learning situation. This area of inquiry provides fertile ground for further research. Another more basic question for researchers is whether the two parameters that we have chosen for classifying OLMs adequately capture their character and variety. There may be different and more useful ways of understanding and describing different kinds of OLMs.

Before we walk out the door, we strongly suggest that you think of OLMs as "cultural islands" that generate and disseminate knowledge for the organization. This idea helps explain how organizational learning is possible despite apparent conflicts between the dominant cultures of most organizations and the values and norms required for productive learning. If managers wish to promote organizational learning, they need to aim at fostering norms of inquiry, issue orientation, transparency, integrity, and accountability in OLMs. By carefully defining and illustrating these cultural norms, we have tried to provide clear targets that managers can shoot for. The starting point will differ in each organization, and each OLM for that matter. In addition, the strength of these norms required for productive learning will vary, depending on the complexity of problems, the uncertainty involved, the extensiveness of the changes that need to be made, and the degree of psychological threat raised by the particular issues at hand.

The idea of cultural islands and the five norms of a learning culture provide fertile ground for further research. We have based our claim about cultural islands on specific examples of OLMs that are culturally distinct from the surrounding organization. However, we still know very little about the conditions that enable such islands to emerge, how they coexist with the dominant culture, and how they might influence it over time. The five cultural norms are not meant to reflect ultimate truths but rather a set of hypotheses about what is likely to generate productive learning. Initial studies on the impact of these norms have already been carried out (see Chapters 12 and 13), but there is a need for additional empirical research that looks at both the validity of the norms and at the specific ways in which they can be developed.

Before going, we would also like to say some things about psychological safety and trust. An atmosphere of trust is critically important for enabling people to take the risks involved in productive learning. It represents a kind of social capital that takes time to develop and ought to be treated as an invaluable resource to be cultivated and preserved. But trust can be a double-edged sword. Trust may mean that participants in an OLM feel free to challenge the status quo—and each other. Or it may mean that people feel confident that they will not be publicly challenged and that others will protect them when they are. Managers need to be aware of the difference between the two. In any case, it is clear that an atmosphere of genuine interpersonal trust is not something that can be easily engineered. Research on the development of trust in teams and organizations can make a significant contribution to organizational learning.

Keep in mind that the best defense against threat is a collective view of reality that is as accurate and undistorted as possible. Organizational learning sometimes requires facing real threats or challenging shared mental models that preserve a sense of stability, familiarity, and/or predictability. Attempts to introduce doubt and uncertainty mobilize powerful social defenses that push away disturbing information, distort reality, and erode the atmosphere of genuine trust. The way to deal with this threat is to help organizational members understand that the realities they experience are, at least in part, objects of their own construction. This realization can help participants in an OLM become more skillful in collectively constructing their images of reality. It can also help them distinguish between the real threats that need to be faced objectively and those threats that emanate from their own anxieties and group processes. This source of psychological safety and the five norms of a learning culture reinforce each other.

There is another important kind of trust—trust in the system—that is largely in the hands of management. This kind of trust means that employees know that they will be rewarded—or at least not punished—for taking the risks involved in learning. It means that the "rules of the game" are perceived as clear, fair, and relatively stable. It also implies a belief that the organization cares about and is committed to the welfare of its employees. The more strongly employees experience this kind of trust, the more committed they will feel to the organization and the more effort they are likely to invest in learning that goes beyond their own personal benefit.

In our discussion of the channels of leadership influence, we tried to specify the ways in which managers can foster this kind of trust. It requires them to make conscious choices about priorities, allocation of resources, and setting a personal example with learning in mind. Perhaps the most important point is that *blocking* learning is easy. Managers who are seriously committed to promoting organizational learning need to be conscious of how they might unintentionally be doing this. The contextual facet, on the other hand, alerts managers to the factors outside of their control that both facilitate or constrain organizational learning.

Research on leadership in organizational learning has focused largely on mythological, larger-than-life managers, usually CEOs who have transformed their organizations into learning organizations. There is much that can be learned from these exemplars. Indeed, we have drawn many examples from them in illustrating components of the multi-facet model. However, the best practice examples we have used are not meant to be models for imitation but rather illustrations of how the multi-facet model looks in practice. Demystification requires shifting the focus to less heroic figures at every management level. There is a real need for research on the ways in which their behavior promotes or inhibits organizational level learning.

Finally, we would like to say a few last words about both the "learning organization" as a laudatory term and the concept of transformation. In many ways, this book has been a critique of the idea, either explicit or implied, that some organizations learn and that others do not. Our fundamental assumption is that all organizations learn, though the frequency and quality of learning vary widely. In challenging the idea of the learning organization, we are not necessarily rejecting the five disciplines (Senge, 1990), Model II (Argyris & Schön, 1978, 1996), or other types of knowledge and skill deemed essential for learning. Indeed, we considered some of these ideas extremely important and have incorporated them either explicitly or implicitly into our model. However, we do not believe that these disciplines, or any other set of skills, add up to organizational learning.

By the same token, we are not arguing against transformations or that transformations do not occur on the collective or individual levels. However, thinking in terms of organizational transformation distances organizational learning from the areas where most managers have influence and control. It makes it easier to long for the vision of the learning organization rather than to focus on the mundane work necessary to help organizations learn more productively.

Furthermore, we are not arguing that organizational learning may not involve deeply personal, even spiritual, aspects of individual and group transformation. The practice of productive organizational learning can, and should, make your work a more stimulating, interesting, and satisfying experience. Ideally, it should also provide you and others with a greater sense of choice about both the ends and means of your work. Nevertheless, focusing on transformation obscures the fact that pragmatic and instrumental aspects of organizational learning are no less important and demand concerted effort.

In an attempt to follow our own prescriptions, we have tried to speak with you in a tone that is neither overly skeptical nor overly inspiring. Nevertheless, we do want to encourage you to experiment with these ideas. The beauty of experimenting with introducing or improving organizational learning is that the process is the product: Organizational learning interventions are themselves organizational learning.

References

Abegglen, J. C., & Stalk, G. (1985). *Kaisha: The Japanese corporation.* New York: Basic Books.

Abelson, E., Aronson, W. J., McGuire, T. M., Newcomb, M. J., Rosenberg, P. H., & Tannenbaum, R. P. (Eds.). (1968). *Theories of cognitive consistency.* Chicago: Rand McNally.

Adler, P. S., & Cole, R. E. (1993). Designed for learning: A tale of two auto plants. *Sloan Management Review, 34,* 85–94.

Allen, N. J., & Meyer, J. P. (1990). The measurement and antecedents of affective, continuance and normative commitment to organization. *Journal of Occupational Psychology, 63,* 1–18.

Amitay, M., Popper, M., & Lipshitz, R. (2005). The effects of leadership style on organizational learning in community clinics. *Learning Organization 12*(1), 57–70.

Argote, L. (1999). *Organizational learning: Creating, retaining, and transferring knowledge.* Norwell, MA: Kluwer.

Argyris, C. (1980). *Inner contradictions of rigorous research.* New York: Academic.

Argyris, C. (1982). *Reasoning, learning, and action: Individual and organizational.* San Francisco: Jossey-Bass.

Argyris, C. (1991). Teaching smart people how to learn. *Harvard Business Review, 69*(3), 99–109.

Argyris, C. (1993). *Knowledge for action: A guide to overcoming barriers to organizational change.* San Francisco: Jossey-Bass.

Argyris, C. (1996). Unrecognized defenses of scholars: Impact on theory and research. *Organization Science, 7,* 79–87.

Argryis, C., Putnam, R., & Smith, D. (1985). *Action science: Concepts, methods, and skills for research and intervention.* San Francisco: Jossey-Bass.

Argyris, C., & Schön, D. A. (1974). *Theory in practice: Increasing professional effectiveness.* San Francisco: Jossey-Bass.

Argyris, C., & Schön, D. A. (1978). *Organizational learning: A theory of action perspective.* Reading, MA: Addison-Wesley.

Argyris, C., & Schön, D. A. (1996). *Organizational learning II: Theory, methods and practice.* Reading, MA: Addison-Wesley.

Armstrong, H. (2000). The learning organization: Changed means to an unchanged end. *Organization, 7*(2), 355–361.

Arrow, K. (1974). *The limits of organizations.* New York: Norton.

Arthur, J. B., & Aiman-Smith, L. (2002). Gainsharing and organizational learning: An analysis of employee suggestions over time. *Academy of Management Journal, 44*(4), 737–754.

Baer, M., & Frese, M. (2003). Innovation is not enough: Climates for initiative and psychological safety, process innovations, and firm performance. *Journal of Organizational Behavior, 24*, 45–68.

Baird, L., Henderson, J. C., & Watts, S. (1997). Learning from action: An analysis of the Center for Army Lessons Learned (CALL). *Human Resource Management 36*, 385–395.

Baldwin, T. T., Danielson, C., & Wiggenhorn, W. (1997). The evolution of learning strategies in organizations: From employee development to business redefinition. *Academy of Management Executive, 11*(4), 47–58.

Banfield, E. (1958). *The moral basis of a backward society.* New York: Glenco Free Press.

Barnett, C. (2001). *Rethinking organizational learning theories: A review and synthesis of the primary literature.* Unpublished manuscript.

Barrow, D. C. (2001). Sharing know-how at BP Amoco. *Research Technology Management, 3*, 8–25.

Bass, B. M. (1985). *Leadership and performance beyond expectations.* New York: Free Press.

Bateson, G. (1979). *Mind and nature.* New York: Dutton.

Baum, J. A. C., Xiao Li, S., & Usher, J. M. (2000). Making the next move: How experiential and vicarious learning shape the locations of chains' acquisitions. *ASQ, 45*(4), 766–801.

Becker, T. E. (1998). Integrity in organizations: Beyond honesty and conscientiousness. *Academy of Management Review, 23*, 154–161.

Beer, M., & Spector, B. (1993). Organizational diagnosis: Its role in organizational learning. *Journal of Counseling and Development, 71*, 642–650.

Ben Horin-Naot, Y., Lipshitz, R., & Popper, M. (2004). Discerning the quality of organizational learning. *Journal of Management Learning, 35*, 451–473.

Berthoin-Antal, A., Dierkes, M., Child, J., & Nonaka, I. (2001). Organizational learning and knowledge: Reflections on the dynamics of the field and challenges for the future. In M. Dierkes, A. Berthoin-Antal, J. Child, & I. Nonaka (Eds.), *Handbook of organizational learning and knowledge* (pp. 921–939). Oxford, UK: Oxford University Press.

Berzins, A., Podolny, J., & Roberts, R. (1998). *British Petroleum (B)* (Case S-IB-16B). Stanford, CA: Graduate School of Business, Stanford University.

Bion, W. R. (1961). *Experiences in Groups*, London: Tavistock.

Bowerman, J., & Collins, G. (1999). The coaching network: A program for individual and organizational development. *Journal of Workplace Working, 11*, 201–207.

Brand, A. (1998). Knowledge management and innovation at 3M. *Journal of Knowledge Management, 2*(1), 17–22.

Brown, C., & Reich, M. (1989). When does cooperation work? A look at NUMMI and GM Van Nuys. *California Management Review, 31,* 26–37.

Busby, J. S. (1999). The effectiveness of collective retrospection as a mechanism of organizational learning. *Journal of Applied Behavioral Science, 35,* 109–129.

Cannon, M. D., & Edmondson, A. C. (2001). Confronting failure: Antecedents and consequences of shared beliefs about failures in organizational work groups. *Journal of Organizational Behavior, 22,* 161–177.

Carlzon. J. (1989). *Moments of truth.* New York: Harper & Row.

Carrol, J. S. (1995). Incident reviews in high-hazard industries: Sensemaking and learning under ambiguity and accountability. *Industrial and Environmental Crisis Quarterly, 9,* 175–197.

Carrol, J. S. (1998). Organizational learning activities in high-hazard industries: The logics underlying self-analysis. *Journal of Management Studies, 36,* 699–717.

Carrol, J. S., & Edmondson, A. C. (2002). Leading organizational learning in health care. *Quality and Safety in Health Care, 11,* 51–56.

Carrol, J. S., Rudolph, J. W., & Hatakenaka, S. (2003). Learning from organizational experience. In M. Easterby-Smith & M. A. Lyles (Eds.), *Blackwell handbook of organizational learning and knowledge management* (pp. 575–600). London: Blackwell.

Castillo, J. (2002). A note on the concept of tacit knowledge. *Journal of Management Inquiry, 11*(1), 46–57.

Chen, H. T. (1990). *Theory-driven evaluations.* Newbury Park, CA: Sage.

Cheney, S. (1998, March 22–23). *Evidence of effective learning environments in organizations.* Paper presented at the conference on Organizational Learning: Moving From Theory to Research, George Washington University, Washington, DC.

Chew, B., Bresnaham, T. F., & Clark, K. B. (1986). *Measurement, coordination and learning in a multi-plant network* [Working paper]. Boston: Harvard Business School.

Cohen, M., Friedman, V., & Eran, M. (1996). *Evaluation of the New Education Environment in technological schools of the AMAL Network: First interim report of school characteristics and the initial stages of program implementation.* Jerusalem: Brookdale Institute.

Cohen-Navot, M. (2000). *The New Educational Environment: Promoting achievements of disadvantaged youth through changes in the educational approach: Summary of the evaluation project.* Jerusalem: Brookdale Institute.

Cohen-Navot, M. (2003). *Evaluation of the New Educational Environment project in the AMAL Technological Network: Final report.* Jerusalem: Brookdale Institute.

Cohen-Navot, M., & Lavenda, O. (2003). *Sustainability of an educational intervention program, the New Educational Environment: Institutionalization after seven years of implementation.* Jerusalem: Brookdale Institute.

Coleman, J. S. (1988). Social capital in the creation of human capital. *American Journal of Sociology, 94*(suppl.), 95–120.

Collison, P., & Parcell, G. (1998). Embedding KM into business practices at BP. *Knowledge Management Review, 4*(2), 30–33.

Coné, J. (2000). How Dell does it. *Training & Development, 54*(6), 58–70.

Constant, D., Kiesler, S., & Sproul, L. (2001). What's mine is ours, or is it? A study of attitudes about information sharing. *Information Systems Research, 5,* 400–421.

Craig, S. B., & Gustavson, S. B. (1998). Perceived leader integrity scale: An instrument for assessing employee perceptions of leader integrity. *Leadership Quarterly, 9*(2), 127–145.

Crossan, M. M., & Guatto, T. (1996). Organizational learning research profile. *Journal of Organizational Change Management, 9,* 107–112.

Crossan, M. M., & Hulland, J. (2002). Leveraging knowledge through leadership of organizational learning. In C. W. Choo & N. Bontiss (Eds.), *The strategic management of intellectual capital and organizational knowledge* (pp. 711–723). Oxford, UK: Oxford University Press.

Crossan, M. M., Lane, H. W., & Roderick, E. W. (1999). An organizational learning framework: From intuition to institution. *Academy of Management Review, 24*(3), 522–537.

Cusumano, M. A., & Selby, R. W. (1995). *Microsoft secrets.* New York: Free Press.

Cyert, R. M., & March, J. G. (1963). *A behavioral theory of the firm.* Englewood Cliffs, NJ: Prentice Hall.

Davenport, T. H., De Long, D. W., & Beer, M. C. (1998). Successful knowledge-management projects. *Sloan Management Review, 39*(2), 43–57.

Davenport, T. H., & Prusak, L. (1998). *Working knowledge.* Boston: Harvard Business School Press.

Davies, J., & Easterby-Smith, M. (1984). Learning and developing from managerial work experiences. *Journal of Management Studies, 21,* 169–183.

Dearborn, D. C., & Simon, H. A. (1958, June). Selective perception: A note on the departmental identification of executives. *Sociometry, 140*–148.

De Geus, A. (1988). Planning as learning. *Harvard Business Review, 66*(4), 70–74.

Delbecq, A. (2000). Spirituality for leadership: Reporting on a pilot course for MBAs and CEOs. *Journal of Management Inquiry, 9*(2), 117–128.

Dell takes a stroll in the park. (2001). *Human Resource Management International Digest, 9*(4), 23–25.

De Long, D. W., & Fahey, L. (2000). Diagnosing cultural barriers to knowledge management. *Academy of Management Executive, 14,* 113–127.

Dewey, J. (1933). *How we think.* Boston: D. C. Heath.

Dewey, J. (1938). *Logic: The theory of inquiry.* New York: Holt, Rinehart & Winston.

DiBella, A., Nevis, E. C., & Gould, J. M. (1996). Understanding organizational learning capability. *Journal of Management Studies, 33,* 361–379.

Dierkes, M., Berthoin-Antal, A., Child, C., & Nonaka, I. (Eds.). (2001). *Handbook of organizational learning and knowledge.* Oxford, UK: Oxford University Press.

Dixon, N. M. (1999). The changing face of knowledge. *Learning Organization, 6*(5), 212–216.

Dixon, N. M. (2000). *Common knowledge: How companies thrive by sharing what they know.* Boston: Harvard Business School Press.

Dodgson, M. (1993). Organizational learning: A review of some literatures. *Organization Studies, 14,* 375–394.

Dong, J. (2002, April 10). The rise and fall of the HP way. *Palo Alto Weekly*, p. 7.

Doving. E. (1996). In the image of man: Organizational action, competence, and learning. In D. Grant & C. Oswick (Eds.), *Metaphor and organizations* (pp. 185–199). London: Sage.

Driver, M. (2002). The learning organization: Foucaldian gloom or Utopian sunshine? *Human Relations, 55*(1), 33–53.

Dumaine, B. (1992). Unleash workers and cut costs. *Fortune, 125*(10), 88.

Earl, M., & Scott, I. (1999). What is a chief knowledge officer? *Sloan Management Review, 40*(2), 29–387.

Easterby-Smith, M. (1997). Disciplines of the learning organization: Contributions and critiques. *Human Relations, 50*, 1085–1113.

Edmondson, A. C. (1996). Learning from mistakes is easier said than done: Group and organizational influences on the detection and correction of human error. *Journal of Applied Behavioral Science, 32*, 5–32.

Edmondson, A. C. (1999). Psychological safety and learning behavior in work teams. *Administrative Science Quarterly, 44*, 350–383.

Edmondson, A. C. (2003). Managing the risk of learning: Psychological safety in work teams. In M. West (Ed.), *International handbook of organizational teamwork and cooperative working* (pp. 255–276). London: Blackwell.

Edmondson, A. C., Bohmer, R. M. J., & Pisano, G. (2000). Learning new technical and interpersonal routines in operating root teams: The case of minimally invasive cardiac surgery. In B. Mannix, M. Neal, & T. Griffith (Eds.), *Research on groups and teams* (pp. 29–51). Greenwich, CT: JAI.

Edmondson, A. C., & Moingeon, B. (1997). From organizational learning to the learning organization. *Management Learning, 28*, 499–517.

Elkington J., & Trisoglio, A. (1996). Developing realistic scenarios for the environment: Lessons from Brent Spar. *Long Range Planning, 29*, 762–769.

Eller, D. (1995). Motorola trains VPs to become growth leaders. *HRMagazine, 40*(6), 82–87.

Ellinger, E., & Bostrom, R. P. (1999). Managerial coaching behaviors in learning organizations. *Journal of Management Development, 18*, 751–771.

Ellinger, E., & Bostrom, R. P. (2002). An examination of managers' beliefs about their roles as facilitators of learning. *Management Learning, 33*, 147–179.

Ellis, S., Caridi, O., Lipshitz, R., & Popper, M. (1999). Perceived error criticality and organizational learning: An empirical investigation. *Knowledge and Process Management, 6*, 166–175.

Ellis, S., & Shpielberg, N. (2003). Organizational learning mechanisms and managers' perceived uncertainty. *Human Relations, 56*(10), 1233–1254.

Elmes, M., & Smith, C. (2001). Moved by the spirit: Contextualizing workplace empowerment in American spiritual ideals. *Journal of Applied Behavioral Science, 37*(1), 33–50.

Englehardt, C. S., & Simmons, P. R. (2002). Organizational flexibility for a changing world. *Leadership & Organization Development Journal, 23*(3/4), 113–121.

Ericsson, K. A., Krampe, T., & Tesch-Romer, C. (1993). The role of deliberate practice in the acquisition of expert performance. *Psychological Review, 100*, 363–406.

Extending the learning curve: John Authers examines the growing popularity of corporate universities in the U.S. (1997, September 22). *Financial Times,* p. 15.

Fahey, L., & Randall, R. M. (1998). *Learning from the future: Competitive foresight scenarios.* New York: Wiley.

Farson, R., & Keyes, R., (2002). Failure-tolerant leader. *Harvard Business Review, 79*(4), 65–72.

Festinger, L. (1954). A theory of social comparison processes. *Human Relations, 7,* 117–140.

Fiol, M. C., & Lyles, M. A. (1985). Organizational learning. *Academy of Management Review, 10,* 803–813.

Fisher, S. R., & White, M. A. (2000). Downsizing in a learning organization: Are there hidden costs? *Academy of Management Review, 25,* 244–252.

Ford, D. N., Voyer, J. J., & Gould-Wilkinson, J. (2000). Building learning organizations in engineering cultures: A case study. *Journal of Management in Engineering, 16*(4), 74–83.

Freud, S. (1957). *The standard edition of the complete psychological works of Sigmund Freud.* London: Hogarth Press.

Friedman, V. J. (1997). Making schools safe for uncertainty: Teams, teaching, and school reform. *Teachers College Record, 99*(2), 335–370.

Friedman, V. (2000). Action science: Creating communities of inquiry in communities of practice. In H. Bradbury & P. Reason (Eds.), *Handbook of action research* (pp. 159–170). Thousand Oaks, CA: Sage.

Friedman, V. (2001a). Action Science: Creating communities of inquiry in communities of practice. In P. Reason & H. Bradbury (Eds.), *The handbook of action research* (pp. 159–170). London: Sage.

Friedman, V. J. (2001b). "Designed Blindness": An action science approach to program theory evaluation. *American Journal of Evaluation, 22,* 61–181.

Friedman, V. (2002). The individual as agent of organizational learning. *California Management Review, 44*(2), 70–89.

Friedman, V., & Berthoin-Antal, A. (2004). Negotiating reality: An action science approach to intercultural competence. *Management Learning, 36*(1), 67–84.

Friedman, V., & Lipshitz, R. (1992). Teaching people to shift cognitive gears: Overcoming resistance on the road to Model II. *Journal of Applied Behavioral Science, 28*(1), 118–137.

Friedman, V., & Lipshitz, R. (1994). Human resources or politics: Framing the problem of appointing managers in an organizational democracy. *Journal of Applied Behavioral Science, 30*(4), 438–457.

Friedman, V., Razer, M., & Sykes, I. (2004). Towards a theory of inclusive practice: An action science approach. *Action Research, 2*(2), 183–205.

Friedman, V., & Rothman, J. (2001). Conflict, identity, and organizational learning. In M. Dierkes, A. Berthoin-Antal, J. Child, & I. Nonaka (Eds.), *Handbook of organizational learning* (pp. 582–597). Oxford, UK: Oxford University Press.

Friedman, V., & Sykes, I. (2001). Reflection "in," reflection "on" and action science research. In S. Sankaran, B. Dick, R. Passfield, & P. Swepson (Eds.), *Effective change management through action research and action learning: Concepts, frameworks, processes and applications* (pp. 149–159). Lismore, Australia: Southern Cross University Press.

Fukuyama, F. (1990). *Trust: The social virtues and creation of prosperity.* New York: Free Press.

Garvin, D. A. (1993). Building a learning organization. *Harvard Business Review, 73*(4), 78–91.

Garvin, D. A. (2000). *Learning in action: A guide to putting the learning organization to work.* Boston: Harvard Business School Press.

Gerhardi, S. (1999). Learning as problem-driven or learning in the face of mystery? *Organization Studies, 20,* 101–124.

Goh, S. C. (1998). Toward a learning organization: The strategic building blocks. *Advanced Management Journal, 63*(2), 15–21.

Golding, P. (1995). Public attitudes of social exclusion: Some problems of measurements and analysis. In G. Room (Ed.), *Beyond the threshold.* Bristol, UK: Policy Press.

Greco, J. A. (1999). What is a CKO—and should you have one? *Journal of Business Strategy, 20*(2), 20.

Gulliver, F. R. (1987). Post-project appraisals pay. *Harvard Business Review, 65*(2), 128–132.

Hansen, M., Nohria, N., & Tierney, T. (1999). What's your strategy for managing knowledge? *Harvard Business Review, 77*(2), 106–116.

Hanson, N. R. (1964). Observation and interpretation. *The voice of America forum lectures* (Philosophy Series # 9). Washington, DC: Voice of America.

Hedberg, B. (1981). How organizations learn and unlearn. In P. C. Nystrom & W. H. Starbuck (Eds.), *Handbook of organizational design* (Vol. 1, pp. 3–27), Oxford, UK: Oxford University Press.

Heschel, A. (1955). *God in search of man.* New York: Farrar, Straus and Giroux.

Hirschhorn, L. (1990). *The workplace within: Psychodynamics of organizational life.* Cambridge: MIT Press.

Hixson, J., & Tinzmann, M. B. (1990). *Reconnecting students at risk to the learning process: Who are AT-RISK students of the 1990s?* Oak Brook, IL: NCREL.

Honold, L. (1996). How Johnsonville Foods became a learning organization. *Adult Learning, 7*(2), 27–31.

Hovland, C. I., & Weiss, W. (1951). The influence of source credibility on communication effectiveness. *Public Opinion Quarterly, 15,* 635–650.

HP history and facts. (2006). Retrieved February 18, 2006, from http://www.hp.com/hpinfo/abouthp/histnfacts.

Huber, G. P. (1991). Organizational learning: The contributing processes and the literatures. *Organizational Science, 2,* 88–115.

Isaacs, W. (1999). *Dialogue: The art of thinking together.* New York: Doubleday.

Jackson, B. (2000). A fantasy theme analysis of Peter Senge's learning organization. *Journal of Applied Behavioral Science, 36*(2), 193–209.

Janis, I. L. (1972). *Victims of groupthink: A psychological study of foreign-policy decisions and fiascoes.* New York: Houghton Mifflin.

Johnson, G. (1990). Managing strategic change: The role of symbolic action. *British Journal of Management, 1,* 183–200.

Johnson, J. R. (2002). Leading the learning organization: Portrait of four leaders. *Leadership and Organizational Development Journal, 23,* 241–249.

Kahn W. A. (1990). Psychological conditions of personal engagement and disengagement at work. *Academy of Management Journal, 33,* 692–724.

Kam, J., & Thomas, J. (2002). Project management maturity models: The silver bullets of competitive advantage? *Project Management Journal, 33*(4), 4–14.

Kantrow, J. M. (1986). Wide open management at Chaparral Steel. *Harvard Business Review, 64*(3), 96–102.

Kashti, Y., Arieli, M., & Shlasky, S. (Eds.). (1997). *Teaching and education: An Israeli lexicon.* Tel Aviv: Ramot Press. (In Hebrew)

Katz, N. (2001). Sports teams as a model for workplace teams: Lessons and liabilities. *Academy of Management Executive, 15*(3), 56–67.

Kelley, R. (1993). How Bell Labs creates star performers. *Harvard Business Review, 71*(4), 128–139.

Kim, D. H. (1993). The link between individual and organizational learning. *Sloan Management Review, 34*(1), 37–50.

Klasen, S. (1999). *Social exclusion, children, and education: Conceptual and measurement issues* [Background paper]. Paris: OECD.

Kleiner, A. (1996). *The age of heretics: Heroes, outlaws, and the forerunners of corporate change.* New York: Currency Doubleday.

Kofman, F., & Senge, P. (1993). Communities of commitment: The heart of the learning organization. *Organizational Dynamics, 22*(2), 5–23.

Kolb, D. A. (1984). *Experiential learning.* Englewood Cliffs, NJ: Prentice Hall.

Kotter, J. P. (1982). What effective general managers really do? *Harvard Business Review, 60*(6), 156–167.

Kotter, J. P. (1988). *The leadership factor.* New York: Free Press.

Kotter, J. P. (1990). What do leaders really do? *Harvard Business Review, 68*(3), 103–111.

Kotter, J. P., & Heskett, J. C. (1992). *Corporate culture and performance.* New York: Free Press.

Kramer, R. M., & Tyler, T. R. (1996). *Trust in organizations: Frontiers of theory and research.* Thousand Oaks, CA: Sage.

Lane, P., Koka, B., & Pathak, S. (2002). A thematic analysis and critical assessment of absorptive capacity research. *Academy of Management Proceedings.* Retrieved February 18, 2006, from http://search.epnet.com/direct.asp?an=7516527&db=buh

Lant, T. (2000). Organizational learning: Creating, retaining, and transferring knowledge [Review of the article by L. Argote]. *Administrative Sciences Quarterly, 45,* 622–624.

Lapidot-Raz, Y. (2002). *Factors that contribute to the development and erosion of followers' trust in leaders: A study of cadets in an officer training course.* Unpublished doctoral dissertation, The Hebrew University, Jerusalem.

Laprè, M., & Van Wassenhove, L. N. (2002). Learning across lines: The secret to more effective factories. *Harvard Business Review, 80*(5), 107–111.

Lave, J. (1991). Situating learning in communities of practice. In L. B. Resnick & J. M. Levine (Eds.), *Perspectives on socially shared cognition* (pp. 63–82). Washington, DC: APA.

Leonard-Barton, D. (1992). The factory as a learning laboratory. *Sloan Management Review, 33*(1), 23–38.

Leonard-Barton, D. (1995). *Wellsprings of knowledge.* Boston: Harvard Business School Press.

Lesser, E. L., & Storck, J. (2001). Communities of practice and organizational performance. *IBM Systems Journal, 40,* 831–842.

Levinson, I. (1998). *The link between organizational learning aspects and criticality pf error.* Unpublished master's thesis, Department of Labor Studies, Tel Aviv University.

Ley, D., & Hitt, M. A. (1995). Strategic restructuring and outsourcing: The effect of mergers and acquisitions on building firm skills and capabilities. *Journal of Management, 21,* 835–859.

Liedtke, J. M., Weber, C., & Weber, J. (1999). Creating a significant and sustainable executive education experience: A case study. *Journal of Managerial Psychology, 14,* 404–420.

Lipshitz, R. (2000). Chic, mystique, and misconception: Argyris and Schön and the rhetoric of organizational learning. *Journal of Applied Behavioral Science, 36,* 456–473.

Lipshitz, R., & Popper, M. (2000). Organizational learning in a hospital. *Journal of Applied Behavioral Science, 36,* 345–361.

Lipshitz, R., Popper, M., & Friedman, V. (2002). A multi-facet model of organizational learning. *Journal of Applied Behavioral Science, 38,* 78–98.

Lipshitz, R., Popper, M., & Ron, N. (1999, June 6–8). *Post-flight reviews in the Israel Defense Force as an organizational learning mechanism.* Paper presented at the 3rd International Conference on Organizational Learning, Lancaster, UK.

Lipshitz, R., & Strauss, O. (1997). Coping with uncertainty: A naturalistic decision-making analysis. *Organizational Behavior and Human Decision Processes, 69,* 149–163.

Luthans, F. (1991). Conversation with Gordon Forward. *Organizational Dynamics, 20,* 63–72.

Maimon, D. (1993). *The vincible terror.* Tel Aviv: Steimatzki.

March, J. G. (1991). Exploration and exploitation in organizational learning. *Organizational Science 2,* 71–87.

March, J. G., & Olsen, J. P. (1976). Organizational learning and the ambiguity of the past. In J. G. March & J. P. Olsen, *Ambiguity and choice in organizations* (pp. 54–68). Bergen, Norway: Universitetsforlaget.

Martiny, M. (1998). Knowledge management at HP Consulting. *Organizational Dynamics, 27,* 71–77.

Maslow, A. (1970). *Motivation and personality.* New York: Harper & Row.

May, D. R., Gilson, R. L., & Harter, L. M. (2004). The psychological conditions of meaningfulness, safety and availability and the engagement of the human spirit at work. *Journal of Occupational and Organizational Psychology, 77*(11), 37.

Mayer, R. C., Davis, J. H., & Schoorman, F. D. (1995). An integrative model of organizational trust. *Academy of Management Review, 20*(3), 709–734.

McAllister, D. J. (1995). Affect and cognition-based trust as foundations for interpersonal cooperation in organizations. *Academy of Management Journal, 38,* 24–59.

McDermott, R. M., & O'Dell, C. (2001). Overcoming cultural barriers to sharing knowledge. *Journal of Knowledge Management, 5*(1), 76–85.

McGill, M. E., & Slocum, J. W. (1998). A little leadership please? *Organization Dynamics, 2,* 39–49.

McGill, M. E., Slocum, J. W., & Lei, D. (1993). Management practices in learning organizations. *Organizational Dynamics, 22,* 5–17.

Miller, D., & Mintzberg, H. (1983). The case for configuration. In G. Morgan (Ed.), *Beyond method* (pp. 57–73). Beverly Hills, CA: Sage.

Mintzberg, H. (1973). *The nature of managerial work.* New York: Harper & Row.

Moingeon, B., & Edmondson, A. (1998). Trust and organizational learning. In N. Lazaric & E. Lorenz (Eds.), *Trust, learning and economic expectations.* London: Edward Elgar.

Moreland, R. L., & Argote, L. (2003). Transactive memory in dynamic organizations. In R. Peterson & E. A. Mannix (Eds.), *Understanding the dynamic organization* (pp. 135–162). Mahwah, NJ: Erlbaum.

Murray, S. (2000, April 3). Learning by stealth case study: Dell Learning. *Financial Times,* p. 4.

Nonaka, I., & Takeuchi, H. (1995). *The knowledge-creating company.* Oxford, UK: Oxford University Press.

O'Dell, C., & Grayson, C. J. (1998). If only we know what we know: Identification and transfer of best practices. *California Management Review, 40*(3), 154–174.

O'Reilly, C. A., & Pfeffer, J. (2000). *How great companies achieve extraordinary results with ordinary people.* Boston: Harvard Business School Press.

Orr, J. E. (1990). Sharing knowledge, celebrating identity: Community memory in a service culture. In D. Middleton & D. Edwards (Eds.), *Collective remembering* (pp. 168–189). London: Sage.

Ortenblad, A. (2002). A typology of the idea of the learning organization. *Management Learning, 33*(2), 213–230.

Ouchi, W. G. (1981). *Theory Z.* Reading, MA: Addison-Wesley.

Overmeer, W. (1998). Reflecting on what? Keynote paper for the on-line conference on Don Schön's Reflective Practitioners, *ACTLIST.3.*

Pagano, B., & Pagano, E. (2003). Transparency. *Executive Excellence, 20*(12), 4–5.

Pan, S. L., & Scarborough, H. (1999). Knowledge management in practice: An exploratory case study. *Technology Analysis & Strategic Management, 11,* 259–274.

Papert, S. A. (1980). *Mindstorms: Children, computers, and powerful ideas.* New York: Basic Books.

Parry, K., & Proctor-Thomson, S. (2002). Perceived integrity of transformational leaders in organisational settings. *Journal of Business Ethics, 35*(2), 75–96.

Parskey, P., & Martiny, M. (2000). Hewlett-Packard. In P. Harkins, L. L. Carter, & A. J. Timms (Eds.), *Best practices in knowledge management and organizational learning handbook* (pp. 25–57). Lexington, MA: Linkage.

Paul, M. (1997). Moving from blame to accountability. *The Systems Thinker-Newsletter, 8*(1).

Pawlowsky, P. (2001). The treatment of organizational learning in management science. In M. Dierkes, A. Berthoin-Antal, J. Child, & I. Nonaka (Eds.), *Handbook of organizational learning* (pp. 61–88). Oxford, UK: Oxford University Press.

Peters, T. J. (1978). Symbols, patterns, and settings: An optimistic case for getting things done. *Organizational Dynamics, 7*(2), 3–23.

Pettigrew, A. M. (1987). Context and action in the transformation of the firm. *Journal of Management Studies, 24,* 649–670.

Pfeffer, J. (1981). Management as symbolic action: The creation and maintenance of organizational paradigms. In B. Staw (Ed.), *Research in organizational behavior* (Vol. 3, pp. 1–15). London: JAI.

Pfeffer, J. (1998). *The Human equation: Building profits by putting people first.* Boston: Harvard Business School Press.

Poduska, B. (1992). Money, marriage, and Maslow's hierarchy of needs. *American Behavioral Scientist, 35,* 756–770.

Politis, J. D. (2001). The relationship of various leadership styles to knowledge management. *Leadership and Organizational Development Journal, 22,* 354–364.

Popper, M., & Lipshitz, R. (1998). Organizational learning mechanisms: A cultural and structural approach to organizational learning. *Journal of Applied Behavioral Science, 34,* 161–178.

Preuss, G. (1998). *Chaparral Steel: Rapid product and process development* (Case 9–692–018, rev.). Cambridge, MA: Harvard Business School.

Prokesch, S. E. (1997). Unleashing the power of learning: An interview with British Petroleum's John Browne. *Harvard Business Review, 75*(5), 147–168.

Putnam, R. D. (1993). *Making democracy work: Civic tradition in modern Italy.* Princeton, NJ: Princeton University Press.

Quinn, J. B. (1988a). IBM 360. In J. B. Quinn, H. Mintzberg, & R. M. James (Eds.), *The strategy process* (pp. 189–203). Englewood Cliffs, NJ: Prentice Hall.

Quinn, J. B. (1988b). The Pillsbury company. In J. B Quinn, H. Mintzberg, & R. M. James (Eds.), *The strategy process* (pp. 398–421). Englewood Cliffs, NJ: Prentice Hall.

Rayner, B. (1993). Trial-by-fire transformation: An interview with Globe Metallurgical's Arden C. Sims. In H. R. Howard & R. D. Haas (Eds.), *The learning imperative* (pp. 277–297). Boston: Harvard Business School Press.

Razer, M., & Friedman, V. (2003). *The new education environment: Intervention strategies.* Jerusalem: Joint Distribution Committee-Israel.

Razer, M., Friedman, V., Sulimani, R., & Sykes, I. (2003, August). *Reaching out: A strategy for reversing exclusion in education.* Proceedings of the ALARPM 6th World Congress and PAR 10th World Congress, Pretoria, South Africa.

Razer, M., Warschawsky, B., & Bar Sadeh, E. (2005). *Social exclusion in education: Theory and practice of guiding educational teams.* Jerusalem: Joint Distribution Committee-Brookdale Institute.

Reason, J. (1990). *Human error.* Cambridge, UK: Cambridge University Press.

Redding, J. C., & Catalanello, R. F. (1994). *Strategic readiness: The making of the learning organization.* San Francisco: Jossey-Bass.

Rittel, H. W. J., & Webber, M. M. (1973). Dilemmas in a general theory of planning. *Policy Sciences, 4,* 155–169.

Rogers, G. C. (1995a). *Human resources at Hewlett-Packard* (Case 9–495–051). Boston: Harvard Business School.

Rogers, G. C. (1995b). *Human resources at Hewlett-Packard* (Case 9–495–052). Boston: Harvard Business School.

Rogers, P., Petrosino, A., Huebner, T., & Hacsi, T. (2000). Program theory evaluation: Practice, promise, and problems. *New Directors for Evaluation, 87,* 5–13.

Ron, N., Lipshitz, R., & Popper, M. (in press). How organizations learn: Post-flight reviews in an F-16 fighter squadron. *Organization Studies.*

Rosenfeld, J., & Tardieu, B. (2000). *Artisan of democracy: How ordinary people, families in extreme poverty and social institutions become allies to overcome social exclusion.* Lanham, MD: University Press of America.

Rucker, R. (1999). Maintaining market leadership through learning. *SuperVision, 60*(9), 3–6.

Schein, E. H. (1985). *Organizational culture and leadership.* San Francisco: Jossey-Bass.

Schein, E. H. (1993). How can organizations learn faster? The challenge of entering the green room. *Sloan Management Review, 34*(2), 85–92.

Schein, E. H. (1996). The three cultures of management: The key to organizational learning. *Sloan Management Review, 38*(1), 9–20.

Schoemaker, P. J. H. and Schuurmans, F. (2003). Opportunity in uncertainty: Techniques for turning an unpredictable future to your advantage. *Association Management,* 55, 49–52.

Schön, D. A. (1983). *The reflective practitioner.* New York: Basic Books.

Schön, D. A. (1987). *Educating the reflective practitioner.* San Francisco: Jossey-Bass.

Senge, P. (1990). *The fifth discipline: The art and practice of the learning organization.* New York: Doubleday.

Senge, P., Kleiner, A., Roberts, C., Ross, R., & Smith, B. (1994). *The fifth discipline fieldbook.* New York: Currency Doubleday.

Shani A. B., & Docherty, P. (2003). *Learning by design: Building sustainable organizations.* Oxford, UK: Blackwell.

Shani, A. B., & Mitki, Y. (2000). Creating the learning organization: Beyond mechanisms. *Public Administration and Public Policy, 81,* 911–920.

Shaw, R. B., & Perkins, D. N. T. (1992). Teaching organizations to lead: The power of productive failures. In D. A. Nadler, M. S. Gerstein, & R. B. Shaw (Eds.), *Organizational architecture* (pp. 175–191). San Francisco: Jossey-Bass.

Shrivastava, P. (1983). A typology of organizational learning systems. *Journal of Management Studies, 20,* 7–28.

Skinner, B. F. (1989). *Recent issues in the analysis of behavior.* Columbus, OH: Merrill.

Smith, H. A., & McKeen, J. D. (2003). *Instilling a knowledge-sharing culture* (Working paper 03–11). Queens Center for Knowledge-Based Enterprise, Queens University, Kingston, Ontario, Canada.

Snell, R. S. (2001). Moral foundations of the learning organization. *Human Relations, 54*(3), 319–342.

Soloveitchik, J. (1983). *Halakhic man.* Philadelphia, PA: The Jewish Publication.

Srikantia, P., & Pasmore, W. (1996). Conviction and doubt in organizational learning. *Journal of Organizational Change Management, 9*(1), 42–53.

Stayer, R. (1990). How I learned to let my workers lead. *Harvard Business Review, 68*(6), 66–75.

Stopford, J. M. (2001). Should strategy makers become dream weavers? *Harvard Business Review, 79*(1), 165–169.

Sugarman, B. (2001). A learning-based approach to organizational change: Some results and guidelines. *Organizational Dynamics, 30*(1), 62–76.

Sulimani, R. (2002). *Studying educational intervention: The case study of the New Educational Environment (NEE) programme in Israel.* Unpublished doctoral thesis, University of Sussex, UK.

Swidler, A. (1986). Culture in action: Symbols and strategies. *American Sociological Review, 51/2,* 273–286.

Sykes, I., & Goldman, M. (2000). *Learning from success: Producing actionable knowledge by reflecting on the practice of a successful project* (Kesher Research Report RR-370-00). Jerusalem: Brookdale Institute.

Szulanski, G. (1994). *Intra-firm transfer of best-practices projects.* Houston, TX: American Productivity and Quality Center.

Szulanski, G. (2003). *Sticky knowledge: Barriers to knowing in the firm.* Thousand Oaks, CA: Sage.

Talbot, S. P. (1994). Peer review drives compensation at Johnsonville. *Personnel Journal, 73*(10), 126–130.

Talisayon, S. D. (2001, November 13). Knowledge and people. *Business World,* pp. 1–2.

Tan, T. K., & Heracleous, L. (2001). Teaching old dogs new tricks: Implementing organizational learning in an Asian national police force. *Journal of Applied Behavioral Science, 17*(3), 361–380.

Thomas, J. B., Sussman, S. W., & Henderson, J. C. (2001). Understanding "strategic learning": Linking organizational learning, knowledge management, and sensemaking. *Organization Science, 12*(3), 331–345.

Torbert, W. (1976). *Creating a community of inquiry: Conflict, collaboration, transformation.* New York: Wiley.

Tucker, A., & Edmondson, A. (2003). *Children's hospital and clinics* (Case 9–302–050). Boston: Harvard Business School Press.

Turnley, W. H., & Bolino M. C. (2001). Achieving desired images while avoiding undesired images: Exploring the role of self-monitoring in impression management. *Journal of Applied Psychology, 86,* 351–360.

Vaill, P. (1999). Mapping organizational knowledge. *Knowledge Management Review, 8,* 10–14.

Vaill, P. (2000a). Knowledge mapping: Getting started with knowledge management. *Information Systems Management, 1,* 16–23.

Vaill, P. (2000b). Introduction to spirituality for business leadership. *Journal of Management Inquiry, 9*(2), 115–116.

Van der Heijden, K. (1996). *Scenarios: The art of strategic conversation.* San Francisco: Jossey-Bass.

Vardi, Y., Wiener, Y., & Popper, M. (1989). The value content of organizational mission as a factor of the commitment of members. *Psychological Reports, 65,* 27–34.

Vera, D., & Crossan, M. (2004). Strategic leadership and organization learning. *Academy of Management Review, 29,* 222–240.

Von Krogh, G. (1998). Care in knowledge creation. *California Management Review, 40*(3), 133–153.

Wack, P. (1985). Scenarios: Uncharted waters ahead. *Harvard Business Review, 63*(5), 73–89.

Waldroop, J., & Butler, T. (1996). The executive as coach. *Harvard Business Review, 74*(6), 111–116.

Watkins, K. E., & Marsick, V. J. (Eds.). (1996). *In action: Creating the learning organization.* Alexandria, VA: American Society for Training and Development.

Wegner, D. M., & Erber, R. (1991). Transactive memory in close relationships. *Journal of Personality & Social Psychology, 61,* 923–929.

Weick, K. (1979). *The social psychology of organizing.* New York: McGraw-Hill.

Weick, K. E., Sutcliffe, K. M., & Obstfeld D. (1999). Organizing for high reliability: Processes of collective mindfulness. In B. Staw & L. Cummings (Eds.), *Research in organizational behavior* (pp. 81–123). London: JAI.

Wheatley, M. J. (1994). Can the U.S. Army become a learning organization? *Journal for Quality and Participation, 17*(2), 50–58.

Whitener, E. M., Brodt, S. E., Korsgaard, M. A., & Werner, J. M. (1998). Managers as initiators of trust. An exchange relationship framework for understanding managerial trustworthy behavior. *Academy of Management Review, 23,* 513–530.

Wiegand, M. (1996). *Prozesse organistionalen Lernes.* Wiesbaden, Germany: Gabler.

Wiggenhorn, W. (1990). Motorola U: When training becomes education. *Harvard Business Review, 4,* 71–83.

Wilkins, A. I., & Patterson, K. J. (1985). You can't get there from here: What will make culture-change projects fail. In L. R. Pondy, R. Frost, P. Morgan, & T. Dandridge (Eds.), *Organizational symbolism* (pp. 262–291). Greenwich CT: JAI.

Willett, C. (n.d.). *Knowledge sharing shifts the power paradigm*. Retrieved February 18, 2006, from http://www.providersedge.com/docs/km_articles/Knowledge_Sharing_Shifts_the_Power_Paradigm.pdf

Wong, P. T. P., & Weiner, B. (1981). When people ask why: Questions and the heuristic of attributional search. *Journal of Personality and Social Psychology, 40*, 650–663.

Woodward, J. (1965). *Industrial organization: Theory and practice*. Oxford, UK: Oxford University Press.

Yeung, A. K., Ulrich, P. O., Nason, S. W., & Von Glinow, M. A. (1999). *Organizational learning capability: Generating and generalizing ideas with impact*. Oxford, UK: Oxford University Press.

Zack, M. H. (1999). Managing codified knowledge. *Sloan Management Review, 4*, 45–58.

Zaleznik, A. (1992). Managers and leaders: Are they different? *Harvard Business Review, 72*(2), 126–135.

Zander, U., & Kogut, B. (1995). Knowledge and the speed of transfer and imitation of organizational capabilities: An empirical test. *Organization Science, 6*, 76–92.

Zell, D. (1997). *Changing by design: Organizational innovation at Hewlett-Packard*. Ithaca, NY: Cornell University Press.

Zell, D. (2001). Overcoming barriers to work innovations: Lessons learned at Hewlett-Packard. *Organizational Dynamics, 30*, 77–86.

Index

About the Authors

Raanan Lipshitz is Associate Professor at the Department of Psychology of the University of Haifa. He specializes in organizational learning and naturalistic decision making. He is a graduate of The Hebrew University (BA in psychology and English literature), The University of North Carolina, Chapel Hill (MA in quantitative psychology), and Purdue University (PhD in administrative science). Prior to joining the University of Haifa, he served 10 years in the Israeli Defense Force as a field psychologist and as a behavioral science instructor at the Command and General Staff College. He has been a visiting researcher at Boston University's Center for Applied Social Studies and a visiting scholar at the Naval Postgraduate School in Monterey, California, and the University of Melbourne's Business School. He is a Senior Editor of *Organizational Studies* and *Cognitive Engineering and Decision Making* and member of the editorial board of the *Journal of Behavioral Decision Making*. He has published extensively on organizational learning and naturalistic decision making in *Organization Studies, Management Learning, Journal of Applied Behavioral Science, Journal of Behavioral Decision Making,* and *Organizational Behavior and Human Decision Making.*

Victor J. Friedman is Associate Professor with a joint appointment to the Behavioral Sciences and the Sociology and Anthropology Departments at the Emek Yezreel (Jezreel Valley) College, Israel. His work focuses on an "action science" approach to integrating research with practice in areas characterized by uncertainty, uniqueness, and conflict. He has worked with educational, social service, government, and business organizations and has published papers dealing with organizational learning, program evaluation, social entrepreneurship, and social inclusion. He is a founder and the director of the Action Research Center, an initiative to develop a more responsive mutual relationship between academia and the local community. He received his EdD from Harvard University in counseling, consulting, and community psychology; his MA from Columbia University; and his BA from Brandeis University. He is a senior associate of the Action Evaluation Research Institute and has participated in the Project for Productive Reflection and Learning at Work, sponsored by the Swedish National Institute for Working Life and the International "Kolleg" in Organizational Learning, sponsored by the Daimler-Benz Foundation. He has been a visiting scholar-faculty at the Organizational Learning Center at the Massachusetts Institute of Technology (MIT), the Berlin Social Science Institute (WZB), the Leipzig Graduate School of Management (HHL), and the Theseus Institute in France.

Micha Popper, an Associate Professor and the Head of the Organizational Psychology Program in the Department of Psychology at the University of Haifa, Israel, is the former Commanding Officer of the School for Leadership Development of the Israel Defense Forces. He is the founder and Codirector of the Center for Outstanding Leadership in Zikhron Yaakov, Israel; a scholar of the U.S. Army Research Institute (ARI); and has been a visiting professor at Simon Fraser University in Vancouver, Canada. His research and consulting concern organizational learning and the dynamics of leader-follower relationships and developmental aspects of leaders. He has a PhD from Tel-Aviv University (1986) and is the author and coauthor of five books and numerous articles in journals, including *Political Psychology, Academy of Management Journal, Military Psychology, Leadership Quarterly, Management Learning,* and *Journal of Applied Behavioral Science.*